ELECTORAL POLITICS OF GRASSROOTS DEMOCRACY

About the Authors

Prof. (Dr.) M.R. Biju, is currently Dean, School of Social Sciences, Dean, School of Legal Studies and Head, Department of Public Administration and Policy Studies, Central University of Kerala, Kasaragod. He is also serving as Chairperson of Board of Studies, Public Administration and Policy Studies. He is also a Member of the Court of the University. He is the Editor of *South Asian Journal of Socio-Political Studies* (SAJOSPS) and Editor-in-Chief of *International Journal of Political Science* (IJOPS). He is a prolific writer on socio-political and developmental issues and published twenty-nine books, One Hundred and Seventy research papers, Seventeen book chapters, and has reviewed over Nine Hundred books for South Asian Journal of Socio-political Studies.

His teaching and research experience, spanning more than 26 years, includes several achievements such as completion of three major research projects funded by Ministry of Panchayati Raj, Government of India and University Grants Commission, New Delhi and the Post-doctoral fellowship awarded by the UGC in 2004. He has successfully guided doctoral students of the University of Kerala.

He is consistently making professional academic contributions in the capacity of an Associate Board member of Economics and Management, a prestigious journal published by the Technical University of Liberec, Czech Republic, as the Director and Member Secretary of the Asian Institute of Development Research (AIDR), and is a life Member of several Academic and Professional Bodies. He is also serving on the Editorial Board of International Journal of Business and Innovation, Administration. He is a member of the PG Board of Studies Political Science and Public Administration of the Central University of Rajasthan and Gandhigram Rural Institute, Dindigul.

M.R.B. Anantha Padmanabha, is working as Deputy Editor of South Asian Journal of Socio-Political Studies (SAJOSPS), has to his credit a few books (co-author) and research papers published in International and national journals. He has also presented papers in National Seminars. Currently, he is studying Political Science and International Relations at Pondicherry University.

Electoral Politics of Grassroots Democracy

The Case of Kerala 1953-2015

Prof. Dr. M.R. Biju
M.R.B. Anantha Padmanabha

CONCEPT PUBLISHING COMPANY PVT. LTD.
NEW DELHI-110059

ISBN-13: 978-93-88937-94-8

First Published 2021

Published and Printed by

Concept Since 1974

Concept Publishing Company Pvt. Ltd.
A/15-16, Commercial Block, Mohan Garden,
New Delhi-110059 (INDIA)
T : 91 11 25351460, 91 11 25351794
E : publishing@conceptpub.com; *W* : www.conceptpub.com

Cataloging in Publication Data--Courtesy: D.K. Agencies (P) Ltd. <docinfo@dkagencies.com>

Electoral politics of grassroots democracy : the case study of Kerala 1953-2015 / [editors], Prof. Dr. M.R. Biju, M.R.B. Anantha Padmanabha.
pages cm
Includes bibliographical references and index.
ISBN 9789388937948

1. Local elections—India—Kerala. 2. Democratization—India—Kerala. 3. Decentralization in government—India—Kerala. 4. Local government—India—Kerala. 5. Kerala (India)—Politics and government—20th century. 6. Kerala (India)—Politics and government—21st century. I. Biju, M. R., 1965- editor. II. Anantha Padmanabha, M. R. B., editor.

LCC JS7025.K47E44 2021 | DDC 324.95483 23

Preface

The 73rd and 74th Constitutional Amendments in 1993, mandating the formation and functioning of local bodies (Panchayati Raj and Municipal Bodies) and listing several functions of the government to be handled down to local bodies, marked a watershed in India's quest for democratic development within pluralistic, parliamentary and electoral framework. Decentralization was defended on the grounds of bringing government closer to people and hence ensuring better results. The effectiveness of mandate of decentralization of administration and devolution of powers, however depended on the success of those stages that took up this task seriously. Kerala is one such state. Kerala's attempt at a participatory, systematical and transparent process of decentralization has hailed its unique achievement.

On the Gandhi Jayanti Day of 2020, the state of Kerala would complete two and a half decades of participatory planning and decentralized governance. During its long and fruitful journey, the new generation Panchayati Raj Institutions and other self governing institutions had travelled a long way with its remarkable achievements in participatory planning and governance process, which had evoked genuine interest from the theoreticians and practitioners of decentralization. When the 25th anniversary was approaching, the others felt that it would be a pleasant experience to highlight the strategies, strength and weaknesses of people's participation in the decentralization process and to draw lessons for the future. Certainly quarter a century is an enough period to assess the achievements, to evaluate on the lost opportunities as well as the challenges ahead.

The authors are extremely concerned about the fact that the new generation of local self governing institutions in the nation especially the rural self-governments, which was inaugurated with great expectations and enthusiasm is facing enormous troubles and problems. The gravity and intensity of these negative forces varies from state to state. Kerala is not an exception in this regard. However, it has to be noted that in spite of a number of disturbing elements, Kerala could make a considerable impact in several spheres of LSGs including the electoral fronts.

Keeping this in background an attempt has been made in this handy volume to present a detailed picture of the electoral history of grassroots democracy in Kerala from 1953 to 2015, which will be a pioneering attempt. The whole volume has been categorized under Eight chapters. The introductory chapter brings together the major political and electoral aspects of grassroots democracy in the Indian context in a chronological sequence. Chapter Two presents the theoretical concepts connected with the grassroots democracy in general and people's participation in particular. The focus of attentions in the Third Chapter is the decentralization initiatives and the role of state election commission in conducting local body polls. The electoral history of the PRIs in Kerala from 1953 to 1991 is the topic of discussion in Chapter Four. Chapter Five depicts the significance of 1995 elections to the civic bodies, after the passing of the 73rd and 74th Constitution (Amendment) Act, 1992, Kerala Panchayati Raj Act, 1994 and Kerala Municipality Act, 1994. Chapter Six unfolds the importance of the local body polls held in 2000. Chapter Seven narrates the currents and undercurrents of the civic polls held in 2005 and the concluding Chapter (Eight) projects the facets of 2015 Polls.

The authors have taken keen interest in incorporating all supporting documents to substantiate their electoral analysis. Though the full data regarding ward-wise election results are available with us, due to space constrains we could not present it in this volume. But we have taken extreme care that the mother data has been examined in its totality before presenting the electoral analysis.

M.R. Biju
M.R.B. Anantha Padmanabha

Acknowledgements

We would like to express our deep sense of gratitude to those who have been kind enough to help us in the preparation of this volume. First of all, we thank the State Election Commission, Government of Kerala for providing materials connected with electoral statistics. The volume is the outcome of election data and electoral statistics connected with the state of Kerala from 1953-2015.

The First Author of the volume, while pursuing his doctoral studies in 80s spent weeks and months in the Directorate of Panchayats, Government of Kerala for collecting data which was available in handwritten form. He is recollecting those days with a nostalgic feeling. He spent numerous hours with the then Director of Panchayats, Shri A.K. Appotti IAS, who was kind enough to give direction to his subordinates to extend unconditional support to him. Similar instances can also be recalled from the Library of University of Kerala, Palayam, Thiruvananthapuram. The then Deputy Librarian, Shri Parameshwaran was also so generous to help him. Both the Directorate of Panchayats and University Library of Kerala is a treasure house of information in this area of academic research. It was a time when photocopying was not available. Naturally data had to be written by hand. We also acknowledge with gratitude to the library staff of State Central Library, Thiruvananthapuram for providing materials connected with the theme.

Before conclude, we would like to thank Shri Ashok Kumar Mittal of Concept Publishing Company Pvt. Ltd., New Delhi who brought out this volume in an elegant form.

M.R. Biju
M.R.B. Anantha Padmanabha

Contents

About the Volume

On the Gandhi Jayanti Day of 2020, the state of Kerala has completed two and a half decades of participatory planning and decentralized governance. During its long and fruitful journey, the new generation Panchayati Raj Institutions and other self governing institutions had travelled a long way with its remarkable achievements in participatory planning and governance process, which had evoked genuine interest from the theoreticians and practitioners of decentralization. When the 25th anniversary was approaching, the authors felt that it would be a pleasant experience to highlight the strategies, strength and weaknesses of people's participation in the decentralization process and to draw lessons for the future. Certainly quarter a century is an enough period to assess the achievements, to evaluate on the lost opportunities as well as the challenges ahead.

Keeping this in background an attempt has been made in this handy volume to present a detailed picture of the electoral history of grassroots democracy in Kerala from 1953 to 2015, which will be a pioneering attempt. The whole volume has been categorized under Eight chapters. The introductory chapter brings together the major political and electoral aspects of grassroots democracy in the Indian context in a chronological sequence. Chapter Two presents the theoretical concepts connected with the grassroots democracy in general and people's participation in particular. The focus of attentions in the Third Chapter is the decentralization initiatives and the role of state election commission in conducting local body polls. The electoral history of the PRIs in Kerala from 1953 to 1991 is the topic of discussion in Chapter Four. Chapter Five depicts the significance of 1995 elections to the civic bodies, after the passing of the 73rd and 74th Constitution (Amendment) Act, 1992, Kerala Panchayati Raj Act, 1994 and Kerala Municipality Act, 1994. Chapter Six unfolds the importance of the local body polls held in 2000. Chapter Seven narrates the currents and undercurrents of the civic polls held in 2005 and the concluding Chapter (Eight) projects the facets of 2015 Polls.

1
Introduction

On the Gandhi Jayanti Day of 2020, the state of Kerala would completed two and a half decades of participatory planning and decentralized governance. During its long and fruitful journey, the new generation Panchayati Raj Institutions and other self governing institutions had travelled a long way with its remarkable achievements in participatory planning and governance process, which had evoked genuine interest from the theoreticians and practitioners of decentralization. When the 25th anniversary was approaching, the others felt that it would be a pleasant experience to highlight the strategies, strength and weaknesses of people's participation in the decentralization process and to draw lessons for the future. Certainly quarter a century is an enough period to assess the achievements, to evaluate on the lost opportunities as well as the challenges ahead.

The authors are extremely concerned about the fact that the new generation of local self governing institutions in the nation especially the rural self governments, which was inaugurated with great expectations and enthusiasm is facing enormous troubles and problems. The gravity and intensity of these negative forces varies from state to state. Kerala is not an exception in this regard. However, it has to be noted that in spite of a number of disturbing elements, Kerala could make a considerable impact in several spheres of LSGs including the electoral fronts.

Electoral Milestones in India's Decentralization

It is a sad commentary on India's national commitment to democratic decentralisation that despite the village having a history as the basic unit of administration and despite the nationalist movement commitment to panchayats and Gandhiji's unequivocal propagation of the ideal, the first draft of India's constitution did not include a provision for panchayats. When Gandhiji learnt that the proposed constitution did not provide for panchayats, he remarked that this was certainly an omission calling for immediate attention, if India's independence was to reflect the voice of the people. Apart from the origin of Gandhian ideals there were a number of individuals, committees and commissions played their fruitful role in executing the content of decentralization on Indian soil. Notable among them include the following:

A. Asoka Mehta Committee

The appointment of the Asoka Mehta Committee in 1977 marked a turning point in the concept and practice of Panchayati Raj. The Asoka Mehta committee was set up to enquire into the working of the Panchayati Raj Institutions, and to suggest measures to strengthen them so as to enable a decentralised system of planning and development to be effective. The Committee's report (1978) is a seminal document which seeks to make panchayats an organic, integral part of our democratic process. The Panchayati Raj Institutions which came into being in certain states after the Asoka Mehta Committee's recommendations could be considered the second generation panchayats.

The second generation of Panchayati Raj Institutions can be said to have started when the West Bengal government took the initiative in 1978 to give a new life to its panchayats on the lines of the Asoka Mehta Committee's recommendations. West Bengal, Karnataka, Andhra Pradesh and Jammu & Kashmir either revised their existing panchayat Acts or passed new Act, in theory accepting the Asoka Mehta Committee report. These states adapted the recommendations to suit their conditions and learnt from each other's experience in bringing forth new legislations or amendments to the prevailing Acts. The most important thrust of the second phase was that the panchayats emerged from a development organisation at the local level into a political institution.

The emphasis shifted from the bureaucracy to the political elements. This was a welcome trend. The Balwantrai Mehta study team had made development central to the panchayat system, while in West Bengal, Karnataka, Andhra Pradesh, and later in Jammu & Kashmir following the Asoka Mehta Committee report, the attempt had been to make panchayats into genuine political institutions. Thus, they were a microcosm of the state itself with all its ramifications.

It may be recalled here that the Asoka Mehta Committee made the first official recommendation for including Panchayati Raj in the Constitution in keeping with its approach that panchayats should be regarded as political rather than mere developmental institutions. This committee also favoured participation of political parties in panchayat elections with their symbols.

B. National Commission to Review the Working of the Constitution [NCRW]

In the Report of the NCRW chaired by Justice M.N. Venkatachala had observed: "More than eight long years have passed, but the change brought about by the Amendment has not been radical, nor its implications are found to be far-reaching. For, Panchayats have, till now, failed to emerge as government at the third stratum, up to the expected level. It is not without some justification that the Panchayats that came in the wake of the post-73rd Constitution amendment have been described as democratic institutions without power—a decorative box, as it were, that contains nothing inside". The National Commission recommended several amendments to Part IX of the Constitution, which included giving an overseeing function to the Central Election Commission over the State Election Commission by amending article 243K and 243ZA; substituting the word "endow" with "vest" the panchayats with such powers and authority as to enable them to function as institutions of self-government by amending article 243G; restructuring the Eleventh and Twelfth Schedules in a manner that creates a separate fiscal domain for panchayats and municipalities, and conferring on the Panchayats full powers of administrative and functional control over staff transferred to them and the power to recruit staff required for service in their jurisdiction.

It also recommended constitution of a State Panchayat Council under the chairmanship of the Chief Minister and Comptroller and Auditor-General of India to conduct the audit or lay down accounting standards for panchayats. The relevant portions of the above report is reproduced hereunder.

(A) ISSUES CONNECTED WITH DECENTRALISATION AND DEVOLUTION – PANCHAYATS AND MUNICIPALITIES

Panchayats

(175) *Article 243K and 243Z should be amended on the following lines:*

1. Amendment of Article 243K.—

In article 243K,—

(a) for clause (1), the following clauses shall be substituted, namely:

"(1) Subject to the provisions of clause (1A), the superintendence, direction and control of the preparation of electoral rolls for, and the conduct of, all elections to the Panchayats shall be vested in a State Election Commission consisting of a State Election Commissioner to be appointed by the Governor.

(1A) The Election Commission shall have the power to issue any directions or instructions to the State Election Commission for the discharge of its functions under clause (1)."

(b) after clause (4), the following clause shall be inserted, namely:

"(5) The State Election Commission shall submit its annual report to the Election Commission and to the Governor, every year and it may, at any time, submit special reports on any matter which in its opinion is of such urgency or importance that it should not be deferred till the submission of its annual report."

2. Amendment of Article 243ZA.—

In article 243ZA, for clause (1), the following clauses shall be substituted, namely:

"(1) Subject to the provisions of clause (1A), the superintendence, direction and control of the preparation of electoral rolls for, and the conduct of, all elections to the Municipalities shall be vested in the State Election Commission referred to in article 243K.

(1A) The Election Commission shall have the power to issue any directions or instructions to the State Election Commission for the discharge of its functions under clause (1)." [Para 9.6.2]

(176) Panchayats should be categorically declared to be 'institutions of self-government' and exclusive functions be assigned to them. *For this purpose, article 243G should be amended to read as follows:*

"Powers, Authority and Responsibility of Panchayats

243G. Subject to the provisions of this Constitution, the Legislature of a State shall, by law, vest the Panchayats with such powers and authority as are necessary to enable them to function as institutions of self-government and such law shall contain provisions for the devolution of powers and responsibilities upon Panchayats at the appropriate level, subject to such conditions as shall be specified therein, with respect to—

(a) preparation of plans for economic development and social justice;

(b) the implementation of schemes for economic development and social justice as shall be entrusted to them including those in relation to the matters listed in the Eleventh Schedule."

Similar amendments should be made in article 243W relating to the powers, authority and responsibilities of Municipalities, etc. [Paras 9.7.1 and 9.7.2]

(177) The Eleventh and Twelfth Schedules to the Constitution should be restructured in a manner that creates a separate fiscal domain for Panchayats and Municipalities. Accordingly, articles

243H and 243X should be amended making it mandatory for the legislation of the States to make laws devolving powers to Panchayats and Municipalities. [Para 9.8.2]

(178) *In order to enable the Finance Commission to take a macro-level view, the provisions sub-clauses (bb) and (c) of clause (3) of article 280 should be amended. The words "on the basis of the recommendation" in these sub-clauses should be replaced by the words "after taking into consideration the recommendations."* [Para 9.8.3]

(179) *In the part of clause (1) of article 243-I which calls for constitution of State Finance Commission (SFC) at the expiration of every fifth year, in line with article 280(1), the words "or at such earlier time as the Governor considers necessary" may be added after the words 'fifth year'.* While it is for the State Legislature to ensure that the Government implements fully its assurances, there should be constitutional obligations for placing the Action Taken Report (ATR) before the legislature within 'six months' after the submission of the report. Clause (4) of article 243-I may need to be amended accordingly. [Para 9.8.4]

(180) *The necessary legislative power of fixing upper limit of taxes on professions, trades, callings and employment under article 276 should be vested in Parliament by suitably amending that article.* [Para 9.8.5]

(181) All local authorities may be allowed to borrow from the State Government and financial institutions. [Para 9.8.6]

(182) *An enabling provision should be made in Part IX of the Constitution permitting the State Legislature to make, by law, provisions that would empower the State Government to confer on the Panchayats full power of administrative and functional control over such staff as are transferred following devolution of functions, notwithstanding any right they may have acquired from State Act/Rules.* They should also have the power to recruit certain categories of staff required for service in their jurisdiction. [Para 9.9.1]

(183) *A proviso to clause (1) of article 243E should be inserted to the effect that a reasonable opportunity of being heard shall be given to a Panchayat before it is dissolved.* [Para 9.10]

(184) *A provision for constitution of a State Panchayat Council under the chairmanship of the Chief Minister [on the pattern of Gujarat State Council for Panchayats as provided in the Gujarat Panchayats Act, 1993] should be made in the Constitution on the analogy of the provision in article 263 of the Constitution relating to the Inter-State Council.* The leader of the opposition may be made *ex-officio* vice-chairman of

the Council to provide a consensual approach to the development of Panchayats as fully democratic, efficient and responsible institutions. [Para 9.11]

(185) Necessary provisions should be made for audit of Panchayat accounts to ensure that all works related to audit (conduct of audit, submission of audit report and compliance with audit objections if any) are completed within a year of the close of a financial year. To ensure uniformity in the practice relating to audits of accounts, the Comptroller and Auditor-General of India should be empowered to conduct the audit or lay down accounting standards for Panchayats. [Para 9.12]

Municipalities

(186) Whenever a Municipality is superseded, a report stating the grounds for such dissolution should be placed before the State Legislature. [Para 9.13]

(187) All provisions regarding qualifications and disqualifications for elections to local authorities should be consolidated in a single law and until that is done, each State should prepare a manual of existing provisions for public information. [Para 9.14]

(188) The State Election Commission (SEC) should have the authority to prescribe ceiling of expenses and code of conduct in elections. Further, the State laws should clearly specify the powers of the SEC to disqualify candidates or set aside elections in the event of violations of those laws. [Para 9.15]

(189) It should be the duty of a State and the Union (in case of Panchayats and Municipalities located in Union Territories) to ensure the completion of elections within the stipulated limits. It should also be duty of the State Election Commissioner to ensure this and in the event of possible delay make a report to the Governor of the State drawing his attention to the problems and suggesting remedial action to fulfil the requirements of the Constitution. *Articles 243K and 243ZA should be suitably amended to specify that the responsibility for the conduct of elections shall include all preparatory steps for the same including the electoral rolls and matters connected therewith and the responsibility for the same shall vest with the State Election Commission.* [Para 9.16.2]

(190) The functions and responsibilities of delimitation, reservation and rotation of seats and matters connected therewith should be vested in a Delimitation Commission constituted by law by the appropriate legislature and not in the SEC. [Para 9.16.2]

(191) The Representation of the People Act and State laws should specify that common polling stations should be used for elections to local bodies, State Legislatures and Parliament. [Para 9.17.2]

(192) The State laws should provide guidelines for the delimitation work such as parity, as far as possible, in the ratio between the population of a territorial constituency and the number of seats within the same class of Panchayats or Municipalities. [Para 9.17.3]

(193) State laws should specify that changes in the administrative boundaries of districts, sub-divisions, taluks, police stations, etc., should not be made within six months prior to a panchayat or a municipal election. [Para 9.17.4]

(194) *To remove ambiguities, articles 243D and 243T should be suitably amended to provide for rotation and changes only at the time of delimitation and not in between.* State laws should provide the guidelines for the process of reservation which should ensure transparency and adequate opportunities for eliciting voter response. [Para 9.18.2]

(195) *To clarify the precise position of reservation under clause (6) of article 243D and clause (6) of article 243T to be provided by the State law, the overall total of reserved seats and reserved offices in Panchayats and Municipalities should be specified.* [Para 9.18.3]

(196) The State Election Commissioner should have a fixed term of 5 years. He/she should be equal to a Judge of the High Court. The broad qualifications for a State Election Commissioner may be specified under the State law. [Para 9.19.1]

(197) *The concept of a distinct and separate tax domain for municipalities should be recognised. This concept should be reflected in a list of taxes in the relevant schedule. Carving out items from the existing State lists such as item 49 (taxes on land and buildings) and item 52 (taxes on entry of goods into a local area for consumption) should not be difficult.* [Para 9.21]

Institutions in North East India

(198) The North Eastern part of India with its large number of tribal communities and emerging educated elites has self-governing village councils and organized tribal chiefdoms. Efforts are to be made to give all the States in this region the opportunities provided under the 73rd and 74th Constitution Amendments. However, this should be done with due regard to the unique traditions of the region and the genius of the people without tampering with their essential rights and giving to each State the chance to use its own nomenclature for systems of governance which will have local acceptance. [Para 9.22.3]

(199) Careful steps should be taken to devolve political powers through the intermediate and local-level traditional political organisations, provided their traditional practices carried out in a modern world do not deny legitimate democratic rights to any section in their contemporary society. The details of state-wise steps to devolve such powers will have to be carefully considered in a proper representative meeting of traditional leaders of each community, opinion builders of the respective communities and leaders of State and national stature from these very groups. A hasty decision could have serious repercussions, unforeseen and unfortunate, which could further complicate and worsen the situation. To begin with, the subjects given under the Sixth Schedule and those mentioned in the Eleventh Schedule could be entrusted to the Autonomous District Councils (ADCs). The system of in-built safeguards in the Sixth Schedule should be maintained and strengthened for the minority and micro-minority groups while empowering them with greater responsibilities and opportunities, for example, through the process of Central funding for Plan expenditure instead of routing all funds through the State Governments. The North Eastern Council can play a central role here by developing a process of public education on the proposed changes, which would assure communities about protection of their traditions and also bring in gender representation and give voice to other ethnic groups. [Para 9.23(i)]

(200) Traditional forms of governance should be associated with self-governance because of the present dissatisfaction. However, positive democratic elements like gender justice and

adult franchise should be built into these institutions to make them broader based and capable of dealing with a changing world. [Para 9.23(ii)]

(201) The implementation of centrally funded projects from various departments of the Union Government should be entrusted to the ADCs and to revived village councils with strict monitoring by the Comptroller and Auditor-General of India. [Para 9.23(iii)]

(202) The process of protection of identity and the process of development and change are extremely sensitive. These twin processes need to be understood in the framework of a changing world and the role of all communities, small and large, in that world. Therefore, the North Eastern Council should be mandated to conduct an intensive programme of public awareness, sensitization and education through non-governmental organizations, State Governments, and its own structure to help bring about such an understanding of the proposals. [Para 9.23(iv)]

(203) The provisions of the Anti-Defection Law in the proposed revised form as recommended in para 4.18.2 of the Report should be made applicable to all the Sixth Schedule areas. [Para 9.23(v)]

(204) Given the demographic imbalance which is taking place in the North-East as a result of illegal migration from across the borders, urgent legal steps are necessary for preventing such groups from entering electoral rolls and citizenship rolls of the country. Reservations for local communities and minorities from other parts of the country should be made in the State Legislatures. Issuance of multi-purpose identity cards to all Indian citizens should be made mandatory for all Indian residents in the North East on a *high-priority basis* and the National Citizenship Law to be reviewed to plug the loopholes which enable illegal settlers to become 'virtual' citizens in a short span of time, using a network of touts, politicians and officials. [Para 9.23(vi)]

(205) A National Immigration Council should be set up under law to examine and report on a range of issues including Work Permits for legal migrants, Identity Cards for all residents, a National Migration Law, a National Refugee Law, review of the Citizenship Act, the Illegal Migrants Determination by Tribunal Act and the Foreigners Act. [Para 9.23(vii)]

(206) Local communities should be involved in the monitoring of our borders, in association with the local police and the Border Security Force. [Para 9.23(viii)]

(207) As regards Nagaland, the Naga Councils should be replaced by elected representatives of various Naga society groups with an intermediary tier at the district level. Village Development Boards should be less dependent on State and receive more Centrally-sponsored funds. [Para 9.25]

(208) As regards Assam,—

(i) the Sixth Schedule should be extended to the Bodoland Autonomous Council with protection for non-tribal, non-Bodo groups,
(ii) other Autonomous Councils be upgraded to Autonomous Development Councils with more Central funds for infrastructure development; within the purview of the 73rd Amendment but also using traditional governing systems at the village level. [Para 9.28]

(209) As regards Meghalaya,—

(1) A tier of village governance should be created for a village or a group of villages in the Autonomous District Councils, comprising of elected persons from the traditional systems plus from existing village councils with not more than 15 persons at each village unit.
(2) The number of seats in each of the Autonomous District Councils in Meghalaya should be increased by 10 seats, i.e., to a total number of 40 seats. Of the 10 additional seats, having regard to the non-representation of women and non-tribals, the Governor may nominate up to five members from these categories to each of the ADCs. The other five may be elected as follows:

    (a) By Syiems and Myntris, from among themselves to the Khasi Autonomous Council.
    (b) By Dolois from among themselves to the Jaintia Autonomous District Council; and
    (c) By Nokmas from among themselves to the Garo Autonomous District Council. [Para 9.29]

(210) As regards Tripura,—

(i) The changes which may be made in respect of other Autonomous Councils should also apply in respect of the Autonomous District Council(s) in Tripura.
(ii) The number of elected members in the Council should be increased from 28 to 32.
(iii) The number of nominated members should be increased to six from the current two. The existing non-tribal seats (currently, they have three elected seats) be converted to tribal seats. Three non-tribals may be nominated by the Governor and three tribal women may be nominated by the Chief Executive Member. [Para 9.30]

(211) As regards Mizoram, –

(i) An intermediary elected 30-member tier should be developed at the district level in areas not covered by the Sixth Schedule, *i.e.*, excluding the Chakma, Lai and Mara District Autonomous Councils. There would thus be two tiers below the State Legislature: the District and the Village.
(ii) Village Councils in non-Scheduled areas should be given more administrative and judicial powers; two or more villages be combined to form one village council, given the small population in the State.
(iii) Consideration should be given to groups seeking Sixth Schedule status, depending on viability of the demand, including size of population, territorial and ethnic contiguity.
(iv) Central funding as outlined in general recommendations should be provided to the ADCs.
(v) Nominated seats for women, non-tribals and Sixth Schedule tribes in non-scheduled area (not to exceed six over and above the size of the Councils, making a total of 36 members); current size of ADCs should be increased to 30 with a similar provision for women and non-scheduled tribes. [Para 9.31]

(212) As regards Manipur,

(i) the provisions of the Sixth Schedule should be extended to hill districts of the State,

(ii) the 73rd Amendment should be implemented vigorously in the areas of the plains where, despite elections, the system is virtually non-existent. [Para 9.32]

(B) ISSUES CONNECTED WITH PACE OF SOCIO-ECONOMIC CHANGE AND DEVELOPMENT

(213) The Citizens' Charters be prepared by every service providing department/agency to enumerate the entitlements of the citizens. In case a citizen fails to receive the public goods and the services in the manner and to the extent set out in such charters, he/she should have recourse to an easy and effective system of grievance redressal through chartered Ombudsman. These citizen's charters should include specifically the entitlements of citizens belonging to Scheduled Castes (SCs), Scheduled Tribes (STs) and other deprived classes. In the case of these deprived classes the charters can with advantage provide for National and State Commission for SCs, STs, BCs (Backward Classes), Minorities, women, *safai karamcharis* to function effectively as ombudsman-bodies. The charter of these National and State Commissions and the way they are constituted should be such as to facilitate the role, *inter alia,* as ombudsman-bodies for different deprived classes. [Para 10.3.2]

(214) The Civil Services Boards, recommended to be set up under Chapter 6 for considering promotions and placements, should be directed to specifically consider the performance of officers in promoting the welfare of Scheduled Castes, Scheduled Tribes and other deprived categories. When officers are being considered for promotion and placement economic agencies/ ministries, weightage should be given to officers who have worked conscientiously and efficiently to implement constitutional values and norms under the law and rules and regulations for the welfare, development and empowerment of the above disadvantaged categories and those who have failed in this and those who have not worked at least for five years in the areas and sectors pertaining to these categories should be excluded from placements in economic ministries/agencies. For this purpose, the provision should be made for Social Justice Clearance before an officer of class I or class II is promoted along the lines detailed in para 3.2 at pages 1390-1391 of Book-3, Vol. II. [Para 10.3.3]

(215) Reservation for members of the SCs and the STs should be brought under the purview of a statute covering all aspects of reservation, as detailed in para 8.10 at pages 1406-1408 of Book-3, Vol. II, including setting up *Arakshan Nyaya Adalats* or Tribunal to adjudicate upon all cases and disputes pertaining to reservation in posts and vacancies in Government, Public Sector, Banks and other financial institutions, Universities and all other institutions and organisations to which reservations are and become applicable. These Tribunals should have the status of High Courts, appeals lying only to the Supreme Court. These Tribunals should have their main Bench at Delhi and other Benches in the States. The Chairperson, Vice-Chairperson and other Members of the Tribunal and its benches should be selected on the basis of their record in the implementation of Reservation in their earlier positions. The statute should, *inter alia,* have a penal provision including imprisonment for those convicted of wilfully or negligently failing to implement reservation. The statute and related provisions should be brought under the Ninth Schedule to the Constitution. [Para 10.3.4]

(216) The three Constitution amendments enacted in the last two years to undo the harm done in 1997 to the long pre-existing rights of SCs and STs in reservations should be put into effect forthwith. The Central and State Governments should amend the executive orders issued in 1997 regarding the roster and restore the pre-1996 roster. This should also be brought under the purview of the statute mentioned above. [Para 10.3.5]

(217) The Reservation for backward classes should also be brought under a statute which, while containing the specificities of reservation for BCs should also contain provisions for *Arakshan Nyaya Adalats* or Tribunal for providing Justice in reservation, penal provisions, etc. as recommended in the case of the statute in respect of SCs and STs. [Para 10.3.6]

(218) It should be mandatorily stipulated in the Memoranda of Understanding (M.O.Us.) of privatisation or disinvestment of public sector undertakings that the policy of reservation in favour of SCs, STs and BCs shall be continued even after privatisation or disinvestment in the same form as it exists in the Government and this should also be incorporated in the respective statutes of reservation. As a measure of social integration there should be a half per cent reservation for children of parents one of whom is

SC/ST and the other parent is non-SC/non-ST and this reservation should be termed as reservation for the Casteless. [Para 10.3.7]

(219) In view of the weighty opinion against the formal introduction of reservation in the higher judiciary, and the fact that over fifty years, the progress of education, however tardy, has certainly produced adequate number of persons of the SC, ST and BC in every State who possess the required qualifications, having necessary integrity, character and acumen required for Judges of Supreme Court and High Courts for appointment as Judge of the superior judiciary, a way could and should, therefore, be found to bring a reasonable number of SCs, STs and BCs on to the Benches of the Supreme Court and High Courts in the same way in which, in practice, it is found is followed in respect of advocates from different social segments/regions of the country/States or different religious communities so that on the one hand the overwhelming opinion against formal reservation in the Supreme Court and High Courts is respected and on the other hand, the feeling of alienation of the vast majority of Indians comprising SCs, STs and BCs that, in spite of having persons of requisite calibre and character among them, they are being ignored in the appointment of Judges, is resolved. [Para 10.3.9]

(220) There should be reservation for SCs, STs and BCs (including BC minorities and especially More and Most Backward classes), with a due proportion of women from each of these categories in the matter of allotment of shops under the public distribution system, and other allotments like petrol stations, gas agencies, etc. for distribution of commodities by public authority. There is need for support mechanism to help entrepreneurs among these deprived sections to help them to come up in these business ventures. These measures should be taken on the lines as spelt out in para 4.6 at page 1393 of Book-3 Vol. II. [Para 10.3.10]

(221) Massive programmes of employment should be undertaken and expanded to cover all such people and provide them employment at statutory minimum wage fixed for agricultural labourers at least for 80 days in the year over and above the unsteady employment they normally have. The nature of the work to be undertaken, the mode of payment of wages etc. should be as detailed in para 4.5 at pages 1392 to 1393 of Book-3 of Volume-II. Inclusion of Right to Work as a fundamental right has been recommended in para 3.13.2 of this Report and this will provide

the necessary constitutional base and support for this programme. [Para 10.3.11]

(222) Residential schools for SCs and STs should be established in every district in the country – one each for SC boys and SC girls, and ST boys and ST girls, as one item of an important package of comprehensive measures required for the development and empowerment of SCs and STs. Similarly, the Commission recommends that residential schools should be set up for the BCs in every district, one each for BC boys and BC girls, including minorities who belong to BCs and with special attention to More Backward and Most Backward classes among BCs. The proportion of the students of the specific category of weaker sections (say 75%) and of other social categories (say 25%), the principles of location, methodology of covering the Minority B.C., phasing and funding, mode of selection of the candidates, management etc. should be as detailed in paras 5.4 and 6.2 at pages 1395 to 1397 of Book 3 of Volume II. This system has got the support of the precedent and experience for the last two decades in Andhra Pradesh state, providing ground for hope in this important and indispensable measure. In addition, the Commission recommends that it is also necessary to see that the SCs, STs and BCs especially the More and Most Backward classes of BCs from poor and middle-class families get due benefit of good and prestigious private educational institutions in the country as well as in foreign educational institutions at all levels and in all disciplines, at state cost. Funding for this can be found by measures outlined in sub-para (v) of para 5.4 at page 1396 of Book 3 of Volume II. The measures detailed in sub-para (ii) and (iv) of para 5.4 at pages 1395 and 1396 of Book 3 of Volume II should be followed in the matter. [Para 10.4.1]

(223) Incentives should be offered to students to prepare for such courses of study in technical, vocational, scientific and professional disciplines. Only a massive transfer of resources to the educational programmes for the Scheduled Castes and Scheduled Tribes will enable us to achieve the kind of quantitative expansion needed to bring these communities on par with others in terms of skills and knowledge base to engage with the modern world. It is only then that they would be in a position to compete on the basis of their own strength and rise to the leadership role in different spheres of public life. This aspect of measures for building

up a reservoir of highly educated professional, scientific and technological manpower among these categories in population equivalent proportion should be borne in mind along with its earlier recommendations regarding residential schools of high quality and elementary education, and provisions and outlays should be made accordingly. [Para 10.4.3]

(224) Social policy should aim at enabling the SCs, STs and BCs (including BC minorities and especially the More and Most Backward Classes among BCs) and with particular attention to the girls in each of these categories to compete on equal terms with the general category. This was always necessary but this becomes more important and increasingly urgent in the context of a knowledge society that is emerging. Reservation has helped the above deprived categories to enter state educational institutions from which they had been debarred and/or otherwise excluded in the past. Reservation continues to be necessary since these adverse factors have not ceased to exist. But with the growth of high quality educational institutions built up by the wealthier sections, almost entirely drawn from non-SC, non-ST, non-BC categories, as a high quality stream distinct and separate from the state educational system, it becomes important to ensure that other measures in addition to reservations are introduced. Without these measures, along with the Commissions recommendations on elementary education, the gap between the SC, ST and BC on the one hand and the rest of society will inexorably continue and even be widened. [Para 10.4.4]

(225) The Employment of Manual Scavengers and Construction of Dry Latrines (Prohibition) Act, 1993, should be strictly enforced to bring to an early end to this degrading practice of manual scavenging so offensive to human dignity without abridgement of the employment and income of existing *Safai Karamcharis*. Automatic applicability of the Act to all States should be brought about by the amendment suggested in para 7.2 at page 1399 of Book 3 of Volume II. Further, the specifics and details of the abolition of the manual scavenging system and the liberation and rehabilitation of *safai karamcharis* and protection of *safai karamcharis* during the transition period should be as detailed in para 7.3 of pages 1399 to 1401 of Book 3 of Volume II, including its incorporation in the System of Social Justice Clearance of officers at the time of their consideration for promotion.

Limitations placed on the National Commission for *Safai Karamcharis* should be removed and it should be given the same powers and functional autonomy as is being enjoyed by the National Human Rights Commission; it should be adequately equipped to achieve its objective of total liberation and full rehabilitation of *safai karamcharis*. This should form an integral part of a National Sanitation Policy-cum-National Social Justice Policy. [Para 10.5]

(226) The bleak situation will continue to bedevil the SCs and STs and the nation unless appropriate new institutions are created to take charge of the full quantum of outlay of SCP and TSP (i.e. outlay not less than the population equivalent proportion of the total plan outlay of the Centre/each State) and manned by competent experts of SCs and STs and others genuinely working for them, to formulate Plans in accordance with the developmental needs and priorities of the SCs and STs and ensure that these plans are implemented effectively. This new institutional system should consist of an integrated network of National Development Council for SCs and STs, and National SCs and STs Development Authority, State SCs and STs Development Authorities and District SCs and STs Development Authorities. Out of the total plan outlay of the Centre and of each State, before sectoral allocations are made, an outlay equivalent to the population proportion of SCs and STs should be placed at the disposal of the National and respective State Authorities, as the corpus of SCP and TSP for formulation of plans in accordance with the needs and priorities of SC & ST. For this, the system as detailed in para 9.2 at pages 1409 to 1411 of Book-3, Volume-II should be established. The schemes as illustrated in sub-para (9) of para 9.2 at pages 1410-1411 of Book-3, Volume-II should also be taken up on a massive scale. This will at one stroke remove the various limitations and difficulties faced by the SCP and TSP and create a powerful, integrated instrument of social transformation based on the vision of economic liberation, educational equality and social dignity of the SCs and STs. [Para 10.6.2]

(227) Land reforms involving distribution and allotment of lands from different sources (i.e. Government lands not required for genuine public use, *Bhoodan* lands, ceiling surplus lands, etc.) to the SCs and STs along with supportive mechanism in the shape

of supply of subsidised capital and credit and extension be made, and development of these lands through irrigation and other means be undertaken. In this context, the measures recommended at (b) of sub-para (9) of para 9.2 at page 1410 of Book-3, Volume-II and in para 14 (i) to (vi) at pages 1416 to 1417 of Book-3, Volume-II should be implemented. Similarly, with regard to enforcement of the Minimum Wages Act for agricultural labour, the methodology recommended at (c) of sub-para (9) of para 9.2 of page 1410 Book-3, Volume-II should be followed. Strong legal action is needed to prevent alienation of lands belonging to the tribal communities and effective prior rehabilitation of tribals before displacement due to developmental projects. For this purpose, the measures listed in para 13.2 at pages 1414 to 1415 of Book-3, Volume-II should be undertaken. Additionally, the tribal communities have to be associated with the management of forest resources, for not only their livelihoods, but also for protecting their way of life and cultural identity which are indissolubly linked to forests. For this purpose, action as recommended in sub-paras (10) and (11) of para 13.2 at page 1416 of Book-3, Volume-II should be taken. [Para 10.7.1]

(228) In the matter of harmonising the preservation of the land ownership of STs, industrial and other development, action should be taken as outlined in sub-paras (6), (8) and (9) of para 13.2 of pages 1415 to 1416 of Book-3, Volume-II. [Para 10.7.2]

(229) Special safeguards should be provided to protect the wholesome traditions of the cultural heritage and of the intellectual property rights of the tribal people. This is no less important for the tribal identity than the effort to prevent alienation of land and land-related institutional rights of tribal people. [Para 10.7.3]

(230) *All areas governed by the Fifth Schedule to the Constitution should be forthwith transferred to the Sixth Schedule extending the applicability of the Sixth Schedule to tribal areas other than the North Eastern States to which alone the Sixth Schedule now applies, and all tribal areas which are neither in the Fifth Schedule nor in the Sixth Schedule should also be brought forthwith under the Sixth Schedule.* Special programmes of training and orientation for the elected representatives of the Sixth Schedule bodies and related officials should be undertaken and conducted regularly in order to secure the full potential of local developmental and

administrative autonomy envisaged under the Sixth Schedule. [Para 10.7.4]

(231) The Government should step in firmly and clearly, if the gap is to be bridged between private prejudices, in the name of "efficiency" on the one hand and the just aspirations of the SC, ST, BC including BC minorities, and women. For this, the Government should take the initiative along the lines suggested in para 11.3 at pages 1412 and 1413 of Book-3, Volume-II. [Para 10.7.5]

(232) Further, the Government should examine other economic and activity sectors at every level of each such sector and see whether the SCs and STs are adequately represented in each of them. If they are not, remedial measures either through reservation or through other means should be undertaken to see that they are adequately represented at every level in every such sector. Similar action should also be taken with regard to backward classes including BC minorities, especially More and Most Backward Classes and women of all categories. This is possible, if non-economic prejudices are excluded, without watering down the genuine requirements of efficiency. [Para 10.7.6]

(233) Agriculturists and other traditional producing classes face certain adverse effects of sudden and unprepared exposure to the regimes of WTO, IPR, etc. In order to protect them from these adverse effects while at the same time to secure the benefits of those regimes, a national convention should be convened involving Ministers in charge of Ministries connected with globalisation and Ministers in charge of Agriculture and other sectors of traditional produce and authentic representatives of the peasant organizations as well as organisations of other traditional producing classes, to identify remedial steps arrive at a consensus about them and these should be implemented quickly. There should be a continuing mechanism involving all these to continuously monitor implementation and corrections and modifications required from time to time. [Para 10.7.7]

(234) Agriculturists and many other traditional producing classes suffer from the adverse effects of natural calamities like drought, cyclone, floods, etc. A similar national convention should identify the measures required to protect them from such adverse effects of natural calamities including crop insurance, preparedness etc., arrive at a consensus about these measures and institute a

continuing machinery of continuous monitoring and corrections and modifications. [Para 10.7.8]

(235) On the one hand, there should be an effective legal structure to protect the SCs and STs against atrocities and discriminatory practices based on untouchability and along with such structure and its efficient functioning and on the other hand, there should also be attitudinal change of a profound nature in the general society. [Para 10.8.1]

(236) With regard to legal structure, the Scheduled Castes and Scheduled Tribes (Prevention of Atrocities) Act, 1989 needs to be strengthened and its effective enforcement ensured. This include the establishment of special courts exclusively to try offences under this Act, inclusion of certain crimes in the list of atrocities, certain penal provisions where they do not exist, appropriate plugging of certain loopholes and comprehensive rehabilitation of victims and so on. For this purpose, the measures suggested in para 8.2.1, 8.2.2, 8.2.3, 8.3 and 8.4 (a) to (p) of Book-3, Vol. II at pages 1401 to 1404 should be taken. [Para 10.8.2]

(237) Regarding untouchability which continues to be widely prevalent in old classic forms as well as in new forms in line with modern developments, multi-pronged measures covering human rights education, moral education, building up of a strong democratic movement against untouchability and effective punitive action under the Protection of Civil Right Acts, 1955 (PCR Act) are required. In view of this, the entire gamut of measures suggested in paras 8.6 to 8.8 at pages 1404 and 1405, Book-3, Vol. II should be taken. [Para 10.8.3]

(238) The National Science and Technology Commission referred to in Chapter 6 should also promote measures for extending the umbrella of modern science and technology and higher scientific and technological research to cover SCs, STs and BCs, women and other poor sections of the society, devise means by which they can also be introduced into this field and potential talent among them identified and nurtured so that they also are enabled to contribute to the advancement of higher scientific and technological research in the country and so that there is no feeling that they are shut out from this important area on account of non-scientific prejudices. [Para 10.9]

(239) The Constitution of India contains distinct provisions for the protection and promotion of the interests of Scheduled

Castes and Scheduled Tribes, Backward classes, women, minorities and other weaker sections. It is necessary to strengthen these provisions by amendments, etc. and certain other similar steps. Accordingly, *the amendments to the Constitution listed in para 15 at pages 1417 and 1418 of Book-3, Vol. II, covering articles 46, 335, 16, 15 and List III of the Seventh Schedule should be carried out.* [Para 10.10]

(240) As regards the minorities, the following shall be implemented:

(a) Steps should be taken for improvement of educational standards amongst the minority communities. Special programmes should be drawn up after the widest consultation with the leaders of minority communities including leaders of BCs, SCs and STs among Minorities from academic, professional, business, and socio-political spheres and from low-occupational spheres. Such programmes should be generously funded. Only educational and cultural advancement will help the cause of national integration as well as raise the capabilities of the communities. This is the high road to national cohesion.

(b) At present the political representation of minority communities in legislatures, especially Muslims, has fallen well below their proportion of population. The proportion of BCs among them is next to nil. This can lead to a sense of alienation. It is recommended that in situations of this kind, it is incumbent for political parties to build up leadership potential in the minority communities, including BCs, SCs and STs among them, for participation in political life. The role of the state for strengthening the pluralism of Indian polity has to be emphasised.

(c) Backward classes belonging to religious minorities who have been identified and included in the list of backward classes and who, in fact, constitute the bulk of the population of religious minorities should be taken up with special care along with their Hindu counterparts in the developmental efforts for the backward classes. This should be on the pattern of the approach to the development of Backward Classes formulated by the

Working Group for the Development and Empowerment of Backward Classes in the Tenth Plan referred to separately under Backward Classes.

(d) An effort needs to be made to carry out special recruitment of persons belonging to the underrepresented minority communities in the police forces of States, para-military forces and armed forces. [Para 10.11.2]

(241) In every State, the linguistic minorities should be provided the facility of having instruction for their children at elementary stage of education in their mother tongue. Numerous recommendations in this behalf and other matters have been made by the Commissioner for Linguistic Minorities in his successive Annual Reports regarding the various problems faced by the linguistic minorities. The Government of India in the Ministry of Social Justice and Empowerment and the Ministry of Human Resources Development should collate all these recommendations and see that substantive action is taken on each of them. [Para 10.11.3]

(242) The denotified tribes/communities have been wrongly stigmatized as crime-prone and subjected to highhanded treatment as well as exploitation by the representatives of law and order as well as by the general society. Some of them are included in the list of Scheduled Tribes and others are in the list of Scheduled Castes and list of backward classes. The special approach to their development has been delineated and emphasized in the Reports of the Working Groups for the Development of Scheduled Tribes, Scheduled Castes and Backward Classes in successive Plans and also in the Annual Reports of the Commissioners for Scheduled Castes and Scheduled Tribes, National Commission for Scheduled Castes and Scheduled Tribes and the National Commission for Backward Classes. There are also special reports available on de-notified tribes. Their recommendations have not received attention. The Ministry of Social Justice and Empowerment and the Ministry of Tribal Welfare should collate all these materials and recommendations contained in the reports of the working groups and the reports of the National Commissions and other reports referred to and strengthen the programmes for the economic development, educational development, generation of

employment opportunities, social liberation and full rehabilitation of denotified tribes. Whatever has been said about vimukta jatis also holds good for nomadic and semi-nomadic tribes/ communities. Similar action should be taken in respect of nomadic and semi-nomadic tribes/communities as done in the case of de-notified tribes or *vimukta jatis*. The continued plight of these groups of communities distributed in the list of Scheduled Castes, Scheduled Tribes and backward classes is an eloquent illustration of the failure of the machinery for planning, financial resources allocation and budgeting and administration in the country to seriously follow the mandate of the Constitution including article 46. The setting up of an integrated network of National Scheduled Castes and Scheduled Tribes Development Authority, etc. recommended in para 10.5.2 to 10.5.3 will provide a structural mechanism to deal in a practical way with *the vimukta jatis* as well as nomadic and semi-nomadic tribes/communities within the framework of the SCP and TSP. Similarly, the approach to the development of backward classes referred to at para 10.14 contains the approach to deal in a practical way with the *Vimukta jatis* and nomadic and semi-nomadic tribes/communities who are in Backward Class list. [Para 10.12.1]

(243) The Commission also considered the representations made on behalf of the De-notified and Nomadic Tribal Rights Action Group and decided to forward them to the Ministry of Social Justice & Empowerment with the suggestion that they may examine the same preferably through a Commission. [Para 10.12.2]

(244) The Union legislation for agricultural workers, drafted as far back as 1978-80, should be introduced and passed immediately. A realistic scheme of credible implementation of Minimum Wages Acts with particular attention to agricultural labours, relying to a suitable degree on the District Collectors/Dy. Commissioners and District Superintendents of Police, should be immediately put into action. For this purpose the measures suggested in para 17.2 at page 1413 of Book 3 Vol. II should be followed. [Para 10.13.2]

(245) Despite prohibition of *begar* and other forms of forced labour by the Constitution, the practice of bonded labour has not ended as it is patronised by the most powerful sections in the rural areas. Child labour too is widespread. In order to deal

effectively with this problem in keeping with the mandate of the Constitution, the Commission recommends that a fully empowered National Authority for the Liberation and Rehabilitation of bonded labour, as recommended by the Commission for Rural Labour in 1990-91, should be set up immediately along with similar authorities at the State level. In addition, simultaneous rehabilitation of released Bonded Labourers and education for released bonded child labourers and other measures referred to in para 19.2 at page 1414 of Book 3, Vol. II should be taken. [Para 10.14]

(246) The Government should immediately implement everyone of the recommendations of the Working Group on Employment of Backward Classes in the Tenth Plan which covers all aspects and fields of their development – economic, educational, social, employment, reservation, etc. – taking in with particular care those backward classes who belong to religious minorities along with their Hindu counterparts in a cohesive manner. For example, some of the residential talent schools earmarked for Backward Classes should be located in areas of concentration of Muslim B.Cs. Further there should be residential talent schools for backward classes as separately recommended for SCs and STs at the rate of one each for boys and girls in each district, 75 per cent being taken from backward classes and 25 per cent from other categories. The Government should without any delay introduce reservation for backward classes in seats in educational institutions since absence of promotion of their education through reservation and other means when there is reservation of employment is anomalous. [Para 10.15]

(247) Action in accordance with the suggestions made in para 16.2 at page 1412 of Book 3 Vol. II, covering reservation, development, empowerment, health including malnutrition and maternal anaemia and protection against violence should be taken. [Para 10.16]

(248) The problems relating to prostitution, child prostitutes and children of prostitutes have been the subject of a landmark judgment of the Supreme Court in Gaurav Jain's case of 9th July, 1997 and the Report of Committee of Secretaries on Prostitution, Child Prostitutes and children of Prostitutes set up in 1997 as explained in para 20.1 and 20.2 at pages 1414 to 1415 of Book 3

Vol. II. In respect of this area of problem, the Government should take action according to the suggestion listed at para 20.3 at page 1415 of Book 3 of Vol. II, covering implementation of the judgement and the Secretaries' report, eliminating the Devadasi system, provision of development and education and prevention of HIV/AIDS.

C. The Second Administrative Reforms Commission [ARC]

The Second ARC Chairman M. Veerappa Moily had rightly recommended *inter alia* that:

(a) States should ensure that Gram Panchayats are of an appropriate size to make them viable units of local self-government;
(b) the ward sabha should provide a platform where people can directly discuss their needs and prepare area-specific local plans;
(c) state governments should not have the power to suspend or rescind any resolution passed by the Panchayati Raj Institutions or take action against the elected representatives or to supersede/dissolve the panchayats. The powers to investigate and recommend action should lie with the local Ombudsman;
(d) the flow of funds for all public development schemes in rural areas should be exclusively routed through panchayats with Local Area Development Authorities and other organizations having similar functions should be wound up and their functions and assets transferred to the appropriate level of the panchayat;
(e) Members of Parliament Local Area Development (MPLAD) and Members of Legislative Assembly Local Area Development (MLALAD) should be abolished; and the centrally sponsored schemes have to shed their separate vertical identity and be part of the overall development plan of the Panchayati Raj system. Details of the Government's decisions of the ARC on the recommendations and 'Action taken' has been reproduced hereunder.

ARC'S 6TH REPORT TITLED "LOCAL GOVERNANCE—AN INSPIRING JOURNEY INTO THE FUTURE" DETAILS OF THE GOVERNMENT'S DECISIONS ON THE RECOMMENDATIONS AND 'ACTION TAKEN' THEREON

Sl. No.	*Recommendations made by Administrative Reforms Commission*	*Government's Decision*
1.	**1. (Para 3.1.1.12) The Principle of Subsidiarity** a. Article 243G should be amended as follows: "Subject to the provisions of this Constitution, the Legislature of a State shall, by law, vest a Panchayat at the appropriate level with such powers and authority as are necessary to enable them to function as institutions of self-government in respect of all functions which can be performed at the local level including the functions in respect of the matters listed in the Eleventh Schedule". **(1)**	(a) Not accepted.
2.	b. Article 243 W should be similarly amended to empower urban local bodies **(2)**	(b) Not accepted.
3.	**2. (Para 3.1.2.4) Strengthening the Voice of Local Bodies** a. Parliament may by law provide for constitution of a Legislative Council in each State, consisting of members elected by the local governments. **(3)**	(a) Not accepted.
4.	**3. (Para 3.1.3.11) Structure of Local Bodies** a. Article 243B(1) should be amended to read as follows: "There shall be constituted in every State, as the State Legislature may by law provide, Panchayats at appropriate levels in accordance with the provisions of this part". **(4)**	(a) Not accepted.
5.	b. The Constitutional provisions relating to reservation of seats (Article 243D) must be retained in the current form to	(b) Accepted. Article 243D would be retained in its present form

Sl. No.	*Recommendations made by Administrative Reforms Commission*	*Government's Decision*
	ensure adequate representation to the underprivileged sections and women. **(5)**	
6.	c. Members of Parliament and State Legislatures should not become members of local bodies. **(6)**	(c) Not accepted.
7.	d. Article 243C (1) should be retained. **(7)**	(d) Accepted
8.	e. Article 243C (2 & 3) should be repealed and supplanted by Article 243C (2) as follows: *243C (2) Subject to the provisions of this part, the Legislature of a State may, by law, make provisions with respect to composition of Panchayats and the manner of elections provided that in any tier there shall be direct election of at least one of the two offices of Chairperson or members:* *Provided that in case of direct elections of members in any tier, the ratio between the population of the territorial area of a Panchayat at any level and the number of seats in such Panchayat to be filled by election shall, so far as practicable, be the same throughout the State. Also, each Panchayat area shall be divided into territorial constituencies in such manner that the ratio between the population of each constituency and the number of seats allotted to it shall, so far as practicable, be the same throughout the Panchayat area.* ***(8)***	(e) to (g) Not accepted.
9.	f. There shall be a District Council in every district with representation from both urban and rural areas. **(9)**	
10.	g. 243B(2) should be substituted by: *"There shall be constituted in every District, a District Council representing all rural and urban areas in the District and exercising powers and functions in accordance with the provisions of Articles 243 G and 243 W of the Constitution."* ***(10)***	

Sl. No.	*Recommendations made by Administrative Reforms Commission*	*Government's Decision*
	4. (Para 3.2.1.12) The Electoral Process	
11.	a. The task of delimitation and reservation of constituencies should be entrusted to the State Election Commissions (SECs); **(11)**	(a) to (d) Accepted.
12.	b. Local government laws in all States should provide for adoption of the Assembly electoral rolls for local governments without any revision of names by SECs. For such a process to be effective it is necessary to ensure that the voter registration and preparation of electoral rolls by Election Commission of India is based on geographic contiguity. Similarly the electoral divisions for elections to local bodies should follow the Building Blocks approach; **(12)**	
13.	c. The Registration of Electors Rules, 1960, should be amended to define a 'Part' as a compact geographical unit.**(13)**	
14.	d. In order to achieve convergence between census data and electoral rolls, the boundaries of a 'Part' and an 'Enumeration Block' should coincide. **(14)**	
15.	e. Reservation of seats should follow any one of the two principles mentioned below: **(15)** i. In case of single-member constituencies, the rotation can be after at least 2 terms of 5 years each so that there is possibility of longevity of leadership and nurturing of constituencies. ii. Instead of single-member constituencies, elections can be held to multi-member constituencies by the List System, ensuring the reservation of seats. This will obviate the need for rotation thus guaranteeing allocation of seats for the reserved categories.	(e) Alternative (ii)) was not accepted
16.	f. The conduct of elections for the elected members of District and Metropolitan	(f) Accepted.

Sl. No.	*Recommendations made by Administrative Reforms Commission*	*Government's Decision*
	Planning Committees should be entrusted to the State Election Commission. **(16)**	
	5. **(Para 3.2.2.6) Constitution of the State Election Commission**	(a) & (b) Accepted.
17.	a. The State Election Commissioner should be appointed by the Governor on the recommendation of a collegium, comprising the Chief Minister, the Speaker of the State Legislative Assembly and the Leader of Opposition in the Legislative Assembly. **(17)**	
18.	b. An institutional mechanism should be created to bring the Election Commission of India and the SECs on a common platform for coordination, learning from each other's experiences and sharing of resources. **(18)**	
19.	6. **(Para 3.2.3.4) Correcting the Urban Rural Imbalance in Representation in Legislative Bodies** a. In order to set right the electoral imbalance between the urban and rural population in view of rapid urbanisation, an adjustment of the territorial constituencies - both for the Lok Sabha and the Legislative Assembly – within a State should be carried out after each census. Articles 81, 82, 170, 330 and 332 of the Constitution would need to be amended. **(19)**	(a) Not accepted.
	7. **(Para 3.3.1.7) Devolution of Powers and Responsibilities**	
20.	a. There should be clear delineation of functions for each level of local government in the case of each subject matter law. This is not a one-time exercise and has to be done continuously while working out locally relevant socio-economic programmes, restructuring organisations and framing subject-matter laws. **(20)**	(a) to (c) Accepted.

Sl. No.	Recommendations made by Administrative Reforms Commission	Government's Decision
21.	b. Each subject-matter law, which has functional elements that are best attended to at local levels, should have provision for appropriate devolution to such levels – either in the law or in subordinate legislation. All the relevant Union and State laws have to be reviewed urgently and suitably amended. **(21)**	
22.	c. In the case of new laws, it will be advisable to add a 'local government memorandum' (on the analogy of financial memorandum and memorandum of subordinate legislation) indicating whether any functions to be attended to by local governments are involved and if so, whether this has been provided for in the law. **(22)**	
23.	d. In case of urban local bodies, in addition to the functions listed in the Twelfth Schedule, the following should be devolved to urban local bodies: – School education; – Public health, including community health centres/area hospitals; – Traffic management and civic policing activities; – Urban environment management and heritage; and – Land management, including registration. These, however, are only illustrative additional functions and more such functions could be devolved to urban local bodies by the respective States. **(23)**	(d) Accepted.
24.	**8. (Para 3.4.20) Framework Law for Local Bodies** a. Government of India should draft and place before Parliament, a Framework Law for local governments. The Framework Law could be enacted under Article 252 of the Constitution on the lines of the South African Act, for the States to adopt. This Law should lay down the broad principles of devolution of powers,	(a) Not accepted.

Sl. No.	*Recommendations made by Administrative Reforms Commission*	*Government's Decision*
	responsibilities and functions to the local governments and communities, based on the following: • Principle of Subsidiarity • Democratic Decentralisation • Delineation of Functions • Devolution in Real Terms • Convergence • Citizen Centricity. **(24)**	
	9. (Para 3.5.2.18) The State Finance Commission (SFC)	
25.	a. This Commission endorses and reiterates the views of the Twelfth Finance Commission regarding the working of the SFCs as listed in paragraph 3.5.2.8. **(25)**	(a) to (j) Accepted.
26.	b. Article 243 I (1) of the Constitution should be amended to include the phrase "at such earlier time" after the words "every fifth year". **(26)**	
27.	c. Each State should prescribe through an Act, the qualifications of persons eligible to be appointed as Members of the State Finance Commission. **(27)**	
28.	d. SFCs should evolve objective and transparent norms for devolution and distribution of funds. The norms should include area-wise indices for backwardness. State Finance Commissions should link the devolution of funds to the level/quality of civic amenities that the citizens could expect. This could then form the basis of an impact evaluation. **(28)**	
29.	e. The Action Taken Report on the recommendations of the SFC must compulsorily be placed in the concerned State Legislature within six months of submission and followed with an annual statement on the devolution made and grants given to individual local bodies and the implementation of other recommendations through an appendix to the State budget documents. **(29)**	

Sl. No.	*Recommendations made by Administrative Reforms Commission*	*Government's Decision*
30.	f. Incentives can be built into devolution from the Union to the States to take care of the need to improve devolution from the States to the third tier of governments. **(30)**	
31.	g. Common formats, as recommended by the Twelfth Finance Commission (TFC) must be adopted, and annual accounts and other data must be compiled and updated for use by the SFCs. **(31)**	
32.	h. SFCs should carry out a more thorough analysis of the finances of local bodies and make concrete recommendations for improvements in their working. In case of smaller local bodies such recommendations could be broad in nature, but in case of larger local bodies, recommendations should be more specific. With historical data being available with the SFC, and with the improvement in efficiency of data collection, the SFC would be in a position to carry out the required detailed analysis. The special needs of large urban agglomerations particularly the Metropolitan cities should be specially addressed by the SFC. **(32)**	
33.	i. SFCs should evolve norms for staffing of local bodies. **(33)**	
34.	j. It is necessary that a mechanism be put in place which reviews the implementation of all the recommendations of the SFCs. If considered necessary, devolution of funds could be made conditional to local bodies agreeing to implement the recommendations of the SFCs. **(34)**	
35.	**10. (Para 3.6.16) Capacity Building for Self-Governance** a. Capacity building efforts in rural and urban local self-governing institutions must attend to both the organisation building requirements as also the professional and skills upgradation of individuals associated with these	(a) to (g) Accepted.

Sl. No.	Recommendations made by Administrative Reforms Commission	Government's Decision
	bodies, whether elected or appointed. Relevant Panchayat and Municipal legislations and manuals framed thereunder must contain clear enabling provisions in this respect. There should be special capacity building programmes for women members. **(35)**	
36.	b. State Governments should encourage local bodies to outsource specific functions to public or private agencies, as may be appropriate, through enabling guidelines and support. Outsourcing of activities should be backed by development of in-house capacity for monitoring and oversight of outsourced activities. Likewise, transparent and fair procurement procedures need to be put in place by the State Government to improve fiscal discipline and probity in the local bodies. **(36)**	
37.	c. Comprehensive and holistic training requires expertise and resources from various subject matter specific training institutes. This can be best achieved by 'networking' of institutions concerned with various subjects such as financial management, rural development, disaster management and general management. This should be ensured by the nodal agencies in State Governments. **(37)**	
38.	d. As an aid to capacity building, suitable schemes need to be drawn up under State Plans for Rural and Urban Development for documentations of case studies, best practices and evaluation with reference to the performance of the prescribed duties and responsibilities of such bodies. **(38)**	
39.	e. Training of elected representatives and personnel should be regarded as	

Sl. No.	Recommendations made by Administrative Reforms Commission	Government's Decision
	a continuing activity. Expenditure requirement on training may be taken into account by the State Finance Commissions while making recommendations. **(39)**	
40.	f. Academic research has a definite role to play in building long-term strategic institutional capacity for greater public good. Organisations like the Indian Council of Social Science Research must be encouraged to fund theoretical, applied and action research on various aspects of the functioning of local bodies. **(40)**	
41.	g. A pool of experts and specialists (e.g. engineers, planners etc.) could be maintained by a federation/consortium of local bodies. This common pool could be then accessed by the local bodies whenever required for specific tasks. **(41)**	
	11. (Para 3.7.5.6) Decentralised Planning	
42.	a. A District Council should be constituted in all districts with representation from rural and urban areas. It should be empowered to exercise the powers and functions in accordance with Articles 243G and 243W of the Constitution. In that event, the DPCs will either not exist or become, at best, an advisory arm of the District Council. Article 243 (d) of the Constitution should be amended to facilitate this. **(42)**	(a) Not accepted.
43.	b. In the interim and in accordance with the present constitutional scheme, DPCs should be constituted in all States within three months of completion of elections to local bodies and should become the sole planning body for the district. The DPC should be assisted by a planning office with a full time District Planning Officer. **(43)**	(b) to (h) Accepted. It was noted that the Planning Commission had already issued guidelines which the States need to implement.
44.	c. For urban districts where town planning functions are being done by Development	

Sl. No.	*Recommendations made by Administrative Reforms Commission*	*Government's Decision*
	Authorities, these authorities should become the technical/planning arms of the DPCs and ultimately of the District Council. **(44)**	
45.	d. A dedicated centre in every district should be set up to provide inputs to the local bodies for preparations of plans. A two-way flow of information between different levels of government may also be ensured. **(45)**	
46.	e. The guidelines issued by the Planning Commission pertaining to the preparation of the plan for the district and the recommendations of the Expert Group regarding the planning process at the district level should be strictly implemented. **(46)**	
47.	f. Each State Government should develop the methodology of participatory local level planning and provide such support as is necessary to institutionalize a regime of decentralised planning. **(47)**	
48.	g. States may design a planning calendar prescribing the time limits within which each local body has to finalise its plan and send it to the next higher level, to facilitate the preparation of a comprehensive plan for the district. **(48)**	
49.	h. State Planning Boards should ensure that the district plans are integrated with the State plans that are prepared by them. It should be made mandatory for the States to prepare their development plans only after consolidating the plans of the local bodies. The National Planning Commission has to take the initiative in institutionalising this process. **(49)** **(Para 3.7.6.2.4)**	
50.	a. The function of planning for urban areas has to be clearly demarcated among the local bodies and planning committees. The local bodies should be responsible for plans at the layout level. The	(a) to (e): Accepted.

Sl. No.	Recommendations made by Administrative Reforms Commission	Government's Decision
	DPCs/District Councils – when constituted – and MPCs should be responsible for preparation of regional and zonal plans. The level of public consultation should be enhanced at each level. **(50)**	
51.	b. For metropolitan areas, the total area likely to be urbanised (the extended metropolitan region) should be assessed by the State Government and an MPC constituted for the same which may be deemed to be a DPC for such areas. As such an area will usually cover more than one district, DPCs for those districts should not be constituted (or their jurisdictions may be limited to the rural portion of the revenue district concerned). The MPCs should be asked to draw up a Master Plan/CDP for the entire metropolitan area including the peri-urban areas. **(51)**	
52.	c. The planning departments of the Development Authorities (DAs) should be merged with the DPCs and MPCs who will prepare the master plans and zonal plans. **(52)**	
53.	d. The task of enforcement and regulation of the master plans/CDPs drawn up by the MPCs should be the specific statutory responsibility of all the local bodies falling within the extended metropolitan region concerned. **(53)**	
54.	e. The monopoly role of Development Authorities (DAs) in development of land for urban uses, wherever it exists, should be done way with. However, public agencies should continue to play a major role in development of critical city level infrastructure as well as low cost housing for the poor. For this purpose, the engineering and land management departments of the DAs should be merged with the concerned Municipality/Corporation. **(54)**	

Sl. No.	*Recommendations made by Administrative Reforms Commission*	*Government's Decision*
	12. (Para 3.8.6) Accountability and Transparency	
55.	a. Audit committees may be constituted by the State Governments at the district level to exercise oversight regarding the integrity of financial information, adequacy of internal controls, compliance with the applicable laws and ethical conduct of all persons involved in local bodies. These committees must have independence, access to all information, ability to communicate with technical experts, and accountability to the public. For Metropolitan Corporations, separate audit committees should be constituted. Once the District Councils come into existence, a special committee of the District Council may examine the audit reports and other financial statements of the local bodies within the district. Such committee may also be authorised to fix responsibility for financial lapses. In respect of the audit reports of the District Council itself, a special committee of the Legislative Council may discharge a similar function. **(55)**	(a) to (j) Accepted except that the constitution of the District Council is not acceptable [11(a)] as it would alter the existing structure of PRIs.
56.	b. There should be a separate Standing Committee of the State Legislature for the local bodies. This Committee may function in the manner of a Public Accounts Committee. **(56)**	
57.	c. A local body Ombudsman should be constituted on the lines suggested below. The respective State Panchayat Acts and the Urban Local Bodies Acts should be amended to include provisions pertaining to the local body Ombudsman. i. Local body Ombudsman should be constituted for a group of districts to look into complaints of corruption and maladministration against functionaries of local bodies, both elected members and officials. For this, the term 'Public Servant' should be defined appropriately in the respective State legislations.	

Sl. No.	*Recommendations made by Administrative Reforms Commission*	*Government's Decision*
	ii. Local body Ombudsman should be a single member body appointed by a Committee consisting of the Chief Minister of the State, the Speaker of the State Legislative Assembly and the Leader of the Opposition in the Legislative Assembly. The Ombudsman should be selected from a panel of eminent persons of impeccable integrity and should not be a serving government official. iii. The Ombudsman should have the authority to investigate cases and submit reports to competent authorities for taking action. In case of complaints and grievances regarding corruption and maladministration against local bodies in general and its elected functionaries, the local body Ombudsman should send its report to the Lokayukta who shall forward it to the Governor of the State with its recommendations. In case of disagreement with the recommendations of the Ombudsman, the reasons must be placed in the public domain. iv. In case of a Metropolitan Corporation, a separate Ombudsman should be constituted. v. Time limits may be prescribed for the Ombudsman to complete its investigations into complaints. **(57)**	
58.	d. In case of complaints and grievances related to infringement of the law governing elections to these local bodies, leading to suspension/ disqualification of membership, the authority to investigate should lie with the State Election Commission who shall send its recommendations to the Governor of the State. **(58)**	
59.	e. In the hierarchy of functionaries under the control of local bodies, functions	

Sl. No.	*Recommendations made by Administrative Reforms Commission*	*Government's Decision*
	should be delegated to the lowest appropriate functionary in order to facilitate access to citizens. **(59)**	
60.	f. Each local body should have an in-house mechanism for redressal of grievances with set norms for attending and responding to citizens' grievances. **(60)**	
61.	g. For establishing robust social audit norms, every State Government must take immediate steps to implement the action points suggested in para 5.9.5 of the Report of the Expert Group on 'Planning at the Grass roots Level'. **(61)**	
62.	h. It should be ensured that suo motu disclosures under the Right to Information Act, 2005 should not be confined to the seventeen items provided in Section 4(1) of that Act but other subjects where public interest exists should also be covered. **(62)**	
63.	i. A suitable mechanism to evolve a system of benchmarking on the basis of identified performance indicators may be adopted by each State. Assistance of independent professional evaluators may be availed in this regard. **(63)**	
64.	j. Evaluation tools for assessing the performance of local bodies should be devised wherein citizens should have a say in the evaluation. Tools such as 'Citizens' Report Cards' may be introduced to incorporate a feedback mechanism regarding performance of local bodies. **(64)**	
	13. (Para 3.9.22) Accounting and Audit	
65.	a. The accounting system for the urban local bodies (ULBs) as provided in the National Municipal Accounts Manual (NMAM) should be adopted by the State Governments. **(65)**	(a) to (e) Accepted.
66.	b. The financial statements and balance sheet of the urban local bodies should be	

Sl. No.	Recommendations made by Administrative Reforms Commission	Government's Decision
	audited by an Auditor in the manner prescribed for audit of Government Companies under the Companies Act, 1956 with the difference that in the case of audit of these local bodies, the C&AG should prescribe guidelines for empanelment of the Chartered Accountants and the selection can be made by the State Governments within these guidelines. The audit to be done by the Local Fund Audit or the C&AG in discharge of their responsibilities would be in addition to such an audit. **(66)**	
67.	c. The existing arrangement between the Comptroller & Auditor General of India and the State Governments with regard to providing Technical Guidance and Supervision (TGS) over maintenance of accounts and audit of PRIs and ULBs should be institutionalised by making provisions in the State Laws governing local bodies. **(67)**	
68.	d. It should be ensured that the audit and accounting standards and formats for Panchayats are prepared in a way which is simple and comprehensible to the elected representatives of the PRIs. **(68)**	
69.	e. The independence of the Director, Local Fund Audit (DLFA) or any other agency responsible for audit of accounts of local bodies should be institutionalised by making the office independent of the State administration. The head of this body should be appointed by the State Government from a panel vetted by the C&AG. **(69)**	
70.	f. Release of Finance Commission Grants to the local bodies may be made conditional on acceptance of arrangements regarding technical supervision of the C&AG over audit of accounts of local bodies. **(70)**	(f) Not accepted
71.	g. Audit reports on local bodies should be placed before the State Legislature and	(g) to (k) Accepted.

Sl. No.	*Recommendations made by Administrative Reforms Commission*	*Government's Decision*
	these reports should be discussed by a separate committee of the State Legislature on the same lines as the Public Accounts Committee (PAC). **(71)**	
72.	h. Access to relevant information/records to DLFA/designated authority for conducting audit or the C&AG should be ensured by incorporating suitable provisions in the State Laws governing local bodies. **(72)**	
73.	i. Each State may ensure that the local bodies have adequate capacity to match with the standards of accounting and auditing. **(73)**	
74.	j. The system of outcome auditing should be gradually introduced. For this purpose the key indicators of performance in respect of a government scheme will need to be decided and announced in advance. **(74)**	
75.	k. To complement institutional audit arrangements, adoption and monitoring of prudent financial management practices in the local bodies should be institutionalised by the State Governments by legislating an appropriate law on Fiscal Responsibility for local Bodies. **(75)**	
76.	**14. (Para 3.10.1.2) Information and Communication Technology** a. Information and Communication Technology should be utilised by the local governments in process simplification, enhancing transparency and accountability and providing delivery of services through single window. **(76)**	(a) Accepted
	15. (Para 3.10.2.8) Space Technology	
77.	a. Space technology should be harnessed by the local bodies to create an information base and for providing services. **(77)**	(a) & (b) Accepted
78.	b. Local governments should become one point service centres for providing various web-based and satellite-based services. This would however require capacity building in the local governments. **(78)**	

Sl. No.	*Recommendations made by Administrative Reforms Commission*	*Government's Decision*
	16. (Para 4.1.3.5) Size of the Gram Panchayat	
79.	a. States should ensure that as far as possible Gram Panchayats should be of an appropriate size which would make them viable units of self-governance and also enable effective popular participation. This exercise will need to take into account local geographical and demographic conditions. **(79)**	(a) Accepted.
	17. (Para 4.1.4.4) Ward Sabha - its Necessity	
80.	a. Wherever there are large Gram Panchayats, States should take steps to constitute Ward Sabhas which will exercise in such Panchayats, certain powers and functions of the Gram Sabha and of the Gram Panchayat as may be entrusted to them. **(80)**	(a) Accepted.
	18. (Para 4.1.5.4) Personnel Management in PRIs	
81.	a. Panchayats should have power to recruit personnel and to regulate their service conditions subject to such laws and standards as laid down by the State Government. Evolution of this system should not be prolonged beyond three years. Until then, the Panchayats may draw upon, for defined periods, staff from departments/agencies of the State Government, on deputation. **(81)**	(a) & (b) Accepted. However, any fresh recruitment should not result in an increase in the overall administrative cost.
82.	b. In all States, a detailed review of the staffing pattern and systems, with a zero-based approach to PRI staffing, may be undertaken over the next one year in order to implement the policy of PRI ownership of staff. The Zila Parishads, particularly, should be associated with this exercise. **(82)**	
	19. (Para 4.1.6.8) PRIs and the State Government	
83.	a. The provisions in some State Acts regarding approval of the budget of a	(a) to (e) Accepted.

Sl. No.	*Recommendations made by Administrative Reforms Commission*	*Government's Decision*
	Panchayat by the higher tier or any other State authority should be abolished. **(83)**	
84.	b. State Governments should not have the power to suspend or rescind any resolution passed by the PRIs or take action against the elected representatives on the ground of abuse of office, corruption etc. or to supersede/dissolve the Panchayats. In all such cases, the powers to investigate and recommend action should lie with the local Ombudsman who will send his report through the Lokayukta to the Governor. **(84)**	
85.	c. For election infringements and other election related complaints, the authority to investigate should be the State Election Commission who will send its recommendations to the Governor. **(85)**	
86.	d. If, on any occasion, the State Government feels that there is need to take immediate action against the Panchayats or their elected representatives on one or more of the grounds mentioned in 'b' above, it should place the records before the Ombudsman for urgent investigation. In all such cases, the Ombudsman will send his report through Lokayukta to the Governor in a specified period. **(86)**	
87.	e. In all cases of disagreements with the recommendations made by the local Ombudsman/Lokayukta, the reasons will need to be placed in the public domain. **(87)**	
	20. (Para 4.1.7.8) Position of Parastatals	
88.	a. Parastatals should not be allowed to undermine the authority of the PRIs. **(88)**	(a) to (e) Accepted.
89.	b. There is no need for continuation of the District Rural Development Agency (DRDA). Following the lead taken by Kerala, Karnataka and West Bengal, the DRDAs in other States also should be	

Sl. No.	*Recommendations made by Administrative Reforms Commission*	*Government's Decision*
	merged with the respective District Panchayats (Zila Parishad). Similar action should be taken for the District Water and Sanitation Committee (DWSC). **(89)**	
90.	c. The District Health Society (DHS) and FFDA should be restructured to have an organic relationship with the PRIs. **(90)**	
91.	d. The Union and State Governments should normally not set up special committees outside the PRIs. However, if such specialised committees are required to be set up because of professional or technical requirements, and if their activities coincide with those listed in the Eleventh Schedule, they should, either function under the overall supervision and guidance of the Panchayats or their relationship with the PRIs should be worked out in consultation with the concerned level of Panchayat. **(91)**	
92.	e. Community level bodies should not be created by decisions taken at higher levels. If considered necessary the initiative for their creation should come from below and they should be accountable to PRIs. **(92)**	
	21. (Para 4.2.3.10) Activity Mapping	
93.	a. States must undertake comprehensive activity mapping with regard to all the matters mentioned in the Eleventh Schedule. This process should cover all aspects of the subject viz. planning, budgeting and provisioning of finances. The State Government should set up a task force to complete this work within one year. **(93)**	(a) Accepted.
94.	b. The Union Government will also need to take similar action with regard to Centrally Sponsored Schemes. **(94)**	(b) Accepted.
	22. (Para 4.2.4.2) Devolving Regulatory Functions to the Panchayats	
95.	a. Rural policing, enforcement of building byelaws, issue of birth, death, caste and	(a) & (b) Accepted. However, control of local bodies over police functions

Sl. No.	Recommendations made by Administrative Reforms Commission	Government's Decision
	residence certificates, issue of voter identity cards, enforcement of regulations pertaining to weights and measures are some of the regulatory functions which should be entrusted to Panchayats. Panchayats may also be empowered to manage small endowments and charities. This could be done by suitably modifying the laws relating to charitable endowments. **(95)**	was not agreed to.
96.	b. Regulatory functions which can be performed by the Panchayats should be identified and devolved on a continuous basis. **(96)**	
	23. (Para 4.3.5.3) Resource Generation by the Panchayats	
97.	a. A comprehensive exercise needs to be taken up regarding broadening and deepening of the revenue base of local governments. This exercise will have to simultaneously look into four major aspects of resource mobilisation viz. (i) potential for taxation (ii) fixation of realistic tax rates (iii) widening of tax base and (iv) improved collection. Government may incorporate this as one of the terms of reference of the Thirteenth Finance Commission. **(97)**	(a) to (j) Accepted.
98.	b. All common property resources vested in the Village Panchayats should be identified, listed and made productive for revenue generation. **(98)**	
99.	c. State Governments should by law expand the tax domain of Panchayats. Simultaneously it should be made obligatory for the Panchayats to levy taxes in this tax domain. **(99)**	
100	d. At the higher level, the local bodies could be encouraged to run/manage utilities such as transport, water supply and power distribution on a sound financial basis and viability. **(100)**	

Sl. No.	*Recommendations made by Administrative Reforms Commission*	*Government's Decision*
101	e. The expanded tax domain could inter alia include levies on registration of cattle, restaurants, large shops, hotels, cybercafés and tourist buses etc. **(101)**	
102	f. The role of State Governments should be limited to prescribing a band of rates for these taxes and levies. **(102)**	
103	g. PRIs should be given a substantial share in the royalty from minerals collected by the State Government. This aspect should be considered by the SFCs while recommending grants to the PRIs. **(103)**	
104	h. State Governments should consider empowering the PRIs to collect cess on the royalty from mining activities. In addition they should also be given power to impose and collect additional/special surcharge from such activities (mines/ minerals/plants). **(104)**	
105	i. Innovative steps taken by the States and the PRIs to augment their resources must be rewarded by linking Central Finance Commission and State Finance Commission grants to such measures. States may reward better performing PRIs through special incentives. **(105)**	
106	j. In the tax domain assigned to PRIs, Village Panchayats must have primary authority over taxation. However, where such taxation has inter-Panchayat remifications, the local government institutions at higher levels. - Intermediate Panchayat and Zila parishad could be given concurrent powers subject to a ceiling. Whenever a tax/fee is imposed by the higher tier, such taxes should be collected by the concerned Village Panchayats. **(106)**	
	24. (Para 4.3.7.5) Transfer of Funds to the Panchayats	
107	a. Except for the specifically tied, major	(a) to (e) Accepted.

Sl. No.	*Recommendations made by Administrative Reforms Commission*	*Government's Decision*
	Centrally Sponsored Schemes and special purpose programmes of the States, all other allocations to the Panchayati Raj Institutions should be in the form of untied funds. The allocation order should contain only a brief description of broad objectives and expected outcomes. **(107)**	
108	b. State Governments should modify their rules of financial business to incorporate the system of separate State and District sector budgets, the later indicating district-wise allocations. **(108)**	
109	c. There should be a separate Panchayat sector line in the State budget. **(109)**	
110	d. State Governments should make use of the software on "fund transfer to Panchayats" prepared by the Union Panchayati Raj Ministry for speedy transfer of funds. **(110)**	
111	e. State Governments should release funds to the Panchayats in such a manner that these institutions get adequate time to use the allocation during the year itself. The fund release could be in the form of equally spaced instalments. It could be done in two instalments; one at the beginning of the financial year and the other by the end of September of that year. **(111)**	
112	**25. (Para 4.3.8.2) PRIs and Access to Credit** a. For their infrastructure needs, the Panchayats should be encouraged to borrow from banks/financial institutions. The role of the State Government should remain confined only to fixing the limits of borrowing. **(112)**	(a) Accepted.
113	**26. (Para 4.3.9.5) Local Area Development Schemes** a. The flow of funds for all public development schemes in rural areas should be exclusively routed through Panchayats. Local Area Development Authorities, Regional Development Boards	(a) GoM deferred decision on recommendation relating to flow of funds.

Sl. No.	Recommendations made by Administrative Reforms Commission	Government's Decision
	and other organization having similar functions should immediately be wound up and their functions and assets transferred to the appropriate level of the Panchayat. **(113)**	
114	b. As recommended by the Commission in its report on "Ethics in Governance", the Commission reiterates that the schemes of MPLAD and MLALAD should be abolished. **(114)**	(b) Not accepted
	27. (Para 4.4.7) Rural Development	
115	a. The Commission while endorsing the views of the Expert Group on Planning at the Grass roots Level as given at Annexure-IV (2) to this Report, recommends that there has to be territorial/jurisdictional/functional convergence in implementing Centrally Sponsored Schemes. **(115)**	(a) to (d) Accepted.
116	b. The centrality of PRIs in these schemes must be ensured if they are to deal with the matters listed in the Eleventh Schedule. (i) In all such schemes, the Gram/Ward Sabha should be accepted as the most important/cutting edge participatory body for implementation, monitoring and audit of the programmes. (ii) Programme committees dealing with functions under the Eleventh Schedule and working exclusively in rural areas need to be subsumed by the respective panchayats and their standing bodies. Some others having wider roles may need to be restructured to have an organic relationship with the Panchayats. (iii) In the programmes, where the activities percolate to areas and habitations below a Panchayat/Ward level, a small local centre committee should be formed to support these activities. This Centre committee should be only a deliberative body with responsibility to provide regular feedback	

Sl. No.	*Recommendations made by Administrative Reforms Commission*	*Government's Decision*
	to the Gram Sabha/Ward Sabha and be accountable to it. **(116)**	
117	c. The Ministry sanctioning the programme should issue only broad guidelines leaving scope for implementational flexibility so as to ensure local relevance through active involvement of the Panchayats. **(117)**	
118	d. All Centrally Sponsored programmes should have properly demarcated goals and there should be a mechanism to assess their socio-economic impact over a given period of time. The NSSO may be suitably strengthened and assigned this task. **(118)**	
	28. (Para 4.4.8.6) Information, Education and Communication - IEC	
119	a. A multi-pronged approach using different modes of communication like the print media, the visual media, electronic media, folk art and plays etc. should be adopted to disseminate information and create awareness about Panchayati Raj. It should be ensured that there is a convergence in approach to achieve synergies and maximise reach. **(119)**	(a) to (c) Accepted.
120	b. The Union Ministry of Information and Broadcasting should devise a mechanism in consultation with the Union Ministry of Panchayati Raj, Ministry of Rural Development and Ministry of Agriculture and other concerned Ministries for effectively implementing this activity. **(120)**	
121	c. Rural broadcasting should become a full-fledged independent activity of the All India Radio. Rural broadcasting units should be based in the districts and the broadcasts should be primarily in the local language(s) prevalent in the district. These programmes should focus on issues related to Panchayati Raj Institutions, rural development, agriculture,	

Sl. No.	Recommendations made by Administrative Reforms Commission	Government's Decision
	Right to Information and relevant ones on public health, sanitation, education etc. **(121)**	
	29. (Para 4.5.4) Rule of Panchayats in Delivery of Services	
122.	a. In terms of the Eleventh Schedule of the Constitution, local level activities of elementary education, preventive and promotive health care, water supply, sanitation, environmental improvement and nutrition should immediately be transferred to the appropriate tiers of the PRIs. **(122)**	(a) & (b) Accepted.
123.	b. State Governments need to prepare an overarching Service Delivery Policy outlining the framework within which each department could lay down detailed guidelines for preparation of Service Delivery Plans. **(123)**	
	30. (Para 4.5.5.6) Resource Centre at the Village Level	
124	a. Steps should be taken to set up Information and Communication Technology (ICT) and Space Technology enabled Resource Centres at the Village and Intermediate Panchayat levels for local resource mapping and generation of local information base. **(124)**	(a) to (c) Accepted. However, it would need to be ensured that these Centres take into account the Department of Information Technology's initiative to set up 1,00,000 Common Service Centres (CSCs).
125	b. These Resource Centres should also be used for documenting local traditional knowledge and heritage. **(125)**	
126	c. Capacity building should be attempted at the local level by shifting the currently available post-school generalistic education to a skill and technology based system having focus on farm and animal husbandry practices, computer applications, commercial cropping and soil and water management. **(126)**	
	31. (Para 4.6.1.2.3) Local Government in the Fifth Schedule Areas	
127	a) The Union and State legislations that impinge on provisions of PESA should be immediately modified so as to bring them	(a) Accepted.

Sl. No.	Recommendations made by Administrative Reforms Commission	Government's Decision
	in conformity with the Act. **(127)**	
128	b) If any State exhibits reluctance in implementing the provisions of PESA, Government of India may consider issuing specific directions to it in accordance with the powers given to it under Proviso 3 of Part A of the Fifth Schedule. **(128)**	(b) Not accepted.
	32. (Para 4.6.1.4.4) Effective Implementation of PESA	
129	a. Regular Annual Reports from the Governor of every State as stipulated under the Fifth Schedule, Part A (3) of the Constitution must be given due importance. Such reports should be published immediately and placed in the public domain. **(129)**	(a) to (c) Accepted subject to the views of MHA being obtained in this matter.
130	b. In order to ensure that women are not marginalised in meetings of the Gram Sabha, there should be a provision in the PESA Rules and Guidelines that the quorum of a Gram Sabha meeting will be acceptable only when out of the members present, at least thirty-three per cent are women. **(130)**	
131	c. Each State should constitute a group to look into strengthening of the administrative machinery in Fifth Schedule areas. This group will need to go into the issues of (i) special administrative arrangements, (ii) provision of hardship pay, (iii) other incentives, and (iv) preferential treatment in accommodation and education. All expenditure in this regard should be treated as charged expenditure under Article 275 of the Constitution. **(131)**	
	33. (Para 4.6.1.5.3) Effictive Implementation of the Tribal Sub-Plan (TSP)	
132	a. Keeping in view the inadequacy of the past efforts, State Governments should form a special planning unit (consisting of professionals and technically qualified personnel) to prepare their Tribal-Sub Plan. **(132)**	(a) to (c) Accepted subject to consultation with the Ministry of Finance and the Ministry of Tribal Affairs on the recommendations.

Sl. No.	Recommendations made by Administrative Reforms Commission	Government's Decision
133	b. A certain portion of the allocation under TSP should be made non-lapsable on the pattern of the Non Lapsable Central Pool of Resources (NLCPR) created for the North-Eastern States. A special cell may be set up in the Ministry of Tribal Affairs to monitor expenditure from this fund. **(133)**	
134	c. The government may consider preparing an impact assessment report every year with respect to the States covered under PESA. This exercise may be assigned to a national level institute which has done similar work in the past e.g. National Council for Applied Economic Research (NCAER), National Institute of Public Finance and Policy (NIPFP), National Sample Survey Organisation (NSSO) or some other suitable agency. This agency will rate the performance of the State on predetermined indices. **(134)**	
	34. (Para 5.1.4) Urbanisation and Growth	
135	a. A new National Commission on Urbanisation should be constituted by Government to suggest measures to deal with the rapid urbanisation, including the large cities and bring about more balanced and efficient urbanisation in the country. **(135)**	(a) Accepted.
	35. (Para 5.2.2.4) Proposed Basic Structure - Ward Committees and Area Sabhas	
136	a. Government may consider the adoption of a common categorisation of urban bodies across the country to improve clarity in their definition so as to assist a systematic planning process and devolution of funds. A categorisation on the lines proposed given in Table 5.6 could be adopted. **(136)**	(a) to (j) Accepted.
137	b. There should be three tiers of administration in urban local governments, except in the case of Town Panchayats, where the middle level would not be required. The tiers should be: i. Municipal Council/Corporation (by whatever name it is called);	

Sl. No.	*Recommendations made by Administrative Reforms Commission*	*Government's Decision*
	ii. Ward Committees; and iii. Area Committees or Sabhas. **(137)**	
138	c. Each Area Sabha comprising all citizens in one or two (or more) polling station areas, should elect, once in five years, a small Committee of Representatives. The Committee of Representatives would elect one person who would chair the meetings of the Area Sabha and would represent the Area Sabha in the relevant Ward Committee. The State may, by law, prescribe the procedure and other details for such election; **(138)**	
139	d. Ward Committees should be set up in every Ward/Corporator's Division. The present system of having more than one ward in a Ward Committee needs to be given up; **(139)**	
140	e. Ward Committees need to be given legitimate functions which can be handled at that level. These functions could include street lighting, sanitation, water supply, drainage, road maintenance, maintenance of school buildings, maintenance of local hospitals/dispensaries, local markets, parks, playgrounds, etc; **(140)**	
141	f. Funds allocated for the functions entrusted to the Ward Committee should be transferred en-bloc to the Ward Committee. The budget proposed by the Ward Committee in respect to the functions allotted to it should be taken into account in formulating the overall municipal budget; **(141)**	
142	g. Meetings of the Ward Committee should be widely publicised to ensure maximum citizens' participation; **(142)**	
143	h. Ward Committees should be given a share of the property taxes collected from the ward, depending on the locality; **(143)**	
144	i. The allocation of functional responsibilities between the tiers must be clearly spelt	

Sl. No.	*Recommendations made by Administrative Reforms Commission*	*Government's Decision*
	out. While doing so, the principle of subsidiarity should be followed. Broadly, the Area Sabha should perform functions similar to the Gram Sabha such as prioritising developmental activities and identifying beneficiaries under various schemes; and **(144)**	
145	j. A process of activity mapping similar to the one taken up for PRIs should be carried out for all ULBs within one year. **(145)**	
	36. (Para 5.2.3.2) Zonal System for Large Cities	
146	a. Zonal offices with all administrative powers delegated to them may be set up immediately in Metropolitan Corporations and Municipal Corporations and become the main point of contact for people in respect of services and amenities. One zone for every five lakh (or less) population could be considered. Similar zonal offices should also be set up in other big cities within the next three years. **(146)**	(a) Accepted.
	37. (Para 5.2.4.3) The Office of the Mayor/ Chairperson	
147	a. The functions of chairing the municipal council and exercising executive authority in urban local government should be combined in the same functionary, i.e. Chairperson or Mayor. **(147)**	(a) to (e) Not accepted.
148	b. The Chairperson/Mayor should be directly elected by popular mandate through a city-wide election. **(148)**	
149	c. The Chairperson/Mayor will be the chief executive of the municipal body. Executive power should vest in that functionary. **(149)**	
150	d. The elected Council should perform the functions of budget approval, oversight and framing of regulations and policies. **(150)**	

Sl. No.	*Recommendations made by Administrative Reforms Commission*	*Government's Decision*
151	e. In municipal corporations and metropolitan cities, the Mayor should appoint the Mayor's 'Cabinet'. The members of the Cabinet should be chosen by the Mayor from the elected corporators. The Mayor's Cabinet shall not exceed 10 per cent of the strength of the elected Corporators or fifteen, whichever is higher. The Cabinet will exercise executive authority on matters entrusted to them by the Mayor, under his overall control and direction. **(151)**	
	38. (Para 5.2.5.4) Management Structure of Urban Local Governments	
152	a. The Mayor should be the Chief Executive of the municipal body while the Commissioner should perform the functions delegated to him/her. **(152)**	(a) to (c) Not accepted
153	b. The responsibility for selection and appointment of the Commissioner and other staff may be given to the Metropolitan Corporations within a period of two years. For other bodies this may be done within three years. States should, however, by law, lay down the procedure and conditions of such appointment. For the duration that the Commissioner/Chief Officer continues to be drawn from the State Government, selection should be made by the Mayor from out of a panel of names sent by the State Government. **(153)**	
154	c. The Directorates of Municipal Administration, wherever they exist, should be abolished. In case there are State-wide cadres of municipal employees, no fresh appointments to these may be made and the employees should be absorbed in municipal bodies through a due process. **(154)**	
	39. (Para 5.3.3.8) Property Tax Reforms	
155	a. State Governments should ensure that all local bodies switch over to the 'unit area	(a) to (i) Accepted.

Sl. No.	*Recommendations made by Administrative Reforms Commission*	*Government's Decision*
	method' or 'capital value method' for assessment of property tax in a Time-bound manner. **(155)**	
156	b. The categories of exemptions from property tax need to be reviewed and minimised. **(156)**	
157	c. In order to ensure that unauthorised constructions do not escape the tax net, State laws should stipulate that levy of tax on any property would not, in itself, confer any right of ownership, in case the property is found to be constructed in violation of any law or regulation. **(157)**	
158	d. Tax details for all properties should be placed in the public domain to avoid collusion between the assessing authority and the property owner. **(158)**	
159	e. The State law should also provide for tax on properties belonging to the municipal authorities which are given on lease, to be payable by the occupants. **(159)**	
160	f. The law should provide for the levy of service charge on properties belonging to the Union and State Governments. This service charge should be in lieu of various services provided such as solid waste management, sanitation, maintenance of roads, streetlighting and general civic amenities. **(160)**	
161	g. A periodic physical verification of the properties and the taxes levied on them should be carried out in each municipal area by a separate wing directly under the control of the Chief Executive. **(161)**	
162	h. A computerised data base of all properties using GIS mapping should be prepared for all municipal areas. **(162)**	
163	i. Randomly selected cases of assessment should be audited by the government auditors as is done by C&AG in case of Union taxes. **(163)**	

Sl. No.	*Recommendations made by Administrative Reforms Commission*	*Government's Decision*
164	**40. (Para 5.3.4.2) Octroi** a. Octroi should be abolished, but the States should evolve mechanisms to compensate the local governments for the loss of revenue caused by such abolition. **(164)**	(a) Accepted.
165	**41. (Para 5.3.5.2) Other Taxes** a. The following principles should be followed while administering all taxes: i. The manner of determination of tax should be made totally transparent and objective; ii. As far as possible, all levies may be based on self-declaration of the tax payer but this should be accompanied by stringent penalties in case of fraud or suppression of facts by the tax payer; iii. The cost of tax collection and of compliance should be reduced to a minimum; iv. There should be an independent unit under the Chief Executive to monitor the collection of all taxes; and v. The appeal against orders of assessing officers should lie with an independent quasi-judicial authority. **(165)**	(a) Accepted.
166	b. Article 276(2) may be amended to enhance the upper ceiling on Profession Tax and this ceiling should be reviewed periodically. **(166)**	(b) Accepted.
167	**42. (Para 5.3.6.8) Non Tax Revenues** a. A significant portion of grants to the municipalities must be linked with their own efforts at resource raising. **(167)**	(a) to (d) Accepted.
168	b. An impact study should be carried out for all major developments in the city. A congestion charge and/or betterment levy in relation to such projects may be levied wherever warranted. **(168)**	
169	c. The power to impose fines for violation of civic laws should be given to municipal authorities. The relevant laws may be suitably modified. **(169)**	

Sl. No.	*Recommendations made by Administrative Reforms Commission*	*Government's Decision*
170	d. The fines prescribed for civic offences need to be enhanced. The amount of fine should be regulated by Rules under the law so that it could be revised periodically without the necessity of an amendment to the law. **(170)**	
	43. (Para 5.3.7.7) Borrowings	
171	a. The limits of borrowings for various municipal bodies in a State may be fixed on the recommendation of the SFC. **(171)**	(a) Not accepted
172	b. Municipal bodies should be encouraged to borrow without Government Guarantees. However, for small municipalities, pooled financing mechanisms will have to be put in place by the State Government. **(172)**	(b) Accepted.
173	c. The capacity of the municipalities to handle legal and financial requirements of responsible borrowing must be enhanced. **(173)**	(c) Accepted.
	44. (Para 5.3.8.7) Leveraging Land as a Resource	
174	a. Municipal bodies should have a periodically updated database of its properties. IT tools like GIS should be used for this purpose. This database should be in the public domain. **(174)**	(a) to (d) Accepted.
175	b. Land banks available with the municipalities as well as with the development authorities should be leveraged for generating resources for the municipalities. However, such resources should be used exclusively to finance infrastructure and capital expenditure and not to meet recurring costs. **(175)**	
176	c. Until the development authorities are merged with urban local bodies, a proportion of the revenue realised by such agencies from the sale of land, say, 25%, should be made available to the municipalities for meeting their infrastructure financing needs. **(176)**	

Sl. No.	***Recommendations made by Administrative Reforms Commission***	***Government's Decision***
177	d. The respective municipal laws should provide that any built-up property of municipal bodies shall not be given on rent/lease without following a competitive process. Such a lease period shall not exceed five years. **(177)**	
	45. (Para 5.4.2.10) Regulatory Services	
178	a. A time-bound programme for updating and simplification of all regulatory provisions relating to the ULBs should be made mandatory. Each State Government should create a task force to examine and suggest simplification of procedures in local governments. This task force could also suggest steps to be taken to reduce discretion and bring objectivity in the field offices of local governments. The city municipal corporations could undertake such an exercise on their own. **(178)**	(a) to (d) Accepted.
179	b. All service providers in cities should be brought under one umbrella by establishing 'one stop' service centres. This could be completed within two years in all cities. Call centres, electronic kiosks, web-based services and other tools of modern technology should be used by all ULBs to bring speed, transparency and accountability into delivery of services to the citizens. **(179)**	
180	c. Citizens' charters in all Urban Local Bodies should specify time limits for approvals relating to regulatory services such as licenses and permits and these should be scrupulously adhered to. The charter should also specify the relief available to the citizens in case of non-adherence. **(180)**	
181	d. A system of self-certification by registered architects for issue of building permits should be introduced in all ULBs with immediate effect, to start with, for individual residential units. **(181)**	

Sl. No.	*Recommendations made by Administrative Reforms Commission*	*Government's Decision*
	46. (Para 5.4.3.1.5) Creating a Responsive Institutional Framework	
182	a. The local government should be responsible for providing civic amenities in its jurisdiction. **(182)**	(a) & (b) Accepted.
183	b. In respect of all downstream activities of a particular State utility, as soon as it enters the geographical and administrative boundary of an Urban Local Body, the Government utility/parastatal should become accountable to the ULB. **(183)**	
	47. (Para 5.4.3.2.8) Water Supply	
184	a. Urban Local Bodies should be given responsibility for water supply and distribution in their territorial jurisdictions whether based on their own source or on collaborative arrangements with parastatals and other service providers. **(184)**	(a) to (g) Accepted.
185	b. Metropolitan Corporations may be given responsibility for the entire water supply programme from development to distribution. For other urban local bodies, a phased transfer of responsibilities for management of the distribution networks within their territorial jurisdiction while leaving source development to the parastatal agency would appear to be the most feasible approach. **(185)**	
186	c. State Finance Commissions may be entrusted with the task of developing suitable normative parameters for different classes of local governments for arriving at optimum tariff structure. **(186)**	
187	d. Municipal bodies must focus on increasing operational efficiencies – through reduction in pilferage, improving efficiency of staff and use of technology. **(187)**	
188	e. The municipal bodies should meter all water connection within a time frame. Installing a hierarchy of metering system could help in identifying pilferage. Payment of water charges should be made hassle-free through use of	

Sl. No.	*Recommendations made by Administrative Reforms Commission*	*Government's Decision*
	Information Technology. As far as possible all water connections should be metered, and if necessary targeted subsidy should be provided to the poorest sections. **(188)**	
189	f. Infrastructure development plans for water supply should be integrated with the CDPs. **(189)**	
190	g. Municipal bye-laws should provide incentives for adoption of water harvesting measures and recycling of waste water for non-potable purposes. In larger cities, non-potable water (recycled treated water) should be used for industries. **(190)**	
	48. (Para 5.4.3.3.9) Sewerage Management	
191	a. Sanitation, as a matter of hygiene and public health, must be given due priority and emphasis in all urban areas. In all towns, advance action for laying down adequate infrastructure should be taken to avoid insufficiency of services. **(191)**	(a) to (d) Accepted.
192	b. Each municipal body should prepare a time bound programme for providing sewerage facilities in slum areas. This should be brought into action through appropriate allocation in the annual budget. Local bodies may impose a cess on the property tax or development charges in order to raise resources for expansion and capacity enhancement of the existing sewerage systems. In order to motivate the local governments to generate additional resources for sewerage management, matching grants may be provided by the Union and State Governments. **(192)**	
193	c. Community participation and co-production of services should be encouraged by municipal bodies. This should be supplemented by awareness generation. **(193)**	
194	d. A separate user charge should be introduced in all municipalities, even as a	

Sl. No.	*Recommendations made by Administrative Reforms Commission*	*Government's Decision*
	minimum levy, for sanitation and sewerage, as distinct from water charges. State Finance Commissions may be entrusted with the task of developing suitable normative parameters for different classes of local governments for arriving at optimum user charges. **(194)**	
	49. (Para 5.4.3.5.3) Solid Waste Management and Scavenging	
195	a. In all towns and cities with a population above one lakh, the possibility of taking up public private partnership projects for collection and disposal of garbage may be explored. This should, however, be preceded by development of capacity of the municipal bodies to manage such contracts. **(195)**	(a) to (f) Accepted.
196	b. Municipal bye-laws/rules should provide for segregation of waste into definite categories based on its manner of final disposal. **(196)**	
197	c. Special solid waste management charges should be levied on units generating high amount of solid waste. **(197)**	
198	d. Extensive surveys should be carried out by the State Governments to identify manual scavengers and estimate the number of dry latrines in existence within six months. **(198)**	
199	e. Following the survey, adequate funds should be allocated for the purpose of eradication of manual scavenging within one year. **(199)**	
200	f. Central Assistance to States Annual Plan should be tied to eradication of manual scavenging. Funds allocated under the JNNURM should also be linked to it. **(200)**	
	50. (Para 5.4.3.6.4) Power Utilities and Municipal Bodies	
201	a. Municipal bodies should be encouraged to	(a) to (c) Accepted.

Sl. No.	Recommendations made by Administrative Reforms Commission	Government's Decision
	take responsibility of power distribution in their areas. This, however, should be done after adequate capacity building in these organisations. **(201)**	
202	b. Municipal building bye-laws should incorporate power conservation measures. **(202)**	
203	c. Municipal bodies should coordinate the layout plans for the distribution networks of power and other utilities. **(203)**	
	51. (Para 5.4.4.3) Services for Human Development	
204	a. There has to be a shift in emphasis in the crucial service delivery sectors of education and health from centralised control to decentralised action, from Accountability to the State department to accountability to the local communities and from employment guarantee to service guarantee. **(204)**	(a) to (i) Accepted.
205	b. It is necessary that all schools are made functionally self-sufficient, in as much as basic facilities and classroom requirements are provided in all urban schools within the next two years. **(205)**	
206	c. The municipalities, especially the larger ones, should seek the help of NGOs, the corporate sector and individual volunteers for assistance in running schools. Indeed, it would be useful to initiate a voluntary service element in our social sector to improve service delivery. **(206)**	
207	d. The trend in urban areas to shift towards private healthcare needs to be seen as an opportunity by the City authorities to concentrate on public health as distinct from clinical services, and on preventive and not only curative aspects of health care. **(207)**	
208	e. Institution-specific standards should be prescribed for schools and hospitals and	

Sl. No.	Recommendations made by Administrative Reforms Commission	Government's Decision
	third party assessments carried out to monitor performance in service delivery. Performance based incentives should be prescribed at all levels by breaking salary ceilings to guarantee service outcomes and linking permanence in service to performance. **(208)**	
209	f. Recruitment for hospitals and schools should be made to an institution/society, moving away from non-accountable State level recruitment. **(209)**	
210	g. Local bodies should ensure convergence among health systems, sanitation facilities and drinking water facilities. Primary level public health institutions in urban areas should be managed by the urban local bodies. **(210)**	
211	h. For all services provided by local governments there is need to develop a set of performance indicators. The concerned Ministry should lay down broad guidelines for this purpose. Thereafter, the State Governments could lay down norms for this purpose. **(211)**	
212	i. The concerned Ministry should maintain a State-wise database about the performance of various service delivery systems. Similarly, the State should have a database for such services covering all municipal bodies. **(212)**	
	52. (Para 5.4.5.15) Urban Transport Management	
213	a. Urban Transport Authorities, to be called Unified Metropolitan Transport Authorities in the Metropolitan Corporations, should be set up in cities with population over one million within one year, for coordinated planning and implementation of urban transport solutions with overriding priority to public transport. **(213)**	(a) to (g) Accepted.
214	b. UMTAs/UTAs should be given statutory powers to regulate all modes of public	

Sl. No.	Recommendations made by Administrative Reforms Commission	Government's Decision
	transport, decide on complementary routes for each operator, and fix fares as well as service standards, etc. In addition, UMTAs/UTAs should be given financial powers and resources to give or recommend financial support, where necessary, to operators on unviable routes. **(214)**	
215	c. Integration of land use with transport planning should be made mandatory for all ULBs as well as planning bodies such as the DPCs and MPCs. **(215)**	
216	d. Demand for transportation in cities should be managed by adopting demand control measures like: i. Imposition of congestion levies; ii. Pedestrianisation of certain zones; and iii. Reserving access to certain areas only through public transport. **(216)**	
217	e. Revitalisation of public transport services in cities should be taken up as priority projects under JNNURM and by tapping other sources of revenue as has been done in Indore and other cities. The aim should be to promote well-structured public-private initiatives for modernising and redefining public transport. At the same time, the efficiency of the existing State-owned transport systems needs to be improved. **(217)**	
218	f. Public transport systems should generally be multi-modal. The modes should be based on economic viability. High capacity public transport systems like metro rail or high capacity bus systems should form the backbone in mega cities supplemented by other modes like a bus system. **(218)**	
219	g. While building transport infrastructure in cities, it must be ensured that the needs of the pedestrians, the elderly, the physically challenged and other users of non-motorised means of transport are	

Sl. No.	Recommendations made by Administrative Reforms Commission	Government's Decision
	adequately met. **(219)**	
	53. (Para 5.4.6.14) JNNURM - A Reform Process	
220	a. On the basis of projections, the total investment needed for urban renewal appears to be far in excess of the funds available. Government must find ways and means to fund this flagship programme – JNNURM – adequately. **(220)**	(a) to (d) Accepted.
221	b. The conditionalities linking reforms with fund flows should be enforced as per the schedules agreed between the ULBs and the Government of India without exceptions or relaxations. **(221)**	
222	c. There should be sectoral allocations for sanitation and solid waste management. **(222)**	
223	d. Capacity-building measures should not be confined to only the selected towns and should be available for all cities/ towns. **(223)**	
	54. (Para 5.4.7.2) A Critical and Urgent Area of Reform - Real Estate	
224	a. There is urgent need to bring in legislation to regulate the Real Estate sector on the lines mentioned in paragraph 5.4.7.1. **(224)**	(a) Accepted.
	55. (Para 5.5.2.9) Re-Forming Mega Cities	
225	a. Public-Private Partnership projects for redevelopment of inner city areas need to be encouraged through a transparent and well-structured regulatory regime of incentives and penalties. **(225)**	(a) Accepted.
	56. (Para 5.5.3.4) Developing 25-30 World Class Mega Cities in India	
226	a. Government should prepare an action plan to redevelop about 25-30 cities (having a population of more than a million) to achieve international level amenities and services as modern megacities of the future. **(226)**	(a) to (c) Accepted.

Sl. No.	*Recommendations made by Administrative Reforms Commission*	*Government's Decision*
227	b. Reform-linked initiatives like JNNURM are an opportunity to complement physical development with enforcement of civic laws and general law enforcement in order to usher in genuine civic regeneration in our cities. In addition to infrastructure development in our cities, such large capital investment programmes for city development should be invariably linked with a zero tolerance strategy towards civic violations. **(227)**	
228	c. As mentioned in the Commission's report on 'Public Order', a "zero tolerance strategy" can be institutionalised in the enforcement departments of local bodies by using modern technology to monitor the levels and trends in various types of civic offences. These can then be linked to a system of incentives and penalties to hold accountable the officials working in these departments. On the spot fines and other summary penalties should be used to inculcate civic discipline and deter and prevent minor civic violations that are at present largely ignored. **(228)**	
	57. (Para 5.5.4.7) Authorities for Metropolitan Corporations	
229	a. As recommended in the Commission's report on 'Public Order', a Metropolitan Police Authority should be set up in all cities with a population above one million to oversee community policing, improve police-citizen interface, suggest ways to improve quality of policing, approve annual police plans and review the working of such plans. **(229)**	(a) Not accepted.
230	b. As recommended in para 5.4.5.15 of this Report, a Unified Metropolitan Transport Authority should be set up in all mega cities for coordinated planning and implementation of urban transport solutions with overriding priority to public transport. **(230)**	(b) to (d) Accepted.
231	c. For all Metropolitan Corporations, which	

Sl. No.	Recommendations made by Administrative Reforms Commission	Government's Decision
	may be defined as cities with a population exceeding 5 million, MPCs may be constituted with the Chief Minister as the Chairperson in order to give the required impetus to the process of planning for such urban agglomerations. **(231)**	
232	d. In all cities with a population exceeding 5 million, a Metropolitan Environment Authority needs to be set up with powers delegated by the State Government from the State Pollution Control Board and related authorities. It should be vested with adequate powers for urban environmental management within the city limits. **(232)**	
	58. (Para 5.6.2.3) Beneficiary Identification	
233	a. An exhaustive survey to identify the urban poor should be carried out within one year. The parameters to be used for such identification should be simple and easily comprehensible, allowing objective measurement without the use of discretion. The basic parameters should be spelt out at the national level. The identification should be based on a door-to-door survey with the survey teams including at least one person from the Area Sabha concerned. The urban poor so identified may be issued multi-utility identity cards for availing benefits under all poverty alleviation programmes. **(233)**	(a) Accepted.
	59. (Para 5.6.3.2.5) Measures for Poverty Alleviation - Employment	
234	a. After identifying the urban poor through surveys, a mission mode approach would need to be adopted for alleviating urban poverty in a time-bound and systematic manner. The urban local bodies may also have their own poverty alleviation schemes with adequate backward and forward linkages converging with the other poverty alleviation schemes. **(234)**	(a) to (d) Accepted.
235	b. The thrust of the urban poverty alleviation schemes should be on upgradation of	

Sl. No.	Recommendations made by Administrative Reforms Commission	Government's Decision
	skills and training. Training institutes may be set up on the lines of RUDSETIs for imparting training to the urban poor for self-employment. These institutes could also help in developing wage employment related skills. **(235)**	
236	c. In case of setting up of micro-enterprises, the urban poverty alleviation schemes should be flexible in selecting projects and providing financial assistance. **(236)**	
237	d. To maximise the benefits of micro-finance, formation of Self-Help Groups (SHGs) needs to be encouraged. Institutions and NGOs with good track record should be encouraged to promote SHGs for availing micro-finance. **(237)**	
	60. (Para 5.6.3.3.4) Measures for Poverty Alleviation - Literacy	
238	a. The education plan should form an integral part of the development plan for the city. **(238)**	(a) Accepted.
	61. (Para 5.6.3.4.2) Measures for Poverty Alleviation - Health and Nutrition	
239	a. Urban Local Bodies should adopt the concept of 'Primary Health Care, for providing health and medical facilities to the urban poor, particularly to women and children with the help of auxiliary health staff.' These should specifically cater to the population living in slum areas. **(239)**	(a) Accepted.
	62. (Para 5.6.3.6.3) Slums in Urban Areas and Land Use Reservation for the Poor	
240	a. There has to be total redevelopment of slum areas. While redeveloping, it should be ensured that adequate provision has been made for schools, health centres, sanitation etc. **(240)**	(a) to (d) Accepted.
241	b. For slum redevelopment the approach suggested in para 5.6.3.5.11 may be considered while formulating policy or specific schemes. **(241)**	
242	c. It is necessary to earmark and reserve a certain percentage of land projects in each	

Sl. No.	*Recommendations made by Administrative Reforms Commission*	*Government's Decision*
	town and city for the urban poor. If a construction cannot allocate housing for the poor, the developer must, at his own cost, provide suitable housing in any other appropriate place acceptable to the authorities. **(242)**	
243	d. A detailed programme for the provision of night shelters needs to be drawn up in all cities, beginning with large cities having Metropolitan and Municipal Corporations, for implementation. **(243)**	
	63. (Para 5.7.2.12) The Town and Country Planning Act(s)	
244	a. The City Development Plan (CDP) and zoning regulations once approved should remain in force for ten years. No authority should normally have any power to change the CDP. **(244)**	(a) to (e) Accepted.
245	b. Infrastructure plans should be made an integral part of the City Development Plan (CDP) in order to ensure that urban planning in cities become a truly holistic exercise. **(245)**	
246	c. The existing system of enforcement of building regulations needs to be revised. It should be professionalised by licensing architects and structural engineers for assessment of structures and for certification of safe buildings. The units of local bodies dealing with enforcement of building bye-laws and zoning regulations also need to be strengthened. **(246)**	
247	d. Prevention of Disaster Management must find a prominent place in spatial planning. Specific guidelines need to be framed by the Ministry of Urban Development. These should be addressed by including them in the zoning regulations and building bye-laws. **(247)**	
248	e. The standards prescribed by BIS for disaster resistant buildings should be available in the public domain, free of	

Sl. No.	Recommendations made by Administrative Reforms Commission	Government's Decision
	cost. They should also be posted on websites of the concerned government agencies to promote compliance. **(248)**	
249	**64. (Para 5.7.5.3) Development Areas** a. In respect of all townships and satellite towns developed under the development authorities, it should be ensured that as soon as the development process is completed, jurisdiction over the township should be transferred to the local bodies. **(249)**	(a) Accepted.
250 251	**65. (Para 5.7.6.5) Private Townships** a. Private townships and gated communities must be placed under the jurisdiction of the concerned local body and subject to its laws, rules and bye-laws. However, they can have autonomy for provision of infrastructure and services within their precincts and/or for collection of taxes and charges (para 5.7.7.2) **(250)** b. The establishment of private, gated colonies must be allowed only within the broad parameters of the larger regional urban planning process where the development plans must clearly indicate spaces for private expansion make mandatory provision for low cost housing and should be integrated with the availability of infrastructure services. **(251)**	(a) & (b) Accepted.
252 253	**66. (Para 5.7.7.4) Special Economic Zones (SEZs)** a. As in the case of private townships, concerned local bodies should have full jurisdiction with regard to enforcement of local civic laws in the SEZs. **(252)** b. SEZs may be given autonomy for provision of infrastructure and amenities in the SEZ area. A formula for sharing the resources raised in the SEZ area needs to be developed. **(253)**	(a) & (b) Accepted.
254	**67. (Para 5.8.4) Urban Local Bodies and the State Government** a. Municipal governments should have full autonomy over the functions/activities	(a) to (c) Accepted.

Sl. No.	*Recommendations made by Administrative Reforms Commission*	*Government's Decision*
	devolved to them. **(254)**	
255	b. If the State Government feels that there are circumstances that make it necessary to suspend or rescind any resolution passed by the Urban Local Bodies or to dissolve or supersede them, it should not do so unless the matter has been referred to the concerned local body Ombudsman and the Ombudsman recommends such action. **(255)**	
256	c. If, on any occasion, the State Government is in possession of records or has adequate reasons to initiate action against the Urban Local Bodies or its elected representatives, it should place the records before the local body Ombudsman concerned for investigation. **(256)**	

(D) Postponing Panchayat Elections

With regard to the electoral issues connected with grassroots democracy is concerned it is a sad commentary on several state governments that they have not taken the provision of the Constitution to hold elections on the expiry of the five-year term of the panchayats seriously. Article 243-B of the Constitution is categorical that there shall be in every State, Panchayats at the village, intermediate and district level and that

(i) every Panchayat shall continue for five years from the date appointed for its first meeting and no longer, and
(ii) election to constitute a Panchayat shall be completed before the expiry of its five-year duration or within six months of its dissolution [Article 243 E (1) and (3)].

Several states have official political party participation at the District or Block level panchayat elections, but not at the Gram

Panchayat level.

However, political parties are keen to capture panchayats from the village level itself and the ruling party/ies in the States are afraid of facing the people either midway or at the fag end of their term. No ruling party or a party aspiring to come to power in the next Assembly elections wants to be discredited by losing seats at various levels of the Panchayats. It must be said to the credit of India's maturing democracy that every election is unpredictable, parties cannot take people for granted. Therefore, we have now situations where even opposition parties join hands with the ruling party/ies to postpone elections because of their fear of facing the panchayat electorate.

As a result, they sponsor indirectly writ petitions in the High Courts citing a deficiency here or a deficiency there in the existing State Panchayat Acts, or an unfavourable weather or civil conflict in one part of the state, the objective being to obtain injunction of the court on the holding of elections. The State Election Commissions are not acting as independent constitutional bodies. Many of them succumb to the pressures of the state governments. Some of them had withheld elections even after the panchayat election process had been set in motion. However, there have also been exceptions when the State Election Commissions have successfully withstood undue pressure and discharged their constitutional obligations.

Details regarding the status of Panchayati Raj elections held/due in the states and union territories are given under:

Status of Panchayat Elections held/due in India

Sl. No.	*States/UTs*	*Year and month when election held last*	*Year and month when next election due*
1	Andhra Pradesh	GP: August 2013 BP: April 2014 DP: April 2014	GP: August 2018~ BP: April 2019 DP: April 2019
2	Andman & Nicobar Island	September 2015	September 2020
3	Arunachal Pradesh	May 2013	May 2018
4	Assam	December 2018	December, 2023
5	Bihar	April-May 2016	April-May 2021
6	Chhattisgarh	February 2015	February 2020
7	Daman & Diu	September 2015	September 2020

Sl. No.	*States/UTs*	*Year and month when election held last*	*Year and month when next election due*
8	Dadar & Nagar Haveli	October 2015	October 2020
9	Gujarat	December 2016 onward	December 2021 onward
10	Goa	May 2017	May 2022
11	Haryana	January 2015	January 2020
12	Himachal Pradesh	December 2015	December 2020
13	Union Territory of Jammu & Kashmir	December 2018	December 2023
14	Jharkhand	December 2015	December 2020
15	Karnataka	GP: May 2015 BP: January-February 2016 DP: January-February 2016	GP: May 2020 BP: January-February 2021 DP: January-February 2021
16	Kerala	November 2015	November 2020
17	Lakshadweep	December, 2017	December 2022
18	Madhya Pradesh	February 2015	February 2020
19	Maharashtra	GP: May 2017 BP: Jan./Feb., 2017 DP: Jan/Feb., 2017	GP: May 2022 BP: Jan./Feb., 2022 DP: Jan/Feb., 2022
20	Manipur	September 2017	September 2022
21	Odisha	February 2017	February 2022
22	Puducherry	July 2006	July 2011
23	Punjab	December 2018	December 2023
24	Rajasthan	February 2015	February 2020
25	Sikkim	November 2017	November 2022
26	Tamil Nadu	December 2019	December 2024
27	Telangana	GP: January 2019 BP: May 2019 DP: May 2019	GP: January 2024 BP: May 2024 DP: May 2024
28	Tripura	July 2019	July 2024
29	Uttar Pradesh	GP: October 2015 BP: March 2016 DP: January 2016	GP: October 2020 BP: March 2021 DP: Jan 2021
30	Uttarakhand	October 2019 for 12 districts January 2016: Haridwar	October 2024 for 12 Districts January 2021: Haridwar
31	West Bengal	July 2018	July 2023

Source: https://www.panchayat.gov.in/status-of-election-of-pris

2

People's Participation in Decentralization

Related Theories

The concept of decentralisation has emerged as a dominant and vibrant trend in global politics. In 1998, the World Bank estimated that all but 12 out of 75 developing and transitional countries with populations greater than 5 million had embarked on a process of political devolution. At the heart of this transformation are a number of complex yet interrelated themes. One is an ideological shift, in which the legitimacy of central state-led development has been challenged on the grounds that it produces systems of governance that undermine national economic performance and effective public policy (Gore, 2000; Johnson and Start, 2001). A second is a (remarkably widespread) political agenda, which asserts that the decentralisation of public administration and the introduction of local elected bodies will produce systems of governance that are better able to meet the needs of poor and politically marginal groups in society. A third and related theme suggests that democratic decentralisation is a political strategy that national elites have used to maintain legitimacy and control in the face of political disintegration. Here it can be argued that economic liberalisation, political regionalism and the rise of powerful inter- and sub-national actors have weakened the traditional nation-state and created the conditions under which more local identities could emerge (Giddens, 1998).

Assertions in favour of decentralisation are often founded upon a wider critique of central state planning, which holds that large and centrally-administered bureaucracies represent an inefficient and potentially destructive means of allocating resources (and generating wealth) within society. Two assertions are generally used to substantiate this claim: One argues that central state agencies lack the time and place knowledge to implement policies and programmes that reflect people's 'real' needs and preferences. A second and related assertion is that time and place gaps give local officials unlimited ability to distribute resources and extract rent as they see fit. Such outcomes are believed to be particularly prone in poor countries, where government represents a vital source of wealth, and mechanisms to ensure accountable governance are often poorly enforced. In theory, decentralisation would undermine these opportunities by creating institutional arrangements that formalise the relationship between citizens and the state, giving the former the authority to impose sanctions (such as voting, recourse to higher level authorities) on the latter. Decentralisation is also thought to create the conditions for a more pluralist political arrangement, in which competing groups can voice and institutionalise their interests in local democratic forum. Finally, it is argued that decentralisation creates institutions that are more amenable to local needs and preferences.

However, a problem that is well-recognized in the literature on decentralisation is that the devolution of power will not necessarily improve tbe performance and accountability of local government. Indeed, in many cases, decentralisation has simply empowered local elites to capture a larger share of public resources, often at the expense of the poor.

In 1993, the Government of India passed a series of constitutional reforms, which were intended to empower and democratise India's rural representative bodies - the Panchayats. The 73rd Amendment to the Constitution formally recognised a third tier of government at the sub-State level, thereby creating the legal conditions for local self-rule or Panchayati Raj. Since this time, the process of decentralisation has been highly variable ranging from ambitious attempts at Gram Swaraj (or village self-rule) in Madhya Pradesh, political decentralisation in Karnataka and peoples plan in Kerala. Early experiences have also revealed considerable uncertainty and confusion about the precise political, administrative and fiscal powers Panchayats have in relation to the States, line ministries, and local user groups. This, in part reflects the fact that the 73rd Amendment gave the State governments considerable autonomy to interpret and implement the constitutional reforms.

Basic Concepts of Decentralization

Decentralisation can be usefully understood as a political process whereby administrative authority, public resources and responsibilities are transferred from central government agencies to lower-level organs of government or to non-governmental bodies, such as community-based organisations (CBOs), third party non-governmental organisations (NGOs) or private sector actors (Craig Johnson, 2003; Crook and Manor, 1998: 6-7; Rondinelli *et al.*, 1989, Meenakshisundaram, 1999; World Bank, 2000a: 3). Conceptually, important distinctions can be made among Deconcentration, in which political, administrative and fiscal responsibilities are transferred to lower units within central line ministries or agencies (Crook and Manor, 1998: 6-7; Rondinelli *et al.*, 1989; Meenakshisundaram, 1999:55; Devolution, in which sub-national units of government are either created or strengthened in terms of political, administrative and fiscal power (Blair, 2000; Crook and Manor, 1998: 6-7; Rondinelli *et al.*, 1989); Delegation, in which responsibilities are transferred to organisations that are outside the regular bureaucratic structure and are only indirectly controlled by the Central Government, (Meenakshisundaram, 1999: 55); Privatisation, in which all responsibility for government functions is transferred to non-governmental organisations (NGOs) or private enterprises independent of government (Meenakshisundaram, 1999: 56). Such transfers can involve the power to decide the allocation and distribution of public resources, the power to implement programmes and policies and the power to raise and spend public revenues for these and other purposes.

These three powers we can classify broadly as political, administrative and fiscal decentralisation.

Political decentralisation transfers policy and legislative powers from Central Government to autonomous, lower-level assemblies and local councils that have been democratically elected by their constituencies. Administrative decentralisation places planning and implementation responsibility in the hands of locally situated civil servants and these local civil servants are under the jurisdiction of elected local government. Fiscal decentralisation accords substantial revenue and expenditure authority to intermediate and local government.

However, democratic decentralisation implies more than the downward delegation of authority. Crucially, it entails a system of governance in which citizens possess the right to hold local public officials to account through the use of elections, grievance meetings and other democratic means (Blair, 2000: 21) captures the essence of this important idea.

Democratic decentralisation can be defined as meaningful authority devolved to local units of governance that are accessible and accountable to the local citizenry, who enjoy full political rights and liberty. It thus differs from the vast majority of earlier efforts at decentralisation in developing areas, which go back to the 1950s, and which were largely initiatives in public administration without any serious democratic component. A defining feature of any democratic system is that decision-makers are under the effective popular control (Mayo, 1960: 60) of the people they are meant to govern. How this is accomplished, of course, constitutes a major dilemma for theorists and proponents of democratic development. Nevertheless, a number of defining features can be observed. Mayo (1960: 6169) identifies four popular control of policy-makers, both by regular elections and by the pressure of social interest groups; the institutionalization of all adult citizens in voting (i.e. one person, one vote); political freedom in the eyes of the state; policy decisions made on the basis of majority rule.

Beyond these very basic principles, democracy also implies a wide range of rules, norms and customs through which citizens can exercise 'effective popular control' over public officials. Included here would be an independent judiciary, a free press, systems of transparency, and freedom of association and speech (Luckham *et al.*, 2000; Putzel, 1997b).

Citizen Participation in the Developmental Process

Since the late 1960s, the term citizen participation has been acquiring growing popularity, although it has yet to achieve a fuller meaning and depth. It represents a revived interest in the philosophy of participatory democracy promoted by the French political philosopher Alexis de Tocqueville who propounded that individual citizen participation is essential to the survival of a democracy, and that democracy is undermined when citizens are incapable of influencing government decisions. A state that ignores the needs and interests of large sections of the population in setting and implementing policies is not an effective state. Popular participation in government and development is emphasised in the ideals of the United Nations. Article 21 of the Universal Declaration of Human Rights stipulates that, 'Everyone has the right to take part in the government of his country, directly or through freely chosen representative. The will of the people shall be the basis of the authority of government.'

The development process in a developing economy will acquire a fuller meaning of the citizens not only associate themselves with planning development programmes but also participate fully in their implementation. The Eighth Five Year Plan document asserts, "it is necessary to make development a people's movement. People's initiative and participation must become the key element in the whole process of development." Citizen participation, therefore, seems to be of much significance for proper development administration, particularly in relation to measures which require structural changes. It tends to bring the government closer to the people.

Citizens' participation has come to mean the direct involvement of citizens in the process of administrative decision-making, policy formulation, and policy implementation. In relation to development it embraces all forms of action by which they participate in the operation of development administration. It refers to the role of citizens as distinguished from that of public servants (in their official capacity) in exerting influence on the developmental activities of government. "People's Participation" says the Report of the Team for the Study of Community Projects and National Extension Service, "is not merely their providing a certain proportion of the cost of a particular work in cash, kind or manual labour. It is their full realisation that all aspects of community development are their concern and that the Government's participation is only to assist them where such assistance is necessary. It is the gradual development of their faith in the efficacy of their own co-operative action in solving their local problems."

The UNRISD promotes the concept of people's participation as "in the organised efforts to increase control over the resources and regulative Institutions in given social situations on the part of groups and movements of those hitherto excluded from such control." Economic and Social Council of the United Nations in its Resolution 1929, defines it in terms of "involvement of people in contributing to the development effort, sharing equitably in the benefits derived therefrom and in decision-making in respect of setting goals, formulating policies and planning and implementing economic and social development programmes." In practice, different countries attribute different meaning to people or popular participation depending upon their socio-political system and policy choices concerning the importance of economic growth, use of scarce resources and the role of planning and market. These range from people's participation as a strategy to mobilise national human resources for development to genuine transfer of power to people and their involvement in decision-making on matters affecting their welfare.

Citizen Participation is often Used in Conjunction with the Term Participatory Democracy

It may range from the village level (construction of rural roads) to the national level (defence). It may involve only decision-making or extend to actual execution. Again, the participation may be direct (as in community projects) or indirect (through electoral representatives). Direct citizen participation is distinguished from indirect citizen participation, such as voting, in that most citizen participation is at the regional or local level. When participation is willed from top it becomes mobilisation, a means of getting things done. On the other hand, when it arises from bottom it generally focuses on distribution, becoming also a means, from the point of view of the groups able to participate, of obtaining a larger immediate share of the fruits of development. Thus, participation covers every kind of action by which citizens take part in development administration. In a real sense, participation can only be explained when the citizens who take part in the development effort are fully conscious of owning responsibility. In a narrow sense, participation consists in a convergent action by which the citizens take part in the accomplishment of administrative services without, however, belonging to the governing or managing organs. However, in a broader sense, participation comprises all forms of action in the form of decision-making, implementation, and evaluation in the right setting.

It implies greater decentralisation of government power and resources—Citizen's association with or intervention in the development effort of a democratic country like India has several advantages. First, it kindles the interest of local people in imparting a new thrust to programmes of which they are the beneficiaries. In other words, participation is a means of showing, by their behaviour and action, that they are capable of assuming responsibility. Secondly, it is a means of ventilating their feelings and thoughts. Third, it offers them an opportunity to demonstrate their willingness to do constructive work and show that they are good citizens. Fourth, it is a cure for the unresponsiveness and repressiveness of traditional decision-making mechanisms. It enables the citizens, especially the poor, to gain control over decisions affecting their lives through direct participation in programme operations. It is a remedy to check corrupt practices. Another advantage of community-based programmes is that they may be less of a financial burden on governments since they can be managed by volunteers or community-based workers.

Moreover, citizen participation ensures that the accruing benefits of education, health and family planning programmes, for example, reach the residents of remote and rural areas. Participation of citizens in development efforts is gaining ground both through voluntary agencies and through non-governmental organisations. Perhaps this is an indication of the importance that issues of development have drawn attention to the perception of the citizens. Citizen participation differs from country to country depending upon their political, social and economic systems, high developed countries, participation is due to the citizens having become conscious of their responsibility and wanting to be associated in some way or other with the process of governmental decision-making and action. In developing countries, however, participation has not gained much momentum. The government of these countries feel the need to prompt people's participation because it helps them achieve their objectives. They initiate measures in this direction. Participation in both developed and developing countries has grown three reasons.

The first is the expansion of government responsibilities. Governments have assumed increasing responsibilities in regulating the economy, planning for financial resources for accelerating development and exploitation of natural resources. In the social sphere they have the responsibility of improving the well-being of the people and decreasing the level of unemployment and poverty and disease. Politics development relating to the building of the nation-state, modernisation law, strengthening of the judiciary, the legislature and the executive other democratic institutions as well as many other broad aspects of development are among their other responsibilities. The government is today directly and indirectly a trader, industrialist, financier, and entrepreneur. To gain acceptance for its objectives and policies, particularly in the economic and social spheres, it has to rely on the citizens' willingness and understanding. As a result of the increasing functions of the state and government's desire to seek the cooperation of the people for its new policies and decisions, opportunities for contact between government and the people have multiplied. Citizens have become very much active and asserted their right of being heard and of voicing their opinions at various levels of administrative action.

The second reason which has led to the growth of citizen participation is the explosion of knowledge and communication. More new knowledge in science and technology and education has been developed in the last thirty years than in the previous history of mankind. Today people have received an education which has made them better able to understand the problems of life in society and a training which has made them responsible to carry out constructive public work. With the explosion of communications, the means of information have become diversified. These help the citizens of a modern state to exercise critical control over its activities. They feel that if they wish to exert pressure on governmental authorities, they can be better heard through collective action. The pressure will be all the more effective if the group which exerts represents a large number of citizens. The third contributing factor in the citizen participation is the perceived failure of the bureaucracy to meet the growing demands of the citizens at the local level. A continuing struggle is called for against the biases of bureaucracy and technocracy which are among the most widespread and persistent impediments to effective state support of participation.

Against these tendencies, it is desirable that the people, through their own participatory organisations, acquire the capacity to control public officials and themselves undertake many of the present responsibilities of the state.

Representative *vs.* Participatory Decentralisation

Decentralisation has the capacity to bring governance processes closer to the people and to create both representative and participatory forms of governance. There is a tendency to use these terms interchangeably, but they are, in reality, completely separate concepts. Governance processes can be brought closer to the people by devolving administrative responsibility from the centre and the province to bureaucrats at the local level. Such a system is neither representative nor participatory. Similarly, under decentralisation, citizens may be allowed to vote their representatives to office at the local level, but they may have little role beyond that in governance processes. Such a system is representative but not participatory. There is, therefore, a clear distinction between these concepts.

Representative decentralisation requires that citizens' participate in governance by electing their representatives to make decisions for them. Therefore, the requirements of citizens' participation under such a system are met simply by the act of voting. This is also the traditional idea of democracy. Participatory decentralisation as well as the redefined concept of participatory democracy requires much more off its citizens. It requires them, and not just their representatives, to become an active part of decision-making itself. To this end, it requires state agency to provide an enabling environment within which citizens can play out this role, and it requires active social agency to take the decisions that affect people. Within a system that is representative, it may be enough to perceive citizen bodies and local governmental agencies for implementing development, but within a system that is to be considered participatory, citizen bodies need to be political institutions. The differences between both, therefore, are very specific (Shandana Khan Mohmand, 2005).

Participative Development: India's Strategy

Citizen participation in development and nation-building in India has posed a number of crucial issues, such as the adoption of new institutions at different levels between the citizens and the administration. Citizen involvement in development calls for improved mass-communication facilities so that the governmental agency responsible for development can reach the masses and learn their views on different areas of urban/rural development.

In 1959, the Government of India launched the Urban Community Development Programme which was designed to transform, socio-economically, the lives of villagers and urban slum-dwellers. It was called 'people's programme', and included the participation of the people together with the local authorities. Some of the studies relating to urban development in India have shown that citizens involvement can occur, even in a government programme, if those involved as animators are committed to the people and can develop their capacity to organize themselves for social and political actions. Such studies have recognised 'poor people' as the most important social and economic resource in urban development. Urban community development has great potential for building systematic linkages between physical improvements, social services and people's participation.

However, as India was predominantly an agricultural society at Independence, development basically meant the development of rural Indian and rural society, although there is also the concomitant need for improvement in urban and industrial infrastructure for further growth plus work on the problem of linkages between urban and rural development. The discussion of citizen participation in development in India is thus related more to rural than to urban areas. In fact, since Independence, various experiences in participatory development in India have taken place through community development programmes which have established the institutional framework of Panchayati Raj institutions. In addition, there is also an infrastructure of cooperative bodies, government sponsored development agencies and an encouragement of voluntary organisations to help and assist in development programmes.

The Community Development Programme

As part of the strategy to bring about socio-economic and cultural transformation in the rural areas, a massive community development programme was launched throughout the country in 1952. This programme drew its inspiration from the experiments in Albert Mayer's Etawah Project in Uttar Pradesh in 1948 and S.K. Dey's Nilokheri Project in Punjab (now in Haryana) in 1950.

The Community Development Programme was launched throughout the country in 1952. Initially, it covered 55 projects comprising 27,388 villages and 6.4 million people. However, within a very short period of time it was felt that the programme needed to be extended to cover the whole country. Hence, a less intensive programme, called the National Extension Service, was formulated and put into effect on 2 October 1953. The CD programmes were described as "all round rural development programmes, aimed at material development by encouraging rural people to create better living conditions through infrastructural facilities provided by the state)." In fact, it was assumed that as the programme caught on and became acceptable to the rural people it would move from officially motivated self-help to self-motivated self-help. The goals of the Community Development Programme were:

1. to increase employment and production by the application of scientific methods in agriculture, including horticulture, animal husbandry, fisheries, etc. and the establishment of subsidiary and cottage industries;
2. self-help and self-reliance and the largest possible extension of the principle of cooperation, and
3. the need to develop a portion of the vast unutilised time and energy in the countryside for the benefit of the community.

The Panchayati Raj Institutions

During the period of the Second Five Year Plan (1956-61), the National Development Council appointed a Committee on Plan Projects (Balwant Rai Mehta Committee) to examine the work of the Community Development and National Extension Service. The Committee's recommendations mark the beginning of a new experimental phase in people's participation in development through what has come to be known as the process of democratic decentralisation.

The establishment of a three-tier system of rural local self-government with full power to assume responsibility for local development was the core of the Balwant Rai Mehta Committee recommendations. Rajasthan was the first state in India to introduce the Panchayati Raj system on 2 October, 1959, which was followed by a number of other states, including Andhra Pradesh, Uttar Pradesh, Maharashtra, Gujarat and Madhya Pradesh. There were two main variants in the adopted Panchayati Raj model which depended on whether greater authority was delegated to Samitis (groups of villages) or Zila Parishads (the districts). By the 1970s, the Panchayati Raj system had been introduced in practically all parts of the country. The new institutional setup was intended to be as an experiment involving the poorest of the poor in rural areas in the process of self-consciousness or national reconstruction and to channel energies towards the refashioning of community life. The Panchayati Raj Institutions have been in operation in almost all states in India for nearly four decades, but with a number of variants in their structure concerning their decision-making, implementation and resource-allocation, staffing pattern, training and recruitment of staff and the degree of autonomy allowed to different units. A number of research studies have been conducted by various scholars in the functioning of the system on an empirical basis, and these have generally pointed to the limited extent of the involvement of people in decision-making at grass-roots level, the interactional resistance between the official and non-official functionaries, the paradoxical resistance and tensions of the system in operation, the problems of caste-elite domination and political influences, and more significantly the non-achievement of developmental goals.

While the Panchayati Raj Institutions have acquired strong roots in some states such as Gujarat, Maharashtra and Karnataka, these have not made any impact in other states due to a number of reasons, including the postponement of elections, declining and inadequate material and human resources, tensions between the officials and political leaders, and the lack of the very premise of popular participation in development programmes, which has been the raison d'etre of the entire concept.

The Asoka Mehta Committee was set up to examine the forking of Panchayati Raj system in 1977 by the Janata Government which came into power after the short aberration of 19 months of emergency regime imposed by the then Prime Minister Indira Gandhi. It reviewed the Panchayati Raj Institutions at various levels and noted that the system had passed through three distinct phases: the phase of ascendancy (1959-64); the phase of stagnation (1965-69); and phase of decline (1969-77). The Committee proposed some structural and organisational changes to revitalize the PR concept, but with the fall of the Janata Government in 1980, the recommendations were put into the cold storage. However, it is doubtful whether the changes proposed by the Asoka Mehta Committee would have made any impact on the relationship between state and civil society in the absence of the realisation that the decentralisation of power had more deeper cultural problems rather than merely the organisational and managerial efficiency of the PR Institutions. From 1980 until 1989, when a new proposal to revitalize the PR Institutions by giving them a constitutional status was initiated by the Rajiv Gandhi Government, the PR Institutions virtually remained in suspended animation.

The Rajiv Gandhi Congress Government presented the 6th Constitutional Amendment Bill in Parliament in May 1989 providing for a constitutional status of elected local bodies at village, intermediate and district levels. The Bill passed the Lok Sabha, but failed to secure a two-third majority in the Rajya Sabha by two votes in October 1989. Opposition was raised on account of the predominant role of the Centre in dealing with the Panchayats.

Concern was expressed about the little flexibility of state governments to design a system of Panchayati Raj according to the specific present and historical situation of the different states. The 73rd Constitutional Amendment Act, 1993 in order to ensure a more participatory role of Panchayati Raj Institutions and decentralised decision-making development, the Narasimha Rao government, enacted the 73rd and 74th Constitutional Amendment Acts in December 1992 which became effective on 24th April, 1993. Those Acts gave Panchayati Raj Institutions and urban local bodies a constitutional status and made it obligatory for all the states to establish three-tier system of Panchayats at village, intermediate and district levels. The state legislatures were then expected to plan and devolve powers for economic development and social justice. Most of the states have already enacted laws to establish new PR institutions with provision for the reservation of seats for Scheduled Castes, Scheduled Tribes and Women in the elected bodies and ensuring Panchayats a fixed term of five year. Control of elections is vested in the State Election Commission and provision is also made for the audit of accounts under the auspices of the Comptroller and the Auditor General. These legislations have also made a provision for the constitution of State Finance Commission every five years to review the finances of Panchayats and to recommend the principles for apportioning assignment of taxes to the Panchayats.

As a consequence of the Panchayati Raj Act, the number of local self-government institutions with directly elected representatives rose to around 500 bodies at district level, 5000 at block level and 2,25,000 at village level. A district level Panchayat covers a population of approximately 1-2 million, an intermediate level Panchayat a population of approximately 8,02,00,000 and a Gram Panchayat comprising a village or a group of villages, a population of approximately 1,50,08,000 varying from state to state. The Act provides for a mandatory three-tier system of local self-government institutions for states with a population above 20 million. Small states are given the option not to have an intermediate level Panchayat. The Act provides for direct elections of Panchayat members at all levels. The chairpersons of Panchayats at intermediate and district level are to be indirectly elected by, and from amongst the elected members thereof. As a result of the 73rd Amendment Act, almost all states in India have adapted the new pattern of Panchayat Raj Institutions as a primary institutional structure for citizen participation in development administration in rural India. The citizen participation, especially of women at the grassroots level has certainly increased after enactment of such stature by various states. At least people now become much more aware and conscious about the developmental efforts of the state due to the existence of a revamped PR system (R.B. Jain, 2002).

Partyless Democracy at Grassroots: A Historical Backdrop

Soon after the submission of the Balwant Rai Mehta Committee Report of 1957, a controversy started with regard to the participation of political parties in the formation and working of popular bodies, in the beginning the controversy was limited to a few people who were probably very enthusiastic about the implementation of PR according to their own visions and aspirations. With the publication of the privately circulated book *A Plea for Reconstruction of Indian Polity* by Jayaprakash Narayan and later on the publication of his two papers: "Reconstruction of

Indian Polity: Some Clarifications I & II" in the Issues of *Kurukshetra*, the controversy started on a wide scale. The controversy reached to its zenith with the publication of his *Swaraj* for the People.

Since 1958 up to the present day, the controversy has been discussed in one form or other and therefore the issue or problem of political parties and their role in PRIs still appears to be as fresh as it was in the past.

The debate over the issue gave birth to two schools of thought. The one is the Sarvodaya School of thought and the other is of supporters of parliamentary democracy.

Sarvodaya School

Sarvodaya school is influenced and inspired by the ideas of Mahatma Gandhi and Vinoba Bhave, but its most ardent and systematic spokesman was Jayaprakash Narayan. JP being a political thinker had the whole concept of PR in a different perspective. The place and role of political parties in PRIs is an integral part of JP's thesis on the philosophy of partyless democracy. But this does not mean that about the present PRIs, he has different views. He in contrast to the western parliamentary democracy, propounds a new thesis of communitarian democracy or participating democracy.

Relevant Ideas of his Philosophy, in this Context, are:

1. The parliamentary system of government as it is functioning in the country is not satisfactory due to tendency towards capitalism, expansiveness, party system accompanied by rivalries.
2. In reconstructing Indian polity much can be learnt from the past village communities as existed in India.
3. Against atomised society the need is of socially integrated community, community is a territorial contiguity of a number of families.
4. In ancient times there was no election, only consensus or lots. The community ideal should be the basis of future polity in India.
5. Panchayat should be constituted by general consensus. The samiti should be elected by the gram panchayats and so on up to the Lok Sabha.

Second School—Supporters of Parliamentary Democracy

There is yet another school of thought though not well organised as Sarvodaya School having some political philosophy or organised viewpoint—school of supporters of parliamentary democracy.

Some of the major arguments of this school of thought are as follows:

1. Communitarian society may be a good exercise in the field of academic intellectualism, but it is too Idealistic, a utopian view of the present constitutional political structure of Indian society. Partyless democracy may be suited to some heavenly state, in the state of human beings of flesh and bones it seems to be highly impracticable and imaginative.
2. The advocates of partyless democracy specially at grassroot level to have faith in mistaken assumptions. That much can be learnt from the part as regards working of panchayats, seems to be an exaggeration of facts. It is true that representative bodies have existed at the village level from times immemorial.
3. If panchayat of past were so nable to be preserved, why were these forgotten when the dèliberations, for the draft constitution of Independent India were going on?
4. Dr. Ambedkar, who were primarily responsible for the draft constitution, gave no place in it to the panchayats. He spoke clearly and unequivocally condemning the village panchayat as a sink of localism and den of ignorance and narrow-mindedness and communalism.

Role of Political Parties

The political parties have several types of roles to play in relation to community development and PR. Firstly, as electoral organisations they nominate candidates, offer programmes, canvas support for their nominees and control the activities of the epresentatives elected on their tickets.

Secondly, as agencies of political education and watchdog of the people they inform the masses about their own approaches to rural development and criticise the approaches which they consider undesirable. Thirdly, as constructive organisations they urge the workers to participate in the social service activities so as to maintain constant contact with citizens. Fourthly, a guardians of liberty and people's interest they agitate against what they consider to be wrong policies and faulty execution and organise the masses to bring pressure on the government for modifying the same.

Attitude of Political Parties Towards PRIs

The manifesto of the various political parties at different elections is an indication of their attitude towards PRIs. The Indian National Congress, in its election manifesto remarked that PR brings new and great opportunities to the people of the villages and expressed its confidence that they would organise and prepare themselves to assume the new responsibilities. Later in 1967, the party declared that the establishment of PRIs was a revolutionary step promoting mass participation in the administrative process and the economic reconstruction of the country at the village level. Recently, in 1989, a special session of the All-India Congress Committee was held at New Delhi, just before introducing the Panchayati Raj Bill (64th Constitution Amendment) in the parliament, and passed a resolution for a steady and immediate implementation of the Panchayati Raj System.

The Communist Party of India, in its 1962 manifesto remarked that the elected bodies were generally captured by representatives of vested interests and that they enjoyed very little power even in such matters as local planning and development. The real power and authority, according to the party vested with the offices.

The Bharatiya Jana Sangh in 1962 promised to restore local bodies, which it considered as the primary units of democratic system. The Praja Socialist Party in 1962 resolved that decentralisation of administration on the lines suggested by Balwant Rai Mehta team should be effected in all states. Its manifesto in 1967 observed that devolution of political power and decentralisation of economy were vital for the growth of democracy.

The Samyukta Socialist Party made no references to PR in its manifesto 1967; but in 1971 it demanded that power to form local panchayat and to regulate and control them should not rest with central and state governments. In its election manifesto, the Janata Dal (1989) promised the implementation of a new Panchayati Raj system, without affecting the existing federal system of the country.

The Partyless Democracy

The idea of partyless democracy first advocated in India by M.N. Roy has gained momentum by the work of protagonists of the Sarvodaya ideology like Jayaprakash Narayan.

In this thesis on reconstruction of Indian polity he has given cogent arguments why political parties should leave the arena of panchayat politics in the interest of the development of a system of participating democracy. Writing in *Swaraj* for the people he say: "The cry has already gone forth from certain parts of the country that the villagers should better be left as they were, rather than be made cockpits in the name of PR. The reason for this is that electoral contests have already produced such tensions that there is virtual stalemate in the affairs of the panchayat...".

According to him the conditions of self rule is that people agree to work together. Self-government through fact on fighting will not be self-government but self ruination.

The village is a face to face community. The caste and class distinction have made it a divided house to introduce electoral contests in the villages is to threw monkey wrench into the works! His two other arguments, namely that in a party system the candidates look upward to the party bosses to win their favour, in getting the party tickets and thus strengthen centralisation and that system of electoral contests are too costly that it tends to concentrate real power in the hands of economic bosses.

The alternative suggested by him is to bring the Gram Sabha into the picture. According to it, every gram sabha should select two delegates to an electoral college. The councilors will make nomination which might then be voted. Persons receiving less than a certain minimum number of votes would be dropped. In case there is no unanimity, the names of candidates selected in the above manner would be sent to the gram sabhas which would then proceed to vote upon them. The candidate would be declared elected by following either of the two procedures a candidate receiving the highest number of votes, or a candidate receiving the highest number of gram sabha votes, declared elected.

The other major advantages claimed are that, whereas in the existing system organised parties play a decisive role, in the proposed scheme the decisive role is played by the gram sabha and other representative bodies at the intermediate level which can arrest the tendency of the power being sanctioned off towards the top. Secondly, in the existing system there is very little scope for active participation in the political process except through periodical voting, in the proposed scheme such opportunities are abundant. Finally, the proposed system is less expensive to operate.

The Asoka Mehta Committee and Political Parties

The Asoka Mehta Committee recommended that political parties should be allowed to participate effectively at all levels. The committee pointed out that participation of political parties in the PR elections without symbols cause confusion among the electorates and detracts from political accountability.

The open and direct participation of political parties would facilitate healthier linkages with higher level political process. It is also necessary to provide constructive outlet to opposition parties; parties out of power at the state level may be able to chalk out achievement at the district level, district elections coupled with programme-based contests would offer greater scope to weaker sections for availing the opportunities offered by the political system. According to the committee, all political parties are in favour of genuine decentralisation of power to rural local levels. All shades of political opinion are represented in proportion to their strength. This alone will bring about the required consensus in the implementation of developmental programme. According to the committee, the success of the entire scheme would depend on continued interest, goodwill and co-operation of all political parties.

Leadership in Panchayati Raj

Leadership plays an important role in shaping the social, political and economic life of rural communities. Leadership however is an extremely complex social phenomenon. In many developing societies where the process of modernisation of economic structure is going on at a rapid place, the study of existing and emerging pattern of leadership has crucial importance. Although there is evidence for a trend for the emergence of a new type of leadership in most of these countries, a considerable gap exists between their urban and urbanised elites and rural leadership.

Panchayati Raj is regarded as the heart and soul of Indian democracy. The health and strength of India democracy depends on its sound functioning. It is an agency of social progress, economic prosperity and political development. Its institution acts as the catchment areas for the discovery of new leaders.

Leadership in PR cannot be studied in isolation, as it is embedded in the prevailing socio-economic and cultural context. No one can rise to a position of leadership unless he has the support of majority or a sizeable section of the community. Power structure in PR is characterised by groupism which provides the local political system. Every group tries to capture the seat of authority by influencing voters by various means at their disposal.

They know that success in the election alone provides the opportunity to rise to the highest position in public life.

Jawaharlal Nehru had firm faith in Panchayati Raj Institutions, but leaders like Lal Bahadur Shastri, did not have the same faith in the ability of the common people to guide and regulate themselves. Shastri expressed that in Indian situation such leadership might not well. He formed this opinion after studying the working of panchayats in Uttar Pradesh. Most of his successors were also like him. The leader has a difficult task in the villages. He has to see that the villages are motivated to work for their own betterment and that of the community and to attain the material and higher goals of the individual and his fellowmen. All this depends entirely upon the quality of leadership.

Leader and Leadership

Leadership has been defined in various ways, suffice here to take into account the following definitions. Ordway Tead defines it—"Leadership is the activity of influencing people to cooperate towards some common goal which they come to find desirable."

Pigors says, leadership is a process of mutual stimulation which by the successful interplay of relevant individual differences, controls human energy in the pursuit of a common cause. Simply defined, the leader is the individual who holds a leader's office. The term leader has been used to designate many different positions and functions. It is used to indicate a position in an organisation or an individual, who has been designated leader by voluntary action of the group.

The leader may emerge as a means to the achievement of the objectives desired by a group. As stated by Kicherboeker, he may be selected, elected or voluntarily accepted by a group because he possesses, or controls means (skills, knowledge, money, association; property etc.) which the group desires to utilise to attain their objectives. Any person who is more than ordinarily efficient in carrying psychological stimuli to others and is thus effective in conditioning collective responses may be called a leader. E.S. Bogardus, in *Leaders and Leadership* defines a leader as a person who exerts special influence over a number of people. Lastly, in the *International Encyclopedia of the Social Sciences,* Arnold Tannenbaum wrote in 1968:

> Leadership defines, initiates and maintains social structure. The serial system is, so to speak, programmed through leadership. Understanding leadership, then should be a simple and parsimonious approach to understanding the larger social system. Leadership, can have consequences for the lives and welfare of a large number of people and therefore, those who are concerned with the practical consequences of human actions must be accompanied with leadership.

Voting behaviour in Panchayat Polls

David C. Potter after making a study of the political process of rural Rajasthan has observed: "further field research is required to analyse the emerging leadership in rural Rajasthan. Enough is known, however to say that it tends to be the progressive in out look, as benefits comparative young educated and wealthy land-owning agriculturists. To meet panchayat raj leaders in Rajasthan today is to meet on the whole, enthusiastic men willing to devote time and energy to rural development work. Whether or not this sense of enthusiasm has filtered down to the ordinary villager throughout the state is a question to which there is no ready answer as yet.

M.V. Mathur, Iqbal Narain *et al.* have pointed out that in many cases the rural leaders have gone out of their way to divert these political currents to their own advantage. In the context of the Panchayati Raj setup the term political cannot as yet be used to denote divisions along ideological or party lines. It is politics of individual connections and preferences, though political labels and ideologies cannot be relegated completely into the background in a discussion of local politics today. Myron Weiner, a keen observer of Indian government and politics writes, in a study of a constituency in Andhra, it was discovered that virtually every village carried by the swathantra assembly candidate or which gave the swathantra candidate a large vote had a panchayat president who supported him. This constituency may of course, have been idiosyncratic, but conversations with local politicians in other constituencies support the impression that the panchayat president can be an influential, if not decisive voice in lieu the village votes in general election.

References

Ashok Vardhan, *People's Participation in Planning,* 1/PA, XXXVL No. 1, March 1990.

Biju, M.R. *Panchayati Raj System in India: A Symbol of Participatory Democracy and Decentralised Development,* Kanishka, New Delhi, 2008.

Biju, M.R., "State Finance Commission Report (1996) in Kerala and Karnataka: A Report", *Southern Economist,* Vol. 35, No. 14, 15 November, 1996.

Biju, M.R., *Dynamics of New Panchayati Raj System, Reflections and Retrospections,* Kanishka, New Delhi, 1998.

Biju, M.R., "Financial Organisation of Panchayati Raj Institutions in Kerala", *Kurukshetra,* Vol. XLIV, No. 7, April, 1996.

Chaturvedi, H.R. and S.K. Mitra, *Citizen Participation in Rural Development,* Word and IBH, 1982.

Dillon, B. and M. Stiefel, *Reading in Rural Development Communication,* Bulletin 21 University of Reading, 1987.

Dubashi, P.R., *Administrator and the Citizen,* IIPA, Vol. XXI, No, 3, July 1975.

Gangrade, K.D. *Development and People,* University of Delhi, 1985. Geoffrey McNicoll, *Community-Level Population Policy: An Exploration Development Review,* Vol. I, No. 1, September 1975, pp. 1-21.

Ghanshyam Shah and Chaturvedi H.R. *Gandhian Approach to Rural Development,* Ajanta, New Delhi, 1983.

Government of India, *Constitution of India,* Ministry of Law and Justice, New Delhi, 1986, p. 91.

Government of India, *Constitution of India, op. cit.*

Government of India, Planning Commission, Various Years, New Delhi Jain, R.B., NGOs in Development Perspective, New Delhi, 1995. lain, R.B., Public Administration in India, Deep and Deep, 2002.

Government of Kerala, "Administration Report of the Panchayat Department", Government Press, Trivandrum, 1987.

Government of Kerala, "Administration Report of the Panchayat Department 1992-93", Government Press, Trivandrum, 1995.

Government of Kerala, "Report of the Panchayat Finance Commission, (Chairman K. Avukader Kutty Naha), Government Press, Trivandrum, 1985, pp. 15, 18, 26, 65.

Government of Kerala, "Report of the Panchayat Finance Commission", *op. cit.*, and "Administration Report of the Panchayat Department 1986-87", *op. cit.*

Government of Kerala, Kerala Panchayat Act, 1960, Manager of Government Publications, Trivandrum, 1961, p. 47.

Harichandran, C., *Panchayati Raj and Rural Development: A Study of Tamil Nadu,* Concept Publishing Company, New Delhi, 1983, p. 50.

Jain, L.C., *Decentralisation and Local Governance,* Orient Longman, 2005.

Jain, L.C., *Grass without Roots,* Sage, New Delhi, 1985.

Karunakaran Pillai, G., *Local Finance in a Developing Economy: A Study of Panchayat Finance,* B.R. Publishing House, Delhi, 1986, pp. 47, 71, 75.

Narayanan Rao, K.V., "Panchayats and their Finances", In *Kerala, Journal of Rural Development,* N.1.R.D., Hyderabad, September, 1982, p. 753.

Nirmal Mukharji, "Decentralisation Below the State Level", *The Hindustan Times,* May 7, 1989.

Sapru, R.K., *Development Administration,* Sterling, New Delhi, 2002.

Shandana Khan Mohmand, "Representative Decentralisation Vs. Participatory Decentralisation" in Jain L.C., *Decentralisation and LocalGovernance: Essays for George Mathew,* Orient Black Swan, New Delhi, 2004.

Siby Mathew, *Law of Panchayat Elections in Kerala,* Law Times Press, Cochin, 1978, p. 62.

Smith, B.C., *Understanding Third World Politics,* Indiana University Press, 2003.

Uday Bhaskar, *Role of Voluntary Agencies in Rural Development,* DPA, Vol. XXX, No. 3, 1984.

United Nations, *Popular Participation in Economic and Social Development,* New York, 1986.

Visalakshi, N.R., *Administration of Village Panchayats in Kerala,* The Educational Supplies Depot, Trivandrum, 1967, p. 136.

3

Decentralization Initiatives and the Role of State Election Commission

The 73rd and 74th Constitutional Amendments in 1993, mandating the formation and functioning of local bodies (Panchayati Raj and Municipal Bodies) and listing several functions of the government to be handled down to local bodies, marked a watershed in India's quest for democratic development within pluralistic, parliamentary and electoral framework. Decentralization was defended on the grounds of bringing government closer to people and hence ensuring better results. The effectiveness of mandate of decentralization of administration and devolution of powers, however depended on the success of those stages that took up this task seriously. Kerala is one such state. Kerala's attempt at a participatory, systematical and transparent process of decentralization has hailed its unique achievement.

Kerala's decentralisation experience no doubt is unparalleled in the history of the country. It depicts the case of first State-led concerted effort for transferring powers, functions and institutions at one go to the third tier of governance – the local Governments accompanied by a simultaneous bottom up initiative for local level planning and development through the People's Plan Campaign. Devolution of Plan resources on a formula based, non-discretionary and equitable manner to the Local Governments is another hallmark where they now get a portion of the State's investible resources (about 25%) as Development Funds for implementing projects formulated at local level. In addition, the State transfers 3.5 per cent of its State Own Tax Revenue (SOTR) as General Purpose Fund and about 6.00 per cent of SOTR as Maintenance Fund every year. The Local Governments have absolute freedom in formulating and implementing projects based on their priorities subject to Plan guidelines issued by the State Government from time to time. It is also widely recognised that decentralisation, as practised in Kerala, has not only put it on a better development trajectory but also has had significant impact on quality, efficacy and inclusiveness of that development. For one thing, it has opened the public sphere for the hitherto socially excluded groups such as the Scheduled Castes/Scheduled Tribes and the politically excluded women in proportions never seen before.

While the first phase of Decentralised planning was initiated in Kerala in the 9th Five-Year Plan consequent to the enactment of the Kerala Panchayati Raj Act (1994) and Kerala Municipality Act (1994) and the constitutional amendments, the launching of the second phase coincides with the 13th Five-Year Plan. It emphasises deepening people's planning through Local Governments as an important strategy for achieving higher economic growth indicating the crucial role of the Local Governments. It also lays stress on the need for restoration of District Planning Committees to their rightful place in the process of planning and in drafting District Plans. The second phase of decentralised planning focuses on empowering and enabling Local Governments in achieving the objectives outlined in the 13th Plan.

At present, there are 1,200 Local Governments in Kerala, which includes 941 Grama Panchayats, 152 Block Panchayats, 14 District Panchayats, 87 Municipalities and 6 Municipal Corporations. The allocation of Development Fund to Local Governments is being done under three categories – General Sector, Scheduled Caste Sub Plan (SCSP) and Tribal Sub Plan (TSP). The Plan allocation for Development Fund for Local Governments is fixed in accordance with the Action Taken Report (ATR) on the recommendations of State Finance Commission (SFC). As per the ATR on the 5th SFC report, Plan allocation for Local Governments is to be fixed as a per cent of State Plan outlay. Thus, 24 per cent of the State Plan outlay was earmarked as Development Fund for the year 2018-19. This includes devolution from the Union Finance Commission Award. In 2019-20, 24.5 per cent (Rs. 7500 crore) of the State Plan Outlay has been earmarked as Development Fund as per the data provided in the Economic Review, 2019 of the State Planning Board.

MILESTONES IN THE DECENTRALIZATION INITIATIVES

(1) During British rule, following Lord Ripon's resolution on local self-government in 1882, urban local bodies were established in the form of municipal boards, sanitary boards, and the like. On the analogy of urban areas, laws were passed regarding panchayats also. Following the report of the Royal Commission on Decentralisation (1909) and the Government of India Act of 1919, the laws regarding panchayats were revised in 1920 and panchayats became legal entities losing their traditional prerogative powers. Above the village, taluk boards and district boards were formed with limited powers, many schools, public health, medical services and local roads. Starting largely as nominated bodies, their democratic character was gradually improved. On the analogy of legislation in British India, laws on panchayats and urban local governments were passed in the princely states also. Thus, when Kerala State was formed in 1956, there were panchayats and urban local bodies in the three different regions of the state, namely, Travancore, Cochin and Malabar. In addition, there was also a district board in the Malabar region which was then part of the Madras Province. The district board was abolished soon after the formation of Kerala State. The panchayats, municipalities, municipal corporations and townships continued as well established units of local government in the state, even though many of them had been facing financial difficulties during the last three decades and their powers had also been reduced in a number of ways, as part of the general tendency of centralisation. In Kerala, the village panchayats, in particular, were strong and viable units as there were only a thousand panchayats in all for a population of twenty nine million people. The average population of a Village panchayat was thus twenty-one thousand, an unusually large figure for a village panchayat in the country.

(2) In 1957, while the Balwantray Mehta study team was at work at the all-India level, the first elected government in Kerala came to power in April. This government gave top priority to administrative reforms and constituted a committee headed by the then chief minister, E.M.S. Namboodiripad. One of the terms of reference of the committee was to suggest methods for democratisation of the organs of the government at various levels. In its report submitted on 26 July, 1958, the committee

recommended the strengthening of panchayats in the state as viable and basic units of administration, development, and for the collection of land revenue. Above the panchayat, the committee recommended the reconstitution of taluks and blocks in such a way that revenue and development functions could be combined at the level of the taluk. On the district, the committee had two views, both set out in the report. One view was that with the strengthening of panchayats, which would be relatively large-sized, it would have been enough to have a district council with advisory functions, coordinating various development matters. The other view was that there should be an elected district council with executive functions and all the development departments at the district level should work under it. The committee recommended the implementation of the reform in three successive stages.

(3) Following the recommendations of the committee, the Kerala Panchayat Bill and later the District Councils Bill were introduced in the state assembly. The functions of the district council covered development matters which were to be progressively changed from agency functions to full-fledged executive functions. Neither the Kerala Panchayat Bill nor the District Councils Bill could, however, be enacted into law as on 31 July, 1959, the government was dismissed and the Legislative Assembly was dissolved. When the new government was formed after the general elections, the Kerala Panchayat Act, 1960, the Kerala Municipalities Act, 1960, and the Kerala Municipal Corporations Act, 1961, were passed, unifying the laws existing in the Malabar-Travancore-Cochin regions of the state and enlarging the functions and financial resources of these local bodies. In accordance with the objectives and reasons of the Kerala Panchayat Act, 1960, an impressive list of duties and functions were assigned to panchayats. The Act also provided that the government could authorise the panchayats to exercise other functions, such as collection of land revenue, maintenance of survey and village records, collection of village statistics, supervision and control over government primary schools, as also medical, public health, child welfare and maternity institutions and execution of community development works. Over the years, however, while the panchayats could perform most of their mandatory duties, only very few. If any of the development

functions were given to them and none of the responsibilities contemplated in the Act were entrusted to them by any of the government that followed. (In 1979, the specific mention of collection of land revenue and other revenue function was finally deleted from the Act.)

(4) In 1964, the next government which came to power introduced a Kerala Panchayat Union Councils and Zilla Parishads Bill. The draft of the Bill was on the lines of the recommendations of the Balwantray Mehta study team, with the Panchayati Raj system to be introduced being similar to the ones existing in states like Tamil Nadu and Rajasthan. Above the village panchayat, the block was to be the basic unit of planning and development with an elected panchayat union council and with sufficient authority to carry out development tasks. At the district level, there was to be an advisory zilla parishad. This Bill could also not make progress as the government fell within a few months. After a prolonged spell of President's Rule in the state, in March 1967, a ministry, again headed by E.M.S. Namboodiripad, came to power. The Kerala Panchayati Raj Bill, 1967, was introduced in the Legislative Assembly the same year. The Bill contemplated a two-tier system panchayats at the basic level and the zilla parishad at the district level. The zilla parishad was to have executive function and some sources of the supervision and control over the village panchayats. The functions of the zilla parishad contemplated in the Bill were developmental and were an elaboration of those contained in the 1959 Bill. The Bill was considered in detail by a Select Committee which recommended substantial changes. Major modifications were suggested in the functions and powers of zilla parishads, to be called district councils. The earlier wording of the relevant clause in the Bill, according to which the district was to be a unit of planning and development, was changed to the effect that the administration of a district in respect of matters enumerated in the First Schedule shall be vested in the district council." The recommendation came very near to what many others have subsequently referred to as creation of "district governments." The Bill, as recommended by the Select Committee, could not, however, become law and it lapsed in August 1970 when the Legislative Assembly was dissolved and fresh elections were called. In 1971, a new government, under the chief ministership of Achutha Menon, introduced the Kerala District Administration

Bill. The general structure of the Bill was the same as that recommended by the Select Committee in 1968, with greater elaboration of some of the provisions. This Bill also lapsed before it could be enacted into law.

(5) A Kerala District Administration Bill was again introduced in the Legislative Assembly in August 1978, when A.K. Antony was the chief minister. The structure of this Bill was also the same as the 1971 Bill, but the Second Schedule specifically listing such items as police administration, business administration, and the like, was removed and the functions under land revenue were also restricted. The Bill was finally passed by the legislature in 1979 and received the assent of the President on 18 May, 1980, by which time a new government under the chief ministership of E.K. Nayanar had come into power. In the next few months, a number of rules and notifications were issued but thereafter all action to implement the Act was abruptly stopped.

(6) The Kerala government commissioned a study of the defects of the Act of 1979, under S.M. Vijayanand, former Chief Secretary. It was entitled "Report on the Measures to be taken for Democratic Decentralisation at the District and Lower Level." The report was submitted. The acts creating these boards made no mention. Though the report was submitted in July 1988, and though it had specifically recommended the details of the preparatory action to be taken over a period of months before elections to the district councils could be held in 1990, no action was taken until the role of panchayats and, therefore, did not assign end of December. A fear had taken in the state any responsibilities to them as regards village that there was voodoo about decentralisation in Kerala as every government which had attempted it had fallen. Large numbers of people believed that it was because of this that no action was being taken by the government which had come to power in 1987 under the leadership of Nayanar. Suddenly, towards the end of December 1990, the government announced elections to the district councils which were to take office by 5 February of the following year.

(7) In March 1994, the state government introduced a Kerala Panchayat Raj Bill in the state legislature. The provisions in this Bill were very restrictive and led to a great deal of criticism both from intellectuals and public men as a result of strong public opinion, substantial changes were made in the Bill by the Select

Committee. A very much improved-Kerala Panchayat Act was introduced and the District Administration Act, 1979, repealed. The new Act conformed to the mandatory provisions of the Constitution. Gram Sabhas were to be formed ward-wise in Kerala in view of the large size of the panchayats. They were to have a number of supervisory and monitoring powers relating to development activity, and were also to assist in the identification of beneficiaries as well as in mobilisation of community efforts. The village panchayat was bound to place a report before each gram sabha on the development schemes and the development activities of each year and those proposed for the next year, and the reasons for non-implementation of the recommendations of the gram sabhas would have to be explained by the president of the panchayat. As regards village panchayats, there was a proposal to increase their number to 1,093, with 152 intermediate-level panchayats coterminous with the rural development blocks and fourteen district panchayats. The powers and functions of the panchayat at each of these levels had been listed in sufficient detail—there were 126 items for village panchayats, twenty-nine items for block level panchayats and eighty items for district panchayats. If the panchayats under the latest Act are enabled to exercise these functions effectively, a very major change will be brought about in the system of governance in the state. A great deal will, however, depend upon the manner in which funds are made available to the panchayats and on the extent of autonomy granted to enable them to function as an Institution of self-government.

(8) Kerala enacted the Conformity Act in April 1994. The first elections to the new three-tier Panchayat Raj set-up were held in September 1995 and the Panchayats came into being on 2 October. A significant event was the issue of a comprehensive government order in September 1995, transferring various institutions and staff to the three-tier PRIs. Another noteworthy event was the budget of 1996 which had a separate document known as Annexure-IV containing the details of the grants-in-aid and the schemes transferred to the local bodies. Thus, the allocation for the local bodies was seen as an independent subject of the state budget giving it the stamp of legislative approval and protecting it from the vagaries of executive decision-making. There was a change of government in May, 1996 and the Left Democratic Front

government embarked on a policy of massive decentralization. Two landmark events in enlarging and deepening the process of decentralisation need to be mentioned. First is the launching of the People's Planning Campaign on 17 August, 1996. This was spearheaded by the State Planning Board in partnership with the Department of Local Administration (now renamed as the Department of Local Self Government), associating political parties, non-governmental organisations, professional and elected members through an Advisory Committee to guide the campaign. It went beyond a government sponsored programme and soon assumed the nature of a movement resulting in an alliance of all those who reposed faith in decentralisation. It succeeded in harnessing public action for participatory planning at the grass-roots level and created not only a favourable environment for genuine decentralisation but also built up a powerful demand for radical reform in the legislative, administrative and developmental systems, thereby helping to formalise and institutionalise the paradigm shift to a bottom-up approach to planning and development with people's participation. Simultaneously, the Committee on Decentralisation of Powers under the chairmanship of late Dr. S.B. Sen was set up. The Committee laid down clear and coherent first principles in its inception report in August 1996 and they have been accepted as the guiding light of government policy. Later the Committee on Decentralisation of Powers interacted closely with the People's Planning Campaign and this synergy resulted in recommendations for basic restructuring of laws relating to local governance. The Committee's recommendations were incorporated into the Kerala Panchayat Raj Act in February 1999, providing the legal foundation for healthy and accountable institutions of local self-government. These and further recommendations of the Committee (still popularly known as the Sen Committee) have contributed immensely towards institutionalising the gains of People's Planning Campaign and other efforts towards decentralisation into a solid foundation for local self-government.

(9) The scale and magnitude of the decentralisation process in Kerala has been gigantic. In a sense it has followed a "big bang" approach, where a large number of powers and functions along with institutions and staff and resources have been transferred at one go. The government did not wait for the capacity of the local

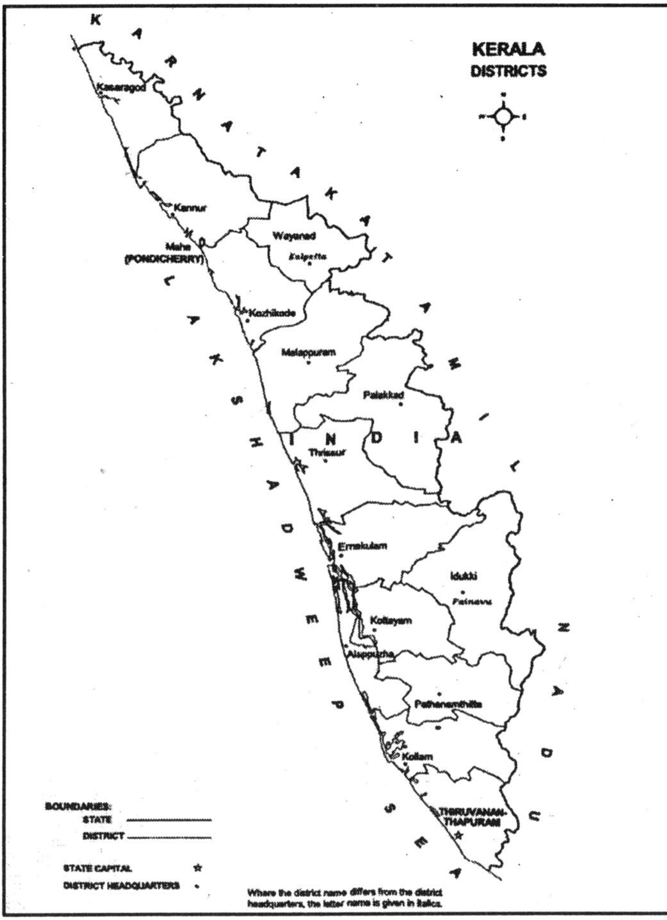

governments to be built up as a pre-condition for transfer of powers and responsibilities. A radically new approach where the capacity building is seen as a process facilitated by on the job responsibilities as well as well-orchestrated execution of public action programme was adopted. Hindsight proves that this approach is sensible where massive decentralisation is envisaged; power obviously can be transferred in small quantums as in this model. It goes to the credit of the government that right from the beginning there was the clear recognition that even if functions and responsibilities can be transferred at one stroke, decentralisation is a process which must be guided with care, and the unexpected issues and challenges thrown up by the process, have to be responded to very promptly with commitment and consistent action. The series of rules and orders issued and corrective action taken speaks of this commitment. (S.M. Vijayanand: *Status of Panchayati Raj*, Concept, New Delhi, 2013).

STATE ELECTION COMMISSION: CONSTITUTIONAL AND ADMINISTRATIVE RESPONSIBILITIES

(1) Constitutional Status: State Election Commission is constituted under Articles 243K and 243ZA of the Constitution of India for the superintendence, direction and control of the preparation of the electoral rolls for, and the conduct of all elections to the Panchayats and the Municipalities in the State. The State Election Commission, Kerala came into existence on 3rd December 1993. The State Election Commissioner is appointed by the Governor of Kerala under clause (1) of Article 243K of the Constitution of India. The Government, as per Notification SRO No. 978/B/2013 issued in GO (Ms) No. 378/2013/LSGD, dated 05.12.2013 have conferred on the State Election Commissioner the status, salary and allowances of a Judge of the High Court. The tenure of the State Election Commissioner is for a period of five years from the date he assumes charge or till he attains the age of 65 years, whichever is earlier. The State Election Commissioner is one of the members of the Delimitation Commission of India, set up under Delimitation Act, 2002, to delimit the boundaries of Assembly and Parliamentary constituencies in the State. State Election Commissioner is also the Chairman of the State Delimitation Commission constituted from time to time, to delimit the constituencies of Panchayats and wards of Municipalities and Municipal Corporations in the State.

(2) Duties and Function: The first and foremost duty of the State Election Commission is to supervise, direct and control of, the preparation of electoral rolls for, and the conduct of, all elections to Panchayats and Municipalities, in accordance with Article 243K and 243ZA of the Constitution of India. As the Chairman of the State Delimitation Commission, the State Election Commissioner plays a vital role in the works connected with delimitation of the wards or constituencies of Local Self Government Institutions in Kerala. In addition to the above, the

State Election Commissioner is vested with the following powers conferred by the Kerala Panchayat Raj Act, 1994, the Kerala Municipality Act, 1994 and the Kerala Local Authority (Prohibition of Defection) Act, 1999:

i. to determine wards/constituencies reserved for Scheduled Caste, Scheduled Tribes or Women.
ii. to determine the seats of President, Vice President, Chairman, Deputy Chairman, Mayor, Deputy Mayor - reserved for SC, ST or Women.
iii. to conduct the election of President/Vice President of Panchayats, Chairperson/Deputy Chairperson of Municipalities, and Mayor/Deputy Mayor of Municipal Corporations.
iv. to conduct the election of members of District Planning Committees.
v. to conduct election to various Standing Committees in the Local Self Government Institutions.
vi. to scrutinise the election expenses/accounts submitted by the candidates, who contested in the election to Local Self Government Institutions, and to disqualify the candidates who failed to submit accounts of election expenses or spent more than the prescribed limit. [According to the Kerala Panchayat Raj (Conduct of Election) Rules, 1995/Kerala Municipality (Conduct of Election) Rule, 1995) the expenditure of a candidate should not exceed Rs. 10,000 to a constituency in a Grama Panchayat, Rs. 30,000 in a Block Panchayat, Rs. 60,000 in a District Panchayat, Rs. 30,000 in a Municipality and Rs. 60,000 in a Municipal Corporation.]
vii. to decide the disqualification of elected members in accordance with the provisions of the Kerala Panchayat Raj Act, 1994 and the Kerala Municipality Act, 1994.
viii. to decide disputes on the question of resignation of Member/Councillor, President/Vice President, Chairperson/Deputy Chairperson, Mayor/Deputy Mayor of Local Self Government Institutions.
ix. to decide whether a member of a local authority has become subject to a disqualification under the provisions of the Kerala Local Authority (Prohibition of Defection) Act, 1999.

x. to conduct meeting in local bodies to discuss and decide on the motion of no-confidence against President/Vice President of Panchayat and Chairperson/Deputy Chairperson of Municipalities and Mayor/Deputy Mayor of Municipal Corporations and Chairman of Standing Committees.

(3) Powers: The State Election Commission has the following powers under Section 139 of the Kerala Panchayat Raj Act, 1994 in respect of enquiry and examination on issues relating to disqualification of a candidate or an elected member as provided under sub-section (2) of Section 34 or Section 36 or section 155 (3) of Kerala Panchayat Raj Act or sub-section (2) of Section 90 or Section 92 or Section 40(3) of Kerala Municipality Act, namely:

(1) (a) summoning and enforcing the attendance of any person and examining him on oath;
(b) requiring the discovery and production of any document or other material object producible as evidence;
(c) receiving the evidence of affidavits;
(d) requisitioning any public record or a copy thereof from any court or office;
(e) issuing summons for the examination of witness or documents.

(2) The Commission shall also have the power to require any person including Government Officials, subject to any privilege which may be claimed by that person under law for the time being in force, to furnish information on such points or matters as in the opinion of the Commission may be useful for, or relevant to, the subject matter of enquiry.

(3) The Commission shall be deemed to be a civil court and when any such offence, as is described in Section 175, Section 178, Section 179, Section 180 or Section 228 of the Indian Penal Code (Central Act 45 of 1860), is committed in the view or presence of the Commission, the Commission may, after recording the facts constituting the offence and the statement of the accused as provided for in the Code of Criminal Procedure, 1973 (Central Act 2 of 1974), forward the case to a Magistrate having jurisdiction to try the same and the Magistrate to whom any such case is

forwarded shall proceed to hear the complaint against the accused as if the case had been forwarded to him under Section 346 of the Code of Criminal Procedure, 1973.

(4) Any proceeding before the Commission shall be deemed to be a judicial proceeding within the meaning of Section 193 and Section 228 of the Indian Penal Code, 1860 (Central Act 45 of 1860).

(4) Disqualification: The Kerala Panchayat Raj Act, 1994 and the Kerala Municipality Act, 1994 enumerate various circumstances under which a member of a local body becomes disqualified. The question whether a member of a local body has become disqualified after having been elected as a member, is decided by the State Election Commissioner. It is a unique provision in the Acts enabling a voter to call back his representative if he fails to perform his statutory obligations and duties to a voter or to the community he represents. Another important function of the Commission is to decide the question of disqualification arising out of the defection under the provisions of the Kerala Local Authority (Prohibition of Defection) Act, 1999. Accordingly, if a member of a political party, after having been elected with the support of that political party, takes a different stand from that of the political party, it is nothing but disloyalty. Such persons are liable to be declared as disqualified from being a member of the local body for six years from the date of such declaration by the State Election Commission. The Commission is vested with judicial powers in deciding the question of disqualifications aforesaid. 714 cases were filed before the Commission for the period from 01.11.2010 to 31.10.2015 out of which, 665 cases have been disposed of by the Commission wherein 230 members of the local bodies have been declared disqualified by the Commission.

(5) Governance: The State Election Commissioner is the head of the office of the Commission. An officer not below the rank of Additional Secretary to Government is appointed as Secretary to the State Election Commission. For the smooth functioning of the Commission, Government have deputed a Senior Administrative Officer and a Senior Finance Manager both in the rank of Additional Secretary to Government and a Law Officer in the rank of Joint Secretary to the Commission. In addition to them, three Additional Secretaries to Government, one Joint Director each from the Department of Panchayats and Department of Urban Affairs and one Deputy Director from the Public Relations Department have been appointed in the Commission. All these officers are also the Nodal officers who supervise the election/by-election process in the district assigned to them. In addition to the above officers, two Section Officers from the Government Secretariat, twelve Assistants, one Data Entry Operator, one Computer Programmer, two Confidential Assistants, five Typists, one Clerical Assistant, eleven Office Attendants, one Watchman, Two Part Time Sweepers and three Drivers are working in the office of the State Election Commission.

(6) Officials:

(a) **District Election Officers:** District Collectors have been designated as District Election Officers in all the 14 districts in the State. There is a Deputy Collector (Election) and an Assistant each in district to assist the District Election Officer. The District Election Officers co-ordinate and supervise all works in the respective districts or in the area within their jurisdiction in connection with preparation or revision of electoral rolls and the conduct of all elections to Local Self Government Institutions subject to the superintendence, direction and control of the State Election Commission. The Commission provides funds to various officials for meeting election expenditure through the District Election Officers. The Election Deputy Collectors have been designated as the Assistant District Election Officers for Municipalities and Corporations and the Deputy Director of Panchayats of the districts as the Assistant District Election Officers for Panchayats.

(b) **Electoral Registration Officers:** As per section 14 of the Kerala Panchayat Raj Act, 1994 and section 72 of the Kerala Municipality Act, 1994, the electoral roll for each constituency or ward, as the case may be, shall be prepared and revised by the Electoral Registration Officers who shall be such officers of Government or of a local body as the State Election Commission may, in consultation with the Government, designate or nominate in this behalf. The Secretaries of the Grama Panchayats and Municipalities are designated as Electoral Registration Officers for the preparation and revision of electoral rolls for all the constituencies comprised in the Grama Panchayats.

ADMINISTRATIVE STRUCTURE OF SEC, KERALA

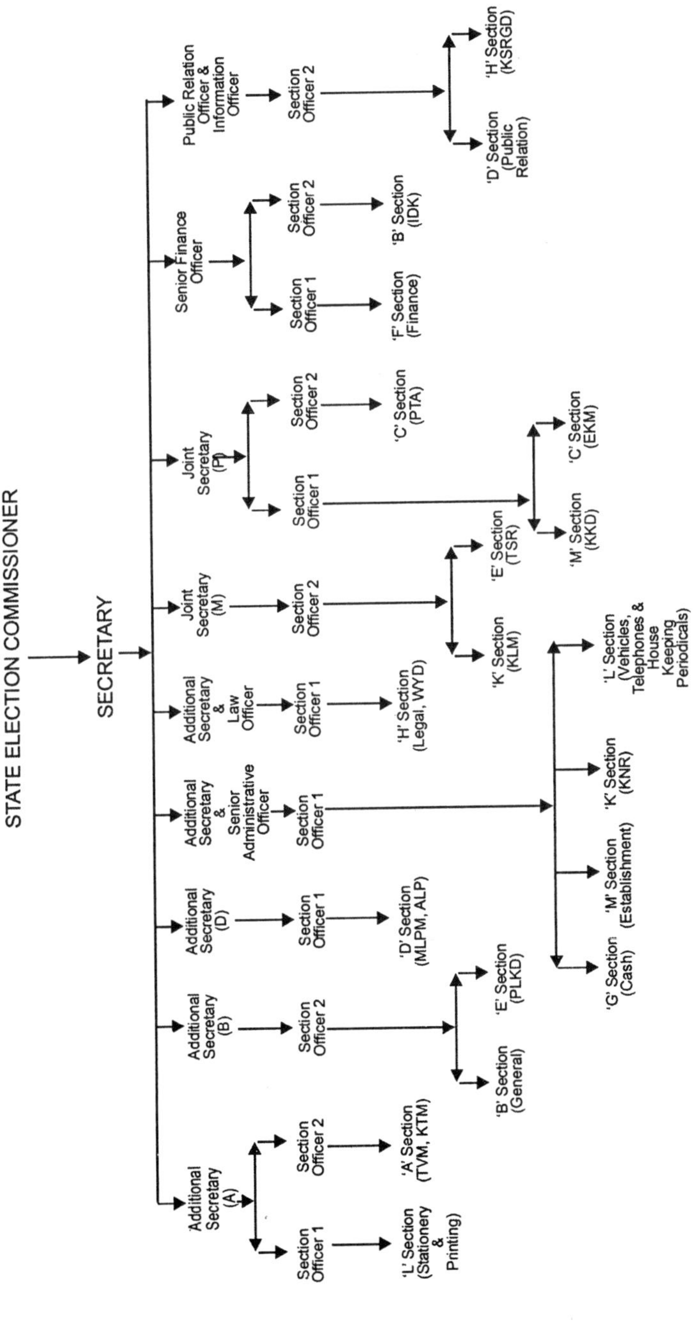

Source: Election Report 2015, Kerala State Election Commission, 2016.

(c) Assistant Electoral Registration Officers: Section 15 of the Kerala Panchayat Raj Act and section 72 of the Kerala Municipality Act provide for the designation of one or more persons as Assistant Electoral Registration Officers to assist the Electoral Registration Officers in the performance for their functions. The Assistant Secretaries, Superintendent/Head Clerk, Accountant of the Grama Panchayat are designated as Assistant Electoral Registration Officers to assist Electoral Registration Officers. For Municipalities, PA to Secretary, Revenue Officer, Municipal Engineer & Superintendent and for Municipal Corporations Deputy Secretary, Revenue Officers, PA to Secretary, Council Secretary, Accounts Officer & Engineers are designated as the Assistant Electoral Registration Officers.

(d) Returning Officers: The State Election Commission shall, in consultation with the Government, designate or nominate one or more Returning Officer who shall be an Officer of the Government or of a Local Self Government Institution for every Panchayat/Municipality for every election to fill a seat or seats in the Panchayat/Municipality. It is the general duty of the Returning Officer to do all such acts and things for conducting the elections as provided by the Act and Rules or Orders made thereunder. In the General Election 2015, the Commission, as per order Nos. from 129/2015/SEC to 132/2015/SEC, dated 03.10.2015 has issued notifications designating Officers of various departments as Returning Offices of Local Self Government Institutions. The State Election Commission appoints one or more persons as Assistant Returning Officers to assist any Retuning Officer in the performance of his function. As per the Notification Nos. from 133/2015/SEC to 136/2015/SEC dated 03.10.2015, the Commission has appointed Assistant Retuning Officers for the above purpose.

(e) Presiding Officers: The District Election Officer shall appoint a Presiding Officer for each polling station and such Polling Officer or Officers as he thinks necessary for the polling duty in any election to Local Self Government Institutions. It is the general duty of the Presiding Officer at a polling station to see that the poll is conducted in free and fair manner.

(f) Election Observers: Section 40A of the Kerala Panchayat Raj Act, 1994 and Section 96A of the Kerala Municipality Act, 1994 provide that the State Election Commission may nominate adequate number of higher officials of Government as Observers in consultation with the Government for observing the election of the Panchayat or Municipality. The Election Observers shall assist the Commission to ensure a fair and equitable election and shall discharge such other functions as may be entrusted by the Commission. During the General Election 2015, the State Election Commission had appointed 14 higher officials in the rank of IAS or IFS as General Observers for 14 districts. Moreover, 60 officials in the rank of Additional Secretary, Joint Secretary, Deputy Secretary in the Finance Department, Joint Director and Deputy Director in the Kerala State Audit Department were appointed as Expenditure Observers for the above purpose.

(g) National Informatics Centre: National Informatics Centre is an organisation under the Ministry of Communication and Information Technology, Government of India in the field of informatics services and information technology application. The State Election Commission had entrusted the NIC, Kerala Circle to provide online facilities for the preparation of electoral roll and all technical support to the Commission for the election activities. Accordingly, the NIC had developed software for Electoral Roll Management System, Online enrollment, e-drop for deployment of staff for polling duties, TREND for online transmission of election result etc. The IC rendered the technical support in a highly appreciable manner.

(h) Reservation for SC, ST and Women: Government notified the total number of constituencies or wards to be filled up by direct election in a Municipality and Municipal Corporation and also the seats to be reserved for Scheduled Caste, Scheduled Tribe and Women. Similarly, the Director of Panchayats on behalf of the Government had notified the total number of constituencies to be filled up in the Panchayats and the number of seats to be reserved for SC, ST and Women. As per Section 10 (2B) of the Kerala Panchayat Raj Act, 1994 and Section 69 of the Kerala Municipality Act, 1994, the State Election Commission had authorised District Election Officers and Regional Joint Directors of Urban Affairs Department to determine the constituencies and wards to be reserved for Scheduled Caste, Scheduled Tribe and Woman according to rotation. The total number of seats reserved in the state in this regards for the purpose of the General Election 2015 is shown in Table 8.5. The Government also notified the number of offices of the Presidents of Grama Panchayat, Block Panchayat,

District Panchayat, Chairman of Municipalities and Mayors of Municipal Corporation to be reserved for Scheduled Caste, Scheduled Tribe and Women. Accordingly, the Commission, as per Notifications No. from 124/2015/SEC to 128/2015/SEC dated 03.10.2015, had reserved the Offices of the Heads of Grama Panchayats, Block Panchayats, District Panchayats, Municipalities and Municipal Corporations for the Scheduled Caste, Scheduled Tribe and Women in connection with the General Election 2015.

References

Status of Panchayti Raj in the State and Union Territories of India, 2013, Institute of Social Sciences and Concept Publishing Company, New Delhi, 2013.

S.M. Vijayanand, Kerala, *Status of Panchayti Raj in the State and Union Territories of India 2013,* Institute of Social Sciences and Concept Publishing Company, New Delhi, 2013.

Government of Kerala, *Kerala: An Authentic Handbook,* Information and Public Relation Department, 2010.

Government of Kerala, *The Kerala Panchayat Raj Bill, 1994,* Government Press, Thiruvananthapuram, 1994.

Government of Kerala, *The Kerala Panchayat Raj Act, 1994,* Government Press, Thiruvananthapuram, 1995.

Government of Kerala, *The Kerala Municipality Act, 1994,* Government Press, Thiruvananthapuram, 1994.

G. Palanithurai, *Third General Election to Local Government in Tamil Nadu,* Concept Publishing Company Pvt. Ltd., New Delhi, 2008.

Government of Kerala, State Election Commission, Election Report 2015, Kerala State Election Commission, 2016.

Biju, M.R. and Pandya, J.N., "Democratic Decentralisation in an Indian State – Kerala", *The Indian Journal of Political Science,* July-September, 1991.

4

Panchayat Polls—1953, 1963, 1979, 1988 and 1995

Kerala was the first in India to have elections on the basis of universal adult franchise when the erstwhile state of Travancore, held it in 1948. Elections were held in Travancore-Cochin state in 1952 and 1954. After the formation of the state of Kerala in 1956, the first elections to the Kerala Legislative Assembly were held in 1957. Through this election, Kerala came to political prominence on becoming the first state in the world to vote Communists to power through parliamentary process.

Kerala, after its formation on November 1, 1956 witnessed fifteen legislative assembly elections, sixteen Lok Sabha elections, and eight panchayat elections. Elections to the legislative assembly were held in 1957, 1960, 1965, 1967, 1970, 1977, 1980, 1982, 1987, 1991, 1996, 2001, 2006, 2011 and 2016. The Lok Sabha elections were held in 1957, 1962, 1967, 1971, 1977, 1980, 1984, 1989, 1991, 1996, 1998, 1999, 2004, 2009, 2014 and 2019.

Panchayat Elections

Since Independence ten panchayat elections were held in the state. The first was in 1953 in Travancore-Cochin under the provisions of the Travancore-Cochin Panchayat Act, 1950. The second election was held in 1963 after the formation of the state (in 1956) and after the passing of Kerala Panchayat Act, 1960. Later, people of Kerala exercised their franchise power, for electing new panchayats was after a long break of sixteen years. The third election was, thus, held in 1979. It was followed by 1988 polls. After 1988 polls Elections to the District Councils were held in 1991. After the district council polls, the efforts and initiatives for the decentralization process started both at the national and state levels. It culminated in the passing of the historic 73rd and 74th Constitution (Amendment) Acts, 1992 and its state level legislation viz., Kerala Panchayati Raj Act, 1994 and Kerala Municipality Act, 1994. After the completion of the constitutional obligations elections to the three-tier PRIs and Municipal Councils and Municipal Corporations were held in 1995. After 1995 polls elections to the rural and urban local bodies were held in 2000, 2005, 2010 and 2015. Next election is due in October 2020.

1. PANCHAYAT POLLS, 1953

The first panchayat poll was held in 1953, under the provisions of the Travancore-Cochin Panchayat Act, 1950 as mentioned earlier. In almost all panchayat elections were fought on party basis. The major parties had their units in their villages. The Congress Party was the most dominant party in the state and also in the rural society generally. The Communists (CPI) had strong, disciplined and well organised party units in many villages. The RSP and the PSP also had their units in certain areas. Panchayat elections gave the non-Congress parties an opportunity to challenge the power position of the Congress among the rural population. The various parties put up their own candidates. In some panchayats they supported independents. The Communist Party did not formally put up its candidates. Their strategy was to forge a broad united front sponsored by it. In the elections this front came next to Congress which bagged the largest number of seats in the 550 panchayats in the Travancore-Cochin state. These elections were keenly contested.

The first elections to the rural representative government since independence witnessed the real political awakening in the villages. The percentage of votes polled ranged between 80 and 85. In 1953, there was no party in the state to challenge seriously the dominant position of the Congress which led the struggle for responsible government in the state. Since 1948 the party had lost its image considerably, but even then it was popular and the dominant elite group in the majority of villages supported it. No political movement or party was able to change the political power structure in the state or to challenge the status quo. Nobody raised the problem of non-partisan rural democracy in 1951. The Congress was quite optimistic about its success. Secondly, the contradictions in the society had not unfolded themselves to the masses very clearly nor were they quite acute. Thirdly, the panchayats had only meagre powers and were circumscribed by many a rule and regulation and by departmental bureaucratic control. The financial resources were very limited. Even though the political parties were enthusiastic in capturing power in rural government, they implicitly recognised the limitations of panchayat administration.

2. PANCHAYAT POLLS, 1963

The second panchayat elections in the state or the first panchayat elections since the formation of the state of Kerala, were held in November-December 1963 exactly from November 16 to December 6. The elections were held on non-partisan basis and the parties were not allowed to use their election symbols. They presented a complex and unique picture of inter-party compromise, understanding and co-operation and conflicts. The elections also reflected to the formalism of a transitional society because parties had agreed to keep the elections free from party politics and their nominees entered the contest without party tickets. The Congressmen, the Communists, the RSP, the NP, the Muslim League, supported and opposed each other in a bewildering variety of combinations. There were total 18,710 candidates, out of it 76 were women. The total number of panchayats in 1963 was 922. Out of it elections were held in 918 panchayats. 535 candidates were elected unopposed throughout the state. It is interesting to note that in 4 panchayat candidates were elected unopposed. The total number of polling stations in the state was 7371. The elections were remarkably peaceful. The candidates on the elections were mainly drawn from the professional classes like teachers, physicians and lawyers from the active cadre of political parties. A number of MLAs and an MP and several ex-MLAs fought for the honour of sitting in the panchayats. Though in the theoretical sense, election was held without party affiliation, the whole scene was permeated with party politics directly or indirectly. The political parties built a number of united fronts, or platforms like the *'Poura Munnani'* (People's Front). There was no uniform pattern of alliances among parties throughout the state. The alliances differed from region to region, panchayat to panchayat. In the Travancore area, the Communists and the RSP generally joined hands to fight the Congress. But this did not prevent them fighting each other in some places. In the Cochin area, peasants and workers party supported the Communists in some panchayats, though it opposed in some others. In Malabar, the Muslim League and the Communist Party forged a front against the Congress and got hold of the majority of the panchayats. A study of the electoral contest and the results shows that even though caste, kinship, personality, money etc. played their role in varying combinations under varying circumstances, party politics and ideology was the most dominant single factor which influenced voting behaviour. In the context of the unique conditions of Kerala, wider issues of party politics were brought bear on electoral politics in rural government. Even before the emergence of the Kerala state in 1956, the political parties were firmly rooted in the rural politics and government.

3. PANCHAYAT POLLS, 1979

After the panchayat poll, 1963 people of Kerala went to polling stations to elect their representatives to panchayat, after a long and historical break of 16 years. Elections were held on two days—September 15, 1979 and September 18, 1979. Significant and historical development in the election was that, the voting age was reduced from 21 to 18. This was made, when A.K. Antony was the Chief Minister. Due to this a large number of youngsters got opportunity to take part in the political destiny of local bodies.

In the districts of Trivandrum, Quilon, Kottayam, Ernakulam, Palaghat and Calicut elections were held on 15 September and in the remaining district—Alleppey, Idukki, Trichur, Malappuram, and Cannanore were held on 18 September. Unlike 1963 election, 1979 election was held on party basis and parties were allowed to use their election symbols. Major fight was between the Congress-led United Democratic Front and the CPI (M)-led Left Front. All major political parties, in the state, both national and regional actively participated in the election process. The major national parties fielded candidates include Congress (I), Congress, CPI (M), Janata, CPI and regional parties include, Muslim League, Muslim League Opposition, Kerala Congress (Pillai), Kerala Congress, RSP and PSP. The district-wise classification of number of panchayats, number of wards, number of candidates, candidates elected unopposed and voting percentage is furnished in Table 4.1.

Table 4.1: Panchayat Polls 1979 – District-wise details

Name of District	*No. of Panchayats*	*No. of Wards*	*No. of Candidates*	*Candidates Elected Uncontested*	*Voting Percentage*
Trivandrum	74	780	3301	2	72%
Quilon	93	960	4714	2	85.90%
Kottayam	67	639	2915	8	75.92%
Ernakulam	76	702	3148	3	72%
Palaghat	85	761	2660	6	70%
Calicut	93	866	8635	8	75.80%
Alleppey	91	861	861	—	78.80%
Idukki	45	385	385	—	78%
Trichur	98	937	937	—	78.80%
Malappuram	83	766	766	—	70%
Cannanore	119	1081	1081	—	78%
Total	931	8738	28403	29	

Source: *Kerala Kaumudi*, Trivandrum dated September 18, 1979, September 19, 1979, September 21, 1979, September 24, 1979.

Table 4.2 depicts the details regarding number of seats contested (ward-wise) and seats won by various political parties.

Table 4.2: Panchayat Polls 1979 – Election Results

Sl. No.	*Party*	*No. of Seats Contested (Wards)*	*Seats Won (Wards)*
1.	CPI (M)	4751	2961
2.	Congress	1687	662
3.	Congress(I)	1795	364
4.	CPI	443	66
5.	Muslim League	982	519
6.	Muslim League (Opp)	278	112
7.	Kerala Congress (Pillai)	68	32
8.	RSP	295	52
9.	Janata	11	1
10.	Independents	23320	3911

Source: Kerala Kaumudi (Trivandrum), September 24, 1979.

Table 4.3 further illustrates the final party position in a detailed manner.

Table 4.3: Panchayat Polls 1979 – Final Party Position

Total number of panchayats	990
Total number of panchayats where election held	931
Total number of wards	8738
Results declared	6370
CPI(M)	2250
Congress	494
Congress(I)	253
CPI	33
Muslim League (Opposition)	106
Muslim League	479
RSP	15
Independents	2700
Others	40
Results countermanded	68

Source: Kerala Kaumudi (Trivandrum), September 21, 1979.

4. PANCHAYAT POLLS, 1988

The third elections to panchayats, were held on 23 January, 1988 after nine years. Out of the 1001 panchayats throughout the state, elections were held in 999. Like 1979 elections, it was held on party basis and all political parties—both national and regional—participated in the election process by using their election symbols. Polls were held in a peaceful manner. 70 per cent to 82 per cent of the electorate exercised their franchise.

A record polling was marked in Kottayam district. More than 92 per cent of the voters exercised their voting right. Next to Kottayam was Quilon, where 85 to 90 per cent electorates exercised their franchise power. A noticeable feature in the poll was that the heavy turnout was reported from the coastal areas of particularly in Trivandrum district. The enthusiasm of the voters in the wards reserved for women were visible throughout the state. In the newly formed Pathanamthitta and Wayanad district, elections were held for the first time, the turnout was impressive. In the both these districts, a festive mood was visible.

In the electoral battle, the Congress-led United Democratic Front (UDF) and the CPI(M)-led Left Democratic Front (LDF) showed more or less same strength. Electoral statistics show, the

UDF got 42.6 per cent of votes and the LDF got 42.93 per cent of votes. In Kerala LDF particularly the Congress (I) strengthened its grassroot level base by capturing more village panchayats than the CPI(M). In this election the Congress and its allies secured a massive mandate in one of the CPI(M) strong tides of northern Kerala. The total difference of votes of both these fronts was less than 6,04,541 votes (0.07).

The panchayat polls in Kerala assumed greater significance mainly due to defeat of the Congress and the UDF in the assembly poll which were held on 23rd March, 1987. But in the previous 1989 parliament elections, the Congress achieved a massive mandate by securing 18 seats out of total 20 seats. This was a disastrous and humiliating defeat for the CPI(M) and its allies. Panchayat poll was declared after these two elections. Out of the two one was won by the Congress and the other by the CPI(M).

The Congress considered the panchayat poll as a means for its revival both at the grassroots and urban areas, whereas the CPI (M) and the left tried its best to vindicate their claim that the party continues to enjoy the overwhelming support of the rural people of Kerala.

Pre-Poll Scene: Ideological Manifestations

The tone of election campaign was set by the CPI(M) by releasing its manifesto. Major features of the CPI(M) manifesto were:

(1) Programme for improving agriculture would be given priority.
(2) It would see the electricity, drinking water and road transport facilities reach every village and improve the existing condition.
(3) It promised loans for the weaker sections of the society for housing, animal husbandry etc.
(4) It emphasised small and minor irrigation, and social forestry projects etc.
(5) It reiterated its commitment to democracy, socialism and secularism.

The Congress manifesto focused on the following principles:

(1) The concept of panchayat raj would be given due weight.
(2) It reiterated its commitment to democracy, socialism, national integration and removal of poverty.
(3) Programme for improving agriculture and allied occupation would be given priority.
(4) Programmes for improving the conditions of small scale industries like cashew, coconut coir etc. were promised.

The manifesto of the CPI contained more or less the same promises like that of the CPI(M) manifesto.

The BJP manifesto also centred its hopes on the following fundamental values, viz.:

(a) National harmony,
(b) Commitment to democracy,
(c) Secularism based on moral principles,
(d) Gandhian socialism, and
(e) Politics based on certain values.

Besides these five principles, the BJP also favoured on more powers to panchayats, elimination of corruption, priorities to the village needs, remunerative prices, protection of Harijans and other weaker sections, removal of red tapism etc. The Janata manifesto tried to project an idyllic picture of rural Kerala. It focused attention on creating facilities for drinking water, link roads, irrigation facilities, removal of literacy etc.

Selection of Candidates

Use of the victory of the CPI(M)-led Left Front in the state assembly elections in March 1987, the rush for tickets in the LDF particularly, in CPI(M) camp was tremendous. Since the CPI(M) had of late became the shelter for all kinds of people, the problem of selection of candidates became more acute. However, compared to other parties, the CPI(M) has started selection process in LDF was a smooth affair. The LDF, particularly, started the preparations for the panchayat poll immediately after the assembly polls held in March 1987. The party engaged a large number of cadres to help prepare the voters' lists and resorted to a mass contact programme. Soon after the assembly polls and a few months before the panchayat polls, the state witnessed one of the most intensive campaigns launched by the CPI(M).

The centre party machinery was geared up for the panchayat poll. The main campaigner for the party was the chief minister E.K. Nayanar and CPI(M) state secretary V.S. Achuthanandan. Their public meetings drew huge crowds indicating what was in store for the CPI(M) in the poll. The UDF particularly the Congress party was a late starter and Kerala Pradesh Congress Committee, took a long time before formally deciding to join the fray. The UDF had little time for election campaigning which was spear-headed by the opposition leader K. Karunakaran. Though the last parliamentary election results gave rise to some hopes in Kerala Pradesh Congress circles of achieving better results this time, but lack of organisation and intra-party squabbles stood in the way of its success in the election. The UDF took a lot of time for selecting their party candidates. There was rift within the UDF, particularly between the Congress and the two factions of the Kerala Congress, and within the front partners, conflict and group rivalries existed up to the polling date. In some panchayats, it is interesting to point out that, the UDF partners fielded their own separate candidates against each other, and led to increased rivalry within the UDF camp.

Compared to the CPI(M) and Congress, the selection process of all other parties particularly BJP was a smooth affair. The BJP made electoral alliance with Hindu Munnani. The Communist Marxist party led by M.V. Raghavan [who was expelled from the CPI(M) for anti-party activities] also fielded their own candidates without joining the LDF or UDF.

Table 4.4 gives the district-wise classification of nomination papers.

Election Campaign

The announcement of panchayat elections had stirred the people and the political parties alike. It had come after six years. As soon as the last date of withdrawal was over, the scene was shifted to poll campaign. The idea is not to discuss the common features of such campaigns but to point out some curious aspects of it. One such was the attitude of the Congress towards the law and order problems in Kerala. It made a series of charges against the LDF particularly against the CPI(M) over its failure in maintaining law and order in the state and raised voice against CPI(M)'s terror

Table 4.4: Panchayat Polls, 1988 – District-wise Classification of Nomination Papers

District	*Total No. of Panchayats*	*Total No. of Wards*	*Total No. of Polling Stations*	*Total No. of Voters*	*No. of Nomination Papers*													*Total*
					BJP	*CPI*	*CPI (M)*	*Cong. (I)*	*Ker. Cong.*	*Ker. Cong. (M)*	*IP*	*Cong. (s)*	*IUML*	*RSP*	*Lok Dal*	*NDP*	*Independent*	
Trivandrum	84	886	1,464	1,432,825	239	163	636	789	23	35	45	88	36	52	62	21	982	3,171
Quilon	71	805	1,367	1,375,018	195	310	431	617	97	40	40	68	61	168	14	3	856	2,900
Pathanamthitta	55	521	719	706,593	74	57	182	319	39	19	25	49	4	39	2	1	1,107	1,917
Alleppey	71	717	1,079	1,089,674	173	158	393	557	35	33	13	45	31	36	2	21	730	2,227
Kottayam	73	733	1,083	1,074,616	61	152	301	321	39	119	9	39	14	3	6	–	1,534	2,598
Idukki	51	480	676	656,652	19	101	206	264	99	93	26	11	19	17	5	1	704	1,565
Ernakulam	86	860	1,302	1,298,201	151	98	381	622	34	53	20	66	49	7		–	1,177	2,658
Trichur	98	1,009	1,592	1,549,930	448	186	525	784	23	37	55	82	55	15	11	10	1,077	3,308
Palaghat	91	894	1302	1,277,299	235	153	718	784	19	39	86	75	152	4	1	1	752	3,019
Malappuram	95	999	1,508	1,467,827	366	60	462	536	4	–	67	80	543	6		–	839	2,963
Calicut	77	804	1,265	1,336,496	309	73	420	480	19	22	133	109	245	–	1	–	427	2,238
Wayanad	25	256	375	366,524	122	18	109	167	11	33	42	27	63	–	–	–	298	890
Cannanore	85	848	1,268	1,250,955	198	77	562	585	28	31	83	57	166	11	–	1	380	2,179
Kasaragod	37	369	567	547,372	168	40	214	206	6	3	14	25	102	–	–	–	294	1,072
Total	**999**	**10,181**	**15,567**	**15,429,982**	**2,758**	**1,646**	**5,540**	**7,031**	**476**	**557**	**658**	**821**	**1,540**	**358**	**104**	**59**	**11,157**	**32,705**

Source: Government of Kerala, Panchayat Directorate, Official file on 1988 Panchayat Poll, Trivandrum, 1988.

tactics and attacks against the Congress workers.

An interesting fall-out of the election was that, both the Kerala Congress, Kerala Congress (I) and Kerala Congress (M), the two major united-front partners, who were embroiled in bitter squabbles with the Congress during the initial stages of the poll, over the selection of candidates, got cooled down considerably, after finalising the list of candidates. Like the Congress party, the BJP-Hindu Munnani alliance, made several charges against the CPI(M) on law and order issues. The campaign of the CPM and the Left concentrated only on certain particular areas, in which they had their committed followers.

Election Results

Never in the past elections to the village panchayats had aroused so much interest in people as they did in 1988. Elections were held in all the fourteen districts of the state. The panchayat poll of 1988 was described as a mini general election. The poll certainly reflected the high level of political consciousness of the state's rural electorates. The state average of voting was 78 per cent whereas there were booths with 95 per cent voting.

Out of the total 999 village panchayats containing 10,181 wards, elections were held in 10,176. In the elections CPI(M) secured the highest number of seats 3,360, followed by the Congress with 2,984 seats. The CPI(M) secured more than 33 per cent of the seats whereas the Congress got 29 per cent. Considering the total number of seats the Left Democratic Front won 42.93 per cent, against the United Democratic Front 42 per cent. The other left front partners CPI. Congress (S), Janata, RSP and Lok Dal secured 594 (5.83%), 191 (1.88%), 155 (1.52%), 64 (0.63%) and 7 (0.069%) respectively. In the UDF, besides the Congress, the other partners—Indian Union Muslim League, Kerala Congress(I), Kerala Congress(M) NDP, secured 1015 (9.97 %), 205 (2.01%), 123 (1.21%) and 10 (0.99%) respectively.

Tables 4.5 to 4.10 give an in-depth picture of the poll results.

Table 4.5: Panchayat Polls 1988 – Total number of Panchayats Won by Various Fronts, BJP and Independents

District	Total No. of Panchayats	Left Demo-cratic Front	United Demo-cratic Front	BJP	Panchayat without absolute majority to any Party	Total No. of Wards	Left Demo-cratic Front	United Democratic Front	BJP	Indepen-dent	Wards where election countermanded
Trivandrum	84	42	30	—	12	886	453	386	—	46	Vellara Panch. Ward No. IV
Quilon	71	32	23	—	16	805	395	351	1	57	Velinallur Panch. Ward No. 11
Pathanamthitta	55	8	9	—	38	521	164	178	3	176	
Alleppey	71	30	24	—	17	717	337	286	1	93	
Kottayam	73	8	18	—	47	733	205	241	1	285	Poonjan Panch Ward No. 1
Idukki	51	11	15	—	25	480	160	216	—	104	Thiruvankulam Panch. Ward II
Ernakulam	86	22	29	—	35	860	324	359	1	175	
Trichur	98	43	28	—	27	1,009	472	393	7	137	
Palaghat	91	45	25	—	21	894	456	349	3	86	
Malappuram	95	8	66	—	21	999	250	638	5	105	Trikkalangode Panch. Ward II
Calicut	77	40	26	—	11	804	413	345	10	36	
Wayanad	25	8	8	—	9	256	100	114	3	39	
Cannanore	85	55	22	—	8	848	505	310	6	27	
Kasaragod	37	12	19	2	4	369	137	171	37	24	
Total	999	364	342	2	291	10,181	4,371	4,337	78	1,390	Total 5 Wards

Source: Government of Kerala, Panchayat Directorate, Official file on 1988 Panchayat Poll, Trivandrum, 1988.

Table 4.6: Panchayat Polls 1988 – Number of Seats Won by Political Parties and Independents – District-wise Picture

District	Total No. of Wards	CPI (M)	CPI	Cong. (S)	Janata Party	Lok Dal	RSP	Total (LDF)	Cong (I)	IUML	Kerala Cong (I)	Kerala Cong (M)	NDP•	Total (UDF)	BJP	Inde-pendent	Wards where election counter-manded
Trivandrum	886	378	46	8	4	6	11	453	370	3	4	4	5	386	—	46	1
Quilon	805	241	110	5	2	—	37	395	282	16	41	10	2	351	1	57	1
Pathanamthitta	521	130	15	11	7	—	1	164	148	1	15	14	—	178	3	175	—
Alleppey	717	254	60	12	2	1	8	337	249	7	11	16	3	286	1	93	—
Kottayam	733	154	38	10	2	—	1	205	156	9	71	5	—	241	1	285	1
Idukki	480	103	49	3	1	—	4	160	126	10	41	39	—	216	—	104	—
Ernakulam	860	252	47	19	5	—	1	324	309	23	15	12	—	359	1	176	1
Trichur	1,009	349	84	25	13	—	1	472	366	24	1	2	—	393	7	137	—
Palaghat	894	392	34	14	16	—	—	456	264	81	—	4	—	349	3	86	—
Malappuram	999	212	14	14	10	—	—	250	187	451	—	—	—	638	5	105	1
Calicut	804	289	27	44	53	—	—	413	190	149	1	5	—	345	10	36	—
Wayanad	256	74	5	4	17	—	—	100	65	45	1	3	—	114	3	39	—
Cannanore	848	417	50	17	21	—	—	505	184	114	3	9	—	310	6	27	—
Kasaragod	369	115	15	5	2	—	—	137	88	82	1	—	—	171	37	24	—
Total	10,181	3,360	594	191	155	7	64	4,371	2,984	1,015	205	123	10	4,337	78	1,390	5

Source: Government of Kerala, Panchayat Directorate, Officials file on 1988 Panchayat Poll, Trivandrum, 1988.

Table 4.7: Panchayat Polls 1988 – Votes Won by Various Political Parties and Independents

District	Total No. of Ward	CPI (M)	CPI	Cong. (s)	Janata Party	RSP	Lok Dal	Total (LDF)	Cong (I)	IUML	Kerala Cong (I)	Kerala Cong. (M)	NDF	Total (UDF)	BJP	Independent	Total No. of Invalid Votes
Trivandrum	886	356,278	65,979	19,746	7,459	14,628	12,676	478,766	432,921	6371	3,474	4,499	5,204	452,669	24,924	131,441	1,087,806
Quilon	805	275,038	150,343	11,434	1,993	54,608	2,855	496,271	385,525	22,048	45,784	9,331	879	443,367	16,781	136,293	1,092,912
Pathanamthitta	521	103,452	22,056	15,703	7,859	3,140	276	152,466	160,802	925	14,473	9,698	149	186,047	7,363	242,476	588,372
Alieppey	717	257,123	73,445	19,300	2,106	13,631	378	365,983	323,752	7,284	13,946	12,384	3,878	361,244	9,787	176,064	913,078
Kottayam	733	166,578	52,420	16,100	4,746	1,387	302	241,533	172,053	8,103	8,670	62,760	—	252,586	6,581	409,988	909,688
Idukki	480	97,427	31,521	3,746	4,561	5,769	61	143,085	126,502	9,951	33,484	52,341	—	222,278	1,582	145,409	512,354
Ernakulam	860	251,530	52,479	33,213	10,816	2,390	—	350,428	358,603	19,564	11,959	12,479	—	402,605	15,181	283,359	105,173
Trichur	1,009	338,551	85,659	39,267	22,355	1,939	714	488,485	463,355	23,449	5,089	5,246	378	497,517	45,003	263,714	1,294,719
Palaghat	894	339,478	39,466	17,540	27,820	286	—	424,590	322,147	72,718	4,477	4,813	—	404,173	21,058	139,748	989,569
Malappuram	999	222,545	23,235	22,089	16,265	38	—	284,172	229,552	380,056	564	97	—	610,269	39,384	222,220	1,156,045
Calicut	804	290,737	30,229	61,504	68,488	—	37	450,995	277,969	147,936	4,488	5,673	—	436,066	41,413	102,926	1,031,400
Wayanad	256	62,616	7,758	8,979	17,708	—	—	97,061	87,181	36,854	2,992	5,610	—	132,637	15,723	58,634	304,055
Cannanore	848	378,443	46,091	32,004	36,106	2,610	—	495,254	'242,839	99,887	4,790	14,164	—	361,680	25,331	80,737	963,002
Kasaragod	369	123,118	20,070	12,466	2,625	78	—	158,357	97,024	61,997	1,651	1,058	—	161,730	46,371	62,512	428,970
Total	10,181	3,262,914	700,751	313,091	230,907	100,504	17,299	4,627,446	3,680,225	897,343	155,841	200,171	10,488	4,924,068	316,482	2,455,52	111,377,143

Source: Government of Kerala, Panchayat Directorate, Officials file on 1988 Panchayat Poll, Trivandrum, 1988.

Table 4.8: Panchayat Polls 1988 – Results in Nutshell

District	Votes Won by Political Groups/Fronts			
	Left Democratic Front	*United Democratic Front*	*BJP*	*Independents*
Trivandrum	4,78,766	4,52,669	24,924	1,31,441
Quilon	4,96,271	4,43,567	16,781	1,36,293
Alleppey	3,65,983	3,61,244	9,787	1,76,064
Pathanamthitta	1,52,466	1,86,047	7,363	2,42,476
Kottayam	2,41,533	2,51,586	6,581	4,09,988
Idukki	1,43,085	2,22,278	1,582	1,45,409
Ernakulam	3,50,428	4,02,605	15,181	2,83,359
Trichur	4,88,485	4,97,517	45,003	2,63,714
Palaghat	4,24,590	4,04,173	21,058	1,39,748
Malappuram	2,84,172	6,10,269	39,384	2,22,220
Calicut	4,50,995	4,36,066	41,413	1,02,926
Wayanad	97,061	1,32,637	15,723	58,634
Cannanore	4,95,254	3,61,680	25,331	80,737
Kasaragod	1,58,357	1,61,730	46,371	65,512
Total	46,27,466	49,24,043	3,16,482	24,55,521

Source: Government of Kerala, Panchayat Directorate, Official file on 1988, Panchayat Poll, Trivandrum, 1988.

Table 4.9: Panchayat Polls 1988 – Details Regarding Percentage of Votes and Total Number of Votes Secured by Political Parties and Fronts

Party	*Seats*	*Percentage of Votes*	*Total No. of Votes*
Left Democratic Front (LDF)			
CPI(M)	3,360	33.0026%	32,62,854
CPI	594	5.03%	7,01,115
Congress(S)	191	1.88%	3,18,209
Janata	155	1.52%	2,31,867
RSP	64	0.63%	1,00,654
Lok Dal	7	0.069%	17,299
Total	**4,371**	**42.93%**	**42,26,498**
United Democratic Front (UDF)			
Congress(I)	2,984	29.31%	36,56,853
IUML	1,015	9.97%	8,94,194
Kerala Congress(J)	205	2.01%	1,55,841
Kerala Congress(M)	123	1.21%	2,00,673
NDP	10	0.99%	10,488
Total	**4,337**	**42.60%**	**49,21,039**
BJP	78	0.77%	3,15,286
Independents	1,390	13.65%	24,68,678

Source: M.R. Biju and J.N. Pandy, 'Panchayat Poll in West Bengal and Kerala: A Comparative Appraisal', *Journal of Political Studies*, No. 1, Vol. XXIII, February 1990, pp. 53-54.

After presenting the election results of 1988 panchayat polls, in varied forms and facets, Table 4.10 depicts voter's participation in the Panchayat, Assembly and Lok Sabha elections in Kerala from 1957 to 1989.

Table 4.10: Voter's Participation in the Panchayat, Assembly and Lok Sabha Elections in Kerala from 1957 to 1989

Year	Assembly Elections		Lok Sabha Elections		Panchayat Elections	
	% of votes polled	% of invalid votes	% of votes polled	% of invalid votes	% of votes	% of invalid votes
1957	66.65	1.05	66.55	0.78	—	—
1960	85.70	1.52	—	—	—	—
1962	—	—	70.23	2.07	—	—
1963	—	—	—	—	73.00	1.01
1965	75.12	1.53	—	—	—	—
1967	75.09	3.63	75.53	3.77	—	—
1970	75.80	1.02	—	—	—	—
1971	—	—	64.50	0.64	—	—
1977	79.21	3.36	79.19	2.43	—	—
1979	—	—	—	—	75.70	1.05
1980	72.01	0.48	62.03	0.92	—	—
1982	73.26	1.02	—	—	—	—
1984	—	—	77.12	1.08	—	—
1987	80.58*	1.01	—	—	—	—
1988	—	—	—	—	76.04	1.01
1989	—	—	74.70	1.02	—	—

Source: *Kerala Kaumudi* (Malayalam daily) Trivandrum, November 23,1989, *Kerala Kaumudi, op. cit.*, September 16, 1989, *The Hindu* (Madras), January 24, 1988.

Conclusion

Thus, the 1988 panchayat polls in Kerala was not an easy walkover for the Left Front particularly for the CPI(M). Both the fronts fought inch by inch for each seat. For the CPI(M) it was a tough time in every way. The Congress Party and the UDF considered the poll as a means for their revival in the grassroots areas whereas the CPI(M)-led left front partners tried their best to vindicate their claim that the party continues to enjoy the overwhelming support of the rural people.

But the Congress strengthened its grassroots level by capturing more village panchayats than the CPI(M). Congress and its allies achieved a thumping victory in some of the strongholds of northern Kerala, which the CPI(M) claimed as the cradle of Indian communism. The UDF particularly, the Congress could shatter and shower the past glories of the CPI(M) in this region. The total difference of votes of both these fronts were less than 0.87 per cent.

A significant development in this poll was the rise of the Bharatiya Janata Party (BJP) in the state politics. Party has won representation in the rural as well as urban areas of the state local government system. It was well known that the cadre strength of BJP is steadily going up in the state largely because of the Congress (I)'s policy of appeasement the Muslim League and the Christian-backed Kerala Congress, particularly under the chief ministership of M.K. Karunakaran.

The BJP which had close links with Hindu Munnani polled 3.5 per cent of the total votes in 1984 parliament election. But it nearly doubled this score in the assembly poll, which held in March 1988, though the party could not capture a single seat. In this background, the BJP has done very well in the panchayat poll. It got absolute majority in three panchayats. By analysing and evaluating the whole, one can point out three major reasons, which to a large extent helped the Congress and the UDF. First internal squabbles were resolved in advance, second high level political consciousness of the rural people i.e. more than 78 per cent of the rural electorate cast their franchise power. Lastly, the unity among the UDF was comparatively strong at the election time.

5. FIRST DISTRICT COUNCIL POLLS, 1991

A great deal of academic interest and political excitement had been generated in Kerala, when the elections to the district councils were declared to be held on 29 January, 1991. The district council poll assumed greater significance mainly due to the humiliating defeat of the then ruling Left Democratic Front (LDF) in the Lok Sabha poll of 1989. The Congress-led United Democratic Front (UDF) considered the poll as a means to strengthen in the rural as well as urban areas and a chance to ventilate their charges against the LDF misrule, whereas the CPI(M)-led LDF tried its best to vindicate their claim that the ruling front continues to enjoy the overwhelming support of the entire Keralites.

Because of the thumping victory of the Congress (I) and its allies in the Lok Sabha poll of November 1989, the rush for tickets in the Congress circle was tremendous. In the election the Congress had fielded so many eminent leaders of the party. They include Presidents of the District Congress Committees, ex-MLA and ex-Ministers. The other major partners of UDF, Kerala Congress(M) and the Muslim League also gave party tickets to the eminent persons who are acceptable to all.

Comparing to the UDF the selection process in the LDF was a smooth affair. All the LDF partners particularly CPI(M) and CPI thought thrice before selecting candidates against the UDF because of the humiliating defeat of the LDF in the Lok Sabha poll of 1989. They took too much precaution in it. But comparing to UDF, they fielded several new faces particularly from youth.

Besides the UDF and the LDF a third front headed by BJP put up candidates in a good number of divisions. The other major parties that tested their political fortunes included were Socialist Congress, Janata Party, NDP, SRP, PSP, Kerala Congress(S), Kerala Congress (B), Janata Dal and RSP. There was an unprecedented increase in the number of Independent candidates.

District-wise classification of the number of candidates is shown in Table 4.11.

A total of 2263 candidates contested for 474 seats, but the total number of nomination papers rose over 6,000. Among the 474 seats, 144 were reserved for women. A total 500 women candidates contested. Table 4.12 shows the district-level number of candidates, more clearly.

Election Campaign

The announcement of district council election had stirred the people and political parties, alike, because these were the first elections after vesting the district councils with enormous powers, which would make Kerala the federation of districts, a unique feature in the Panchayati Raj system in the country. Electioneering reached new heights this time, but the Gulf War which adversely affected the UDF camps particularly in the Gulf pockets.

There were also demands from the UDF to postpone the election. But in the LDF circles, campaign started well in advance and remained systematic throughout. No stone was left unturned

Table 4.11: District-wise Details of Candidates – Party-wise Contested

District	*No. of Divisions*	*Parties and No. of Seats Connected*	
		UDF	*LDF*
1. Kasaragode	20	Cong.(I)-11 ML-9, KC(M) = 4	CPM-9, CPM (Ind.) = 1 CPI-4, Cong(S)-2, RSP-1, JD-3.
2. Kannur	39	Cong(I)-29, KC(M)-14, L-NA KC(B)-6	CPM-26, CPI-1, RSP-1, JD-4, Cong (S)-6
3. Kozhikode	40	Cong.(I)-22 ML-14, NDP-1, KC(M)-1, CMP-1 SRP-1	CPM-21, CPI-4, Ind.-1, Cong(S)-5, KC(J)-1, JD-8
4. Wayanad	20	Cong(1)-13, ML-5, KC(M)-2	CPM-7, JD-4, CPI-3, KC(J)-1, Cong(S)-2, RSP-2, Indp-2
5. Malappuram	40	Cong(I)-14, ML-25 Indp.-1	CPM-20, CPI-6, Cong(S)-6, JD-7, RSP-1
6. Palghat	40	Cong. N.A.	CPM-24, CPI-7, Dal-5, Cong(S)-3, RSP-1
7. Thrissur	40	Cong(I)-29 ML-4, NDP-2, SRP-2, KC(M)-2, CFM-1	CPM-15, Indp. -5, Cong (S) -3, CPI-9, Ind.-8, JD-5.
8. Ernakulam	40	Cong.(I)-26, ML-5, KC(M)-7, NDP-2	CPM-19, Indp-4, RSP-1, CPI-7, JD-5, Cong. (S)-5
9. Alappuzha	38	N.A.	CPM-21, CPI-7, RSP-3, KC(J)2, JD-I4, Cong. (S)-2
10. Idukki	20	Cong(I)-13, KC(M)-14, ML-8, NDP-1, JD(S)-2	CPM-7, CPI-15, Cong(S)-1, JD-2
11. Kottayam	34	Cong(I)-13, KCM(M)-13, NDP-4, ML-2, SRP-1, KC(B)-1	CPM-13, CPI-7 KC(J)-6, JD-3, Cong(S)-16, RSP-6, Ind-1
12. Pathanamthitta	23	Cong(I)-155, KC(M)-5, NDP-2, ML-1	CPM-10. CPI-5, JD-3, KC(J)-3, Cong(S)-2, RSP-1
13. Kollam	40	Cong(I)-25, KC(M)-4, ML-5	CPM-17, CPI-13, RSP-7, Cong(S)-1 JD-1, KC(J)-1
14. Thiruvananthapuram	40	Cong(I)-26, NDP-7, ML-3, KC(M)-2	CPM-20, CPI-6, JD-6, Cong(S)-3, RSP-2, CPM(Ind.) = 1

Note: (ML-Muslim League, KC(M)-Kerala Congress (Mani), KC(J)-Kerala Congress (Joseph), CPM-Communist Party of India (Marxist), JD-Janata Dal)

Source: *Malayala Manorama*, 6 January, 1991.

Table 4.12: District-wise Details of Candidates

Kasaragode	95
Kannur	161
Kozhikode	185
Wayanad	110
Malappuram	170
Palaghat	154
Thrissur	197
Ernakulam	169
Alappuzha	176
Idukki	1133
Kottayam	182
Pathanamthitta	124
Kollam	203
Thiruvananthapuram	224

Source: Malayala Manorama, 30 January, 1991.

by the main rivals. The major national and international issues like the Gulf war, Mandir-Masjid dispute, reservation for backward castes etc. were the issues raised by the LDF to attack UDF.

Both the fronts resorted to street corner meetings and door canvassing in preference to public meetings. Mass rallies were arranged to demonstrate the strength of the parties. Like the previous Lok Ṣabha assembly polls, the electronic media was extensively used by the major political parties especially the ruling CPM. Video films highlighting the achievements of the CPM-led LDF government were shown by the LDF. Multi-coloured pictures of the candidates and huge banners with election symbols were widely used in the campaign. Street dramas, folk songs, cartoons, caricatures, group songs etc. constituted on the media of communication to the people. Congress-led UDF raised the issues like law and order problem in the state, atrocities of the ruling LDF against the UDF workers, political murders, corruption charges against four state ministers, deplorable condition of the traditional industries like cashew and coir. The LDF put Mandir - Masjid dispute and the alleged double stand of the Congress(I) on the Mandal Commission Report, as the major weapon against the UDF particularly against the Congress(I).

People's Verdict

Elections were held in all 474 divisions. But the polling percentage was extremely low. It was the lowest in the whole poll history of the state. Before this time, the lowest polling percentage was recorded in 1957, during the assembly poll—66.62 per cent. But this time it came down to 61.57 per cent. In the assembly poll of 1987, it was 80.58 per cent. In the Lok Sabha poll of 1989, it was 74 per cent and in the elections to the local bodies in 1988 was 78 per cent. The low polling percentage was a shocking-one to the UDF. Table 4.13 shows the details of the district-wise polling percentage.

Table 4.13: Polling Percentage

District	*Polling Percentage*
Kasaragode	61
Kannur	63
Kozhikode	65
Wayanad	71
Malappuram	55
Thrissur	61
Ernakulam	61
Alappuzha	75
Idukki	53
Kottayam	70
Pathanamthitta	60
Kollam	65
Thiruvananthapuram	55

Source: Malayala Manorama, 30 January 1991.

The people's verdict was clearly in favour of the LDF. The results were thumping and startling to the CPM-led LDF. The CPI(M) and its allies swept the poll by capturing 12 out of 14 districts. The Congress(I) could not gain control of even a single district. In one district (Kasaragode) there was tie between the LDF and UDF and the other (Malappuram) district went to the UDF because of the Muslim League.

The electoral statistics shows that the LDF got 64,93,396 votes and the UDF got 58,41,467 votes. In a more clear sense, LDF got 6,51,929 more votes than the UDF. Though the difference between the LDF and the UDF below 7 lakh (6.51 lakh) as was referred above but in the case of number of seats LDF got two times more seats than the UDF. It is a significant development that BJP got two seats and 9,14,826 votes. Independents got elected in 26 divisions. But most of them were having either the support of UDF or LDF. Among the political parties. CPM got the maximum number of councillors, with 175. Table 4.14 provides a clear picture about the number of parties contested and won.

Table 4.14: Performance of Major Political Parties

Party	*Contested Seats*	*Seats Won*
CPI(M)	215	175
CPI	85	59
Congress(I)	303	74
Muslim League	91	47
Janata Dal	55	24
Kerala Congress(M)	60	18
Kerala Congress(J)	25	15
Congress (S)	38	15
RSP	19	11
NDP	14	2
CMP	6	1
SRP	6	0
Independents	829	26

Table 4.15 explains the district-wise voting performance of the UDF, LDF and BJP in a detailed manner.

Table 4.15: District-wise Voting Performance

District	*UDF*	*LDF*	*BJP*
Kasaragode	547080	635426	105167
Kannur	426562	574279	67274
Kozhikode	455834	549273	55788
Wayanad	244277	260614	57492
Malappuram	384537	408965	56798
Palaghat	214708	252540	22418
Thrissur	642385	661381	48518
Ernakulam	583571	637412	105606
Alappuzha	438159	531323	76856
Idukki	606999	486781	87778
Kottayam	547504	618190	167510
Pathanamthitta	134365	140984	26857
Kollam	396208	499764	54917
Thiruvananthapuram	201420	221624	72229

Source: Malayala Manorama, 1 February, 1991.

Representation of the Weaker Sections

The electoral statistics further reveals that the weaker sections of the society got adequate representation in the district council. Seventeen per cent of the elected members belong to the Scheduled Castes and Scheduled Tribes. This is much higher than the state SC/ST population. (The percentage of SCs in the state is 10.02 and that of STs is 1.02) Members belonging to other backward castes are 31 per cent. Women members constitute about 35 per cent of the total elected members, which is above the 30 per cent reservation for women proposed in the national legislation. This means a large number of women fought in the non-reserved constituencies against men and won. Table 4.16 illustrates the representation of weaker sections in the district councils polls.

Table 4.16: Representation of Women and Weaker Sections

District	Total No. of Seats	Women	SC	ST
Kasaragode	20	6	3	1
Kannur	39	12	5	1
Kozhikode	40	12	4	—
Wayanad	20	6	2	1
Malappuram	40	12	4	—
Palaghat	40	12	8	1
Thrissur	40	13	5	—
Ernakulam	40	12	4	—
Alappuzha	38	12	4	—
Idukki	20	6	3	1
Kottayam	34	11	4	1
Pathanamthitta	23	7	4	—
Kollam	40	12	4	1
Thiruvananthapuram	40	12	4	—

Source: Kerala Kaumudi Daily, 16 Sept. 1989.

Representation of Youth

The election results further shows that youth got adequate representation in the district councils. A recently concluded study shows that Kerala has preference for younger leadership. Twenty six per cent of the members belong to the age group 21-35 years. 50 per cent of the members are below 50 years. Those who are 65 and above constitute only a microscopic minority (less than two per cent) comparing to the rest.

Conclusion

The above analysis of the district council election shows that the following factors were responsible for the debacle of the UDF.

1. *Double Stand of the Congress Party*

The UDF particularly the Congress party took a double stand in the vital issues like reservation policy and issues related to Mandir-Masjid disputes. The official stand of the party was absolutely vague up to the last minute of the poll. At the same time, the party leaders tried to satisfy both the backward castes and the upper castes alike. Both these steps, forced the backward communities in Kerala to stand away from the UDF.

2. *Apathy of the Muslim Community*

A large section of the Muslim community were reluctant to accept the official line of the Muslim League. Muslim population of the state constitute 21.25 per cent of the total population. At the same time, a large section of the party particularly its youth with strongly and openly criticised the party's alliance with the Congress.

3. *National and International Issues*

National and international issues were the determining factors which influenced the poll outcome than the local issues. Among the international issues, the Gulf war deserves special attention. The LDF leaders strongly criticised the Congress in their stand in Gulf crisis.

4. *LDF and their Clear Stand on Vital Issues*

The LDF particularly the CPI(M), took a clear stand on vital issues, particularly on matters related to the Mandal Commission report. The party openly supported the implementation of the report. This has helped the backward communities in general and a large section of the Muslim community in particular to parade behind the LDF, TC resolve the problems of the Keralites working in the Gulf areas, both the state government and the LDF supported Central Government when they took appreciable steps.

5. *Low Polling Percentage*

A noticeable feature of the poll was its lowest polling percentage. It was the lowest in the whole electoral history of the state. The state average was 61.57 per cent. Before the district council poll, the lowest polling was recorded in 1957 with 66.62 per cent. The Gulf crisis, was mainly responsible for it.

6. PANCHAYAT POLLS, 1995

The Constitution (73rd Amendment) Act, 1992 by the centre provided a fresh opportunity for re-organisation of the panchayats in the state of Kerala. The new Panchayati Raj Act, 1991 has come into force on 30th April 1994. On the basis of this Act elections to the local bodies were held on 23rd and 25th September 1995. The Panchayati Raj polls assumed greater significance and attention mainly due to two basic reasons—firstly these were the first elections after vesting PRIs with enormous powers, secondly it was the first comprehensive state-wide electoral outing since Mr. A.K. Antony take-over as the Chief Minister of the state. The ruling Congress(I) led UDF considered the poll as a means of vindicate their claim that it continues to enjoy the overwhelming support of the entire Keralites whereas the CPI(M) led LDF considered the poll as chance to ventilate their charges against the UDF rule.

A total number of 58,089 candidates tested their political fortunes in the poll. In it 40,220 were male candidates and the remaining 17,869 were female. The Congress had fielded the maximum number of candidates with 9,644 followed by the BJP with 7,542, CPI(M) with 6,566 and CPI with 1,894 candidates. Detailed illustration is furnished in the Table 4.17.

Table 4.17: Party-wise Distribution of Candidates

Total no. of candidates	58,089
Total no. of male candidates	40,220
Total no. of female candidates	17,869
Congress(I)	9,644
CPI(M)	6,566
CPI	1,894
BJP	7,542

Source: Mathrubhumi, September 23, 1995.

Elections were held in two phases. In the first phase, over 70 per cent of voters in Thiruvananthapuram, Pathanamthitta, Idukki, Ernakulam, Palaghat, Kasaragod and Kozhikode district exercised their franchise on 23rd September, 1995. The remaining districts of Malappuram, Kollam, Wayanad, Alappuzha, Kannur, Kottayam and Trichur went to the poll on 25th September when about 72-75 per cent of voters exercised their right to vote. Table 4.18 shows the district-wise polling percentage.

Table 4.18: District-wise Polling Percentage

Districts	*Panchayat*	*Municipality*	*Corporation*
Thiruvananthapuram	70.0	72.0	71.0
Kollam	72.0	67.0	—
Pathanamthitta	70.0	72.0	—
Alappuzha	72.6	67.0	—
Kottayam	70.8	75.0	—
Idukki	70.0	81.2	—
Ernakulam	72.0	71.0	65.0
Thrissur	72.0	74.0	—
Palakkad	64.0	65.0	—
Malappuram	75.0	78.0	—
Kozhikode	70.0	78.7	65.0
Wayanad	73.0	75.0	—
Kannur	71.8	71.6	—
Kasaragod	74.5	70.0	—

Source: *Mathrubhumi*, September 24, 1995, *Kerala Kaumudi*, September 26, 1995.

People's Verdict

Just like the first district council poll of 1991, the people's verdict was clearly in favour of the LDF. The CPI(M) led LDF completed its victory march by winning 530 out of 990 Gram Panchayats (i.e., 53.53%), 90 out of 152 Block Panchayats (i.e., 59.21%) and 10 out of 14 District Panchayats (i.e., 71.2%). On the other hand, the ruling UDF could establish its dominance in 342 Gram Panchayats (i.e., 34.54%), 45 Block Panchayats (i.e., 29.6%) and 3 District Panchayats (i.e., 21.42%).

The District Panchayats which went to the LDF way are Thiruvananthapuram, Kollam, Ernakulam, Alappuzha, Kottayam, Idukki, Thrissur, Palakkad, Kozhikode and Kannur. The remaining went to the UDF way. Besides the LDF and UDF, the BJP has got absolute majority in three Grama Panchayats—all in Kasaragod. Yet another noticeable feature of the poll was that in 115 Grama Panchayats the voters have not given a clear verdict and things will be decided by the independents. Tables 4.19 to 4.21 clearly illustrate the verdict in an in-depth manner.

Table 4.19: Party Position in Grama Panchayats

Districts	*Total No. of GPs*	*LDF*	*UDF*	*Others*
Thiruvananthapuram	84	61	16	7
Kollam	71	55	11	1
Pathanamthitta	54	13	26	15
Alappuzha	71	35	24	12
Kottayam	73	25	35	13
Idukki	51	21	22	8
Ernakulam	84	50	29	7
Thrissur	98	51	36	11
Palakkad	90	59	24	7
Malappuram	94	29	53	12
Kozhikode	76	48	22	6
Wayanad	24	12	8	4
Kannur	81	56	24	I
Kasaragod	37	13	14	7 (3 BJP)

Source: Kerala Kaumudi, September 30, 1995.

1995 Poll Analysis

In the 1995 poll, the CPI(M)-led LDF established a clear lead in 10 out of 24 District Panchayats, 90 out of 152 Block Panchayats, 530 out of 990 Gram Panchayats. However, the results do not show a wave in favour of the LDF, unlike in the 1991 District Council Polls.

But the UDF, no doubt, has much cause for concern. That its leaders are drawing satisfaction from the 'not-so-bad' verdict shows to what level the party has sunk from the heydays of 1991 when it swept to power with an powerful mandate. One of the wishful thoughts in the UDF camp was that since the front had adopted a stance in favour of the creamy layer section of the backward communities getting the benefit of job reservation and the LDF had criticised this, it would endear it to the voters of these communities.

Table 4.20: Party Position in Block Panchayats

District	*Total Seats*	*LDF*	*UDF*	*Others*
Thiruvananthapuram	12	11	1	—
Kollam	13	12	—	1
Pathanamthitta	9	1	5	3
Alappuzha	12	10	1	1
Kottayam	11	7	3	1
Idukki	8	3	4	1
Ernakulam	15	8	4	3
Trichur	17	11	4	2
Palakkad	13	9	2	2
Malappuram	14	2	12	—
Kozhikkode	12	8	4	—
Wayanad	3	—	3	—
Kannur	9	7	1	1
Kasaragod	4	1	1	1
				1 Equal
				1 Equal
				1 BJP

Source: Kerala Kaumudi, 30 September, 1995.

Table 4.21: Party Position in District Panchayats

District	*Total Seats*	*LDF*	*UDF*	*Others*
Thiruvananthapuram	25	19	5	1
Kollam	25	19	2	4
Pathanamthitta	15	2	13	–
Alappuzha	21	12	9	–
Kottayam	21	11	10	–
Idukki	15	8	6	1
Ernakulam	24	16	8	–
Trichur	25	16	9	–
Palakkad	25	18	7	–
Malappuram	25	3	22	–
Kozhikkode	25	15	9	1
Wayanad	15	6	9	–
Knnnur	24	14	8	No poll in 2 Seats
Kasaragod	15	7	5	3

Source: Kerala Kaumudi, 30 September, 1995.

Such ambitions were specially focused on the Ezhavas, usually seen as the traditional vote bank of the CPM and its allies. But the results belied these hopes as the LDF was the favourite of those districts where the Ezhava community has its dominant presence.

While examining the performance of Panchayati Raj

Institutions in the 1995 polls, it is quite interesting to evaluate the performance of various political parties in the urban local bodies too – city corporation and municipal councils. Tables 4.22 and 4.23 presents the picture in its totality.

Table 4.22: Party Position in City Corporations

	Thiruvananthapuram	*Kochi*	*Kozhikode*
Total seats	50	50	50
Election held	50	49	50
LDF	24	27	37
UDF	20	18	11
PDF	1	2	—
BJP	3	1	2
India	—	1	—
Rebels	2	—	—

District-wise Picture

District-wise poll analysis shows that the LDF got more than 3.75 lakh votes than the UDF. In District Panchayats out of 298 divisions, the LDF got 171 (i.e., 57.38%) whereas the UDF captured 123 divisions (i.e., 41.27%). In Block Panchayat LDF got absolute majority in 59.21 per cent of the Block Panchayats and the UDF got control in 29.21 per cent. In Gram Panchayats, out of 990 (GPs) 53.5 per cent were captured by LDF and 34.5 per cent by UDF. In 115 Gram Panchayats none got absolute majority. Comparing with the last civic poll held in 1988, then UDF got 455 panchayats and the LDF got 469. But this time it has turned to 342 and 530 respectively.

But a noticeable but contradictory point in the poll is that, though the LDF is far ahead of UDF in case of the number of seats, but the UDF has secured more votes than LDF. For example in Kottayam district panchayat, out of 21 divisions the LDF got 11, and it came to power. But the UDF got 27,511 votes more than LDF. Similarly in Alappuzha out of 21 seats, the LDF got 12. But the UDF got 20,305 votes more, than the LDF.

But in Kasaragod, the story is quite reverse in order, where LDF got 11,150 votes more than UDF. But UDF is in power. In Wayanad and Pathanamthitta, UDF got 9,851, and 25,416 votes more than LDF. In Malappuram district, the UDF got more than one lakh votes than the LDF.

Table 4.23: Party Position in Municipalities

Municipality	*Congress (I)*	*CPI (M)*	*BJP*	*CPI*	*Janata Dal*	*IUML*	*KC (M)*	*Ind. and Others*
Neyyatinkara	1	14	0	1	2	0	0	6
Nedumangadu	6	12	0	4	0	0	0	6
Attingal	8	8	0	3	1	0	0	4
Varkala	9	9	0	1	0	0	0	5
Paravoor	8	7	1	1	0	0	0	5
Kollam	11	11	1	2	0	0	1	10
Punalur	9	11	0	5	0	0	0	3
Pathanamthitta	9	2	0	0	0	0	1	12
Thiruvalla	8	3	1	0	0	0	7	13
Adoor	8	2	0	2	0	0	0	8
Alappuzha	10	8	1	4	0	3	1	9
Kayamkulam	9	9	1	2	1	2	1	7
Chengannur	4	2	0	0	0	0	2	13
Mavelikara	8	2-	0	1	0	0	1	7
Cherthala	14	6	0	3	0	0	I	4
Kottayam	11	7	0	0	1	1	1	11
Changanacherry	7	5	0	0	1	0	4	15
Vaikom	5	3	0	0	3	0	0	9
Pala	0	1	0	0	0	0	8	11
Thodupuzha	3	2	0	0	0	2	2	19
Guruvayoor	10	0	0	3	1	1	0	4
Thrissur	15	3	1	3	3	0	0	7
Kodungalloor	6	5	0	7	0	1	0	5
Kunnankulam	5	8	0	0	0	0	0	3
Chavakkadu	6	9	0	1	0	3	1	4
Palakkad	14	5	4	0	0	3	0	10
Shornur	7	9	0	2	0	0	0	4
Ottappalam Chittur	10	14	1	0	0	1	0	2
Thathamangalam	13	2	0	0	0	1	0	8
Malappuram	1	4	0	0	0	9	0	14
Thiroor	0	1.	0	0	0	13	0	14
Ponnani	5	14	0	1	0	10	0	2
Aaluva	16	0	0	0	0	0	0	4
Moovattupuzha	2	6	0	1	0	1	0	10
Kalamassery	13	10	0	0	0	2	0	7
Kothamangalam	8	3	0	o	0	0	3	10
Thrippunithura	13	9	0	2	0	0	0	8
Angamali	10	8	0	0	0	0	1	5
North Paravoor	9	2	0	2	0	0	0	7
Perumbavoor	9	4	0	0	0	0	0	7
Chalakkudy	8	5	0	1	1	0	0	13
Irinjalakuda	4	3	0	2	4	0	0	7
Perinthalmanna	1	6	0	0	0	8	0	9
Manjeri	4	5	0	1	0	12	0	10
Vadakara	4	12	0	2	1	8	0	5

(Contd.)

Table 4.23: (*Contd.*)

Municipality	*Congress (I)*	*CPI (M)*	*BJP*	*CPI*	*Janata Dal*	*IUML*	*KC (M)*	*Ind. and Others*
Koilandi	4	12	2	2	1	9	0	2
Kalpatta	3	5	0	0	3	4	0	5
Thalipparampu	6	4	2	0	0	11	0	1
Kannur	10	4	0	0	0	10	2	6
Thalasserry	3	13	0	2	1	4	0	9
Koothuparampu	3	10	1	2	1	1	0	2
Payyannoor	9	16	0	1	1	3	0	2
Kasaragod	0	2	11	0	0	9	0	10
Kanjangadu	8	7	4	0	1	8	0	4

Source: Kerala Kaumudi, September 29, 1995.

But the LDF established a clear lead in the following District Panchayats. In Kannur LDF got 1,14,000 votes more than UDF. In Thrissur it is 63,842, in Thiruvananthapuram 75,429, in Kollam 92,111, in Palaghat 63,842 and in Kozhikode 93,392.

Performance of BJP, PDF, INL and JSS

As far as their performance are concerned, it is quite difficult to reach a reasonable conclusion. All these parties concentrated their attention in Gram Panchayats and Block Panchayats than District Panchayat.

In the case of BJP, though the party has increased its strength in Kozhikode area, but in Kasaragod, Palaghat and even in Thiruvananthapuram it could not show much strength.

In toto, the party won 76,000 votes in Kasaragod, 46,000 in Kannur, 1,00,000 in Kozhikode, 66,000 in Malappuram, 75,000 in Palakkad, 87,000 in Thrissur, 94,000 in Kollam, 94,000 in Thiruvananthapuram, 47,000 in Pathanamthitta, and 45,000 in Alappuzha. BJP candidates got about 7.5 lakh votes (statewide).

The People's Democratic Party (PDP), formed by Abdul Nassar Madani (in 1993) after a fundamentalist organisation (ISS) led by him was banned, bagged 33,000 votes in Kollam, 45,000 in Malappuram and 20,000 in Palaghat. It shows that the PDP has emerged as a strong contender to the IUML, the IUML is certainly the worst sufferer in the poll, which got a drubbing even in its traditional areas. Both the PDP and Indian National League of

Ibrahim Sulaiman Sait played key role in it. Lastly, the Janathipathya Samrakshana Samiti (JSS) a new party formed by K.R. Gowri Amma could not make much impression even in her home district of Alappuzha.

1995 Poll: Few Comments and Observations

1. Though the overall performance of the ruling UDF in the poll may not add up to a rout, but it certainly amounts to a setback. But when compared with the 1991 elections to the erstwhile district councils, the UDF has of course turned in a better performance by capturing three district level bodies in addition to Malappuram.
2. The UD.F leaders are in a way right when they point out that the CPM success in the Muslim League, the CPM success in the bastions in the north was made possible by its open electoral understanding with the INL led by Sulaiman Sait.
3. It is also a fact that a large number of Hindus who used to vote for the BJP in the past voted for the CPM candidate this time. Moreover, the forward caste people who used to vote for the Congress or the BJP in the recent past decided either choose not to vote or vote for the Left on account of their stand in the Creamy Layer Issue.
4. The Indian National League (INL), a splinter group of UDF's JUMP and People's Democratic Party (PDP) led by radical Muslim leader Abdul Nasser Madani, did bag a lot of votes that would otherwise have gone to the UDF. Even where the candidates of these parties lost out, they indirectly helped the LDF candidates.
5. The poor UDF performance in some of the Syrian Christian dominated areas in Ernakulam and Kottayam districts also indicates a small but perceptible shift in their political allegiance, though it need not be merely on account of the reservation issue.
6. The expectation of the UDF was that, its pro-backward class sloganeering might help it to consolidate Muslim votes and win over the Ezhavas to its fold totally failed. The Madani led PDF equally cut into both CPM and IUML

vote banks in the central and southern districts and the LDF did not lose the Ezhava votes.

7. Voters in the smaller towns of the central and southern districts have not rallied in support of the Left in such a scale ever since the liberation struggle that ousted the first Namboodiripad Ministry.
8. The UDF could still have come up with a better performance if its house was in order. The Congress rebels played havoc with the ruling front fortunes in thousands of constituencies. The two factions of the Kerala Congress led by K.M. Mani and T.M. Jacob fought each other to the advantage of the CPM in Kottayam and Idukki districts.
9. Though the IUML has managed to retain the Malappuram District Panchayat, its urban base has suffered a serious erosion and there is little to suggest that the threat from its rival formations has receded.

Conclusion

The electoral politics in Kerala has always been a topic of special interest for political scientists all over the world. An impartial and scientific analysis of the polls shows that, one of the most important and striking determinants of the voting behaviour of the rural electorates in Kerala is the influence of political ideology. The high level political consciousness, high level literacy, highly developed communication network, the existence of a number of national and local parties and trade unions are some of the factors responsible for this politicisation. Some of the voters who are committed to a particular ideology, usually vote for a candidate who is put up by that party sharing that ideology. The personality of the candidate is more important for the voters than the charisma of the leader. Certainly, the political issues too influence the rural voters. Rural voting behaviour is also influenced by the performance of party in power. Casteism is another major factor which influences the voting behaviour of the rural electorates in the state particularly after the emergence of Muslim League, Kerala Congress, BJP, INL and lastly People's Democratic Party. It is very clear now-a-days that caste and politics both going together in Kerala politics.

References

Bhargava, B.S., *Panchayati Raj System and Political Parties*, Ashish Publishing House, New Delhi, 1979, p. 1

Biju, M.R. and J.N. Pandya, "Panchayat Polls in Kerala and West Bengal: A Comparative Appraisal", *Journal of Political Studies*, No. 1, Vol. X 1990, p. 53.

Biju, M.R. and Pandya J.N., "The Eighth Lok Sabha Poll in Kerala", *The Indian Journal of Political Studies*, Vol. 14, December, 1990.

Biju, M.R., "LDF's Repeat Performance: Kerala's Local Body Polls, *Economic and Political Weekly*, Vol. XXX Nos. 41 and 42, Oct. 14-21, 1995.

Biju, M.R., "Panchayat Elections in Kerala", *Kurukshetra*, Vol. December, 1995.

Biju, M.R., *The First District Council Poll (1991) in Kerala*, 150/2, October-December 1992, No. 4.

Deb, P.C. and Agarwal, B.K., *Rural Leadership in Green Revolution*, Researcher's Publications, New Delhi, 1974, p. 1.

Dey, S.K., *Power to the People*, Orient Longmans, New Delhi, 1969, p. 74.

Dube, S.C., *A Framework for the Study of Rural Leadership in Transitional Societies in Emerging Pattern of Leadership in South East Asia*, National Institute of Community Development, Hyderabad, 1965.

Irving Knickerbocker, *Leadership: A Conception and Some Implications in Browne and Danville, T.S., The Study of Leadership, Interstate*, Publishers, London, 1958, pp. 10-11.

Jayaprakash Narayan, "Swaraj for the People", *op. cit.*, p. 12.

Jayaprakash Narayan, *A Plea for Reconstruction of Indian Polity*. Akhil Bharat Sarva Seva Sangh Prakashan, Rajghat, Kashi, 1959.

Jayaprakash Narayan, *Swaraj for the People*, A.B.S.S. Prakashan, Rajghat, Kashi, 1963.

Kerala Kaumudi, op. cit., November 19, 1989.

Kerala Kaumudi, Trivandrum, November 27, 1989.

Kerala Kaumudi, Trivandrum, September, 15, 1979.

Kurukshetra, Ministry of Community Development and Co-operation, Government of India, New Delhi, April-May, 1961.

Mathur, M.V., Iqbal Narain and Sinha, V.M., *Panchayati Raj in Rajasthan: A Case Study in Jaipur District*, Impes India, New Delhi, 1966, p. 233.

Myron Weiner, *Political Parties and Panchayati Raj, Indian Administration*, D.P.A., New Delhi, October-December, 1962.

Ordway lead, *The Art of Leadership*, Wittiessey House, London, 1935, p. 20.

Potter, David, C., *Government in Rural India: An Introduction to Contemporary District Administration*, London, G. Bell and Sons, 1964, pp. 55-56.

Quoted by Bhargava, B.S., *Grassroots Leadership*, Ashish Publishing House, New Delhi, 1979, p. 2.

Quoted by Francis Abraham, *Dynamics of Leadership in Village India,* India International Publication, Allahabad.

Rajeshwar Dayal, *Panchayati Raj in India,* Metropolitan Book Company, Delhi, 1970, p. 240.

Ralph, W. Nicholas, "Village Factions and Political Parties", Bengal, *Journal of Common Wealth Political Studies,* Vol. 11, 19;

Report of the Committee on PRIs, Government of India, Ministry of Agriculture and Irrigation, New Delhi, 1978, p. 52.

Sukumaran Nair, K., *Rural Politics and Government in Academy of Political Science,* Trivandrum, 1976, p. 73.

The Hindu, Madras, January 24, 1988.

5

Local Body Polls, 2000

Warning Signal for the Left

The announcement of elections to the local bodies scheduled for 25th and 27th September, 2000 had enthused neither the political parties nor the people of the state of Kerala. The major players—the CPM and the Congress(I) and the BJP were rather preoccupied with internal squabbles and this had also affected the functioning of the coalition ministry led by the CPM. Trouble has been brewing in the state unit of the CPM for quite some time over its bid to control the Centre of Indian Trade Union (CITU). When the CITU's bid to keep the party at bay failed the issue was raised on the Central Committee of the CPM; but situation remained unchanged because of the belligerent stand adopted by the State Unit. The issue ultimately led to the alienation of some of the senior most leaders of the CITU and the Party. Just when the dust on it settled, the controversy over a tie-up with the Indian Union Muslim League surfaced. Top leaders of the party openly fought over the issues and the national leadership stopped short of reprimanding the state leaders for advocating the alliance. However, some of the party leaders continued to nurse their close affinity towards the IUML which finally resulted in making tactical.

The four and a half years of Left Democratic Front had offered, political parties of the state an excellent opportunity to measure the extent of their popular support at the local level through their declaration of polls to the local bodies. One of the first tasks of the LDF Government that came to power in 1996 was the radical restructuring of the civic bodies by introducing people's plan campaign programme and allocation enough funds to the local bodies, the LDF government paved the way for local development with maximum participation of the people. In four years, Kerala's devolution experiment has transformed the civic bodies in the state to institutions that rewrote the rules of decentralization and restructured the mode of governance in the panchayat and municipal bodies. A new structure of governance extending from Grama Sabhas to block and district panchayats were established. Thirty five per cent of the state's annual plan funds and the powers to utilise them according to the local needs and to take decisions were transferred to the local bodies. In three years, Rs. 2700 crores were transferred to the civic bodies for their own developmental programmes. In the first two years nearly three million people actively participated in the campaign as volunteers, trainers, expert, resource persons, and so on. So far, the physical achievements of the campaign have been impressive and provide a contrast to the development activities undertaken during the pre-campaign years.

The LDF had to approach the electorate with a truncated Revolutionary Socialist Party. One faction of the RSP led by Baby John left the LDF and joined hands with the UDF. Added to this grave issue, there were general resentment of almost all the partners of the ID over CPM by brother attitude steam bleed the protests of the little brothers who have been grinning and bearing its owing to lack of alternatives. But when the CPM took a unilateral decision on Rajya Sabha seats issue, the CPI, the biggest of the little brother plunked enough courage to twist the arms of the big brother to force it to concede the seat. It accommodated its stalwart, Y.V. Raghavan in whose defeat in the last Lok Sabha elections the CPM had allegedly played a role. Due to the adamant stand of the CPI, the CPM agreed to a seat sharing formula which was highly beneficial to the other constituents of the LDF.

Like the LDF, the situation in the UDF which was equally bad. It took for the worse with the revolt of the veteran congress(I) leader K. Karunakaran. The UDF had not been able to play an effective opposition so far, mainly because of the vacillation on the part of the IUML, second biggest constituent. It was only on the eve of the civic elections that the League finally made up its mind to continue in the UDF and work for its victory in local bodies poll. But T. Karunakaran's revolt had queered the UDF's pitch once again, though his supporters had indicated that they will not rock the boat for the present poll. Things were not well in the BJP camp as well. The party was consolidating its position at the local bodies and was surviving to make it a stepping stone to enter the Assembly, where it is yet to open account.

POLL MANIFESTO: BOTH THE FRONTS VOWED BY PEOPLE'S PLAN

The LDF in its election manifesto, which was released on 5 September, 2000, promised to consolidate its programme of administrative decentralization, besides concentrating more on the productive sectors with tried and tested programmes. The LDF in its poll document sought to build on its thesis of Congress-BJP alliance in the state. It traced out similarities in their approaches to national economic issues like globalization and economic liberalization and suggests that the ties here were merely extension of their national affinity. The document has further stated that the present civic elections were held under the changed circumstances in the context of the achievements under the people's plan campaign. Pointing out that the LDF had done well in the 1995 elections with the UDF in power, the document claimed that the LDF was facing the electorate with more confidence on the strength of the achievements during the past four years.

The document criticized the UDF of spearheading a series of agitations on a horde of issues. Instead of agitating against the center's policies regarding ration subsidy and its globalization policies, the UDF had turned against the state government. It also alleged that, the UDF had staged agitation on the plus two issue in preparation of a grand alliance with the BJP. The UDF was forced to call off the agitation when it found the BJP setting isolated for the violent incidents in the state capital. Moreover, though the Opposition has raised the bogey of corruption, it has failed to bring these changes before the legal machinery like the Lok Ayukta. It has also claimed that the UDF was disintegrating because some sections had started believing that the Congress was weak. The LDF demand also recalled its fight against the imperialism and capitalist force in the dawn of the 20th century. "It was imperative to give new meaning to the objective of the uplift of the poor and downtrodden in the context of vast changes taking place in terms of new ideas and technical know-how."

The LDF leadership also reiterated its stand that the local body elections would be considered as a referendum on the four year rule of the Nayanar Government. Asked about LDF's links and tactical alliance with IUML, the LDF Convener had stated that, the LDF had a definite policy towards the IUML and there was nothing to hide. To him the LDF policy was clear and it had opened its doors for any party which come out of the UDF. Lastly, the LDF leadership had further stated that, the CPM and its allies are committed to fight the threat of communalism and also to work further of people's planning process. Regarding the Local level tie-ups with the groups and individuals outside the orbit of LDF the LDF leadership made it clear that the Front would not enter into any understanding that would harm the interest of coalition.

The UDF local bodies' election manifesto which too indicated that its main poll plank would be the people's planning programme. In the 20-point manifesto, the UDF assured that if it is voted to power it would make people's planning corruption-free, more transparent and development-oriented. However, barring a few points like the auditing of the people's planning accounts, the manifesto has nothing new to offer. Moreover, most of the front assurances sound like guidelines for people's planning or promises of projects which were in fact being implemented now. For instance, the UDF manifesto stated that the UDF would generate new employment opportunities by implementing project in agriculture, food processing, tourism, information technology, bio-technology etc. The manifesto also said that the UDF would tackle the drinking water problem by tapping the local water sources. It also stated about the opening of old age homes. The sanitation and health projects would be made more effective and garbage disposal units would be set up. In this context it has been noted that the UDF's long standing demand of disbanding the expert committee, implementation committee and panel of resource persons have also been included in the manifesto. The text of the 20 point UDF manifesto is as follows:

(1) Administration of local bodies will be made more effective and transparent. (2) Benefits of the decentralisation of power will be ensured to all sections of people irrespective of their political alliance. Collective efforts would be initiated to ensure that the benefit of decentralization reaches all. (3) Expert committee, Implementation committee and panel of resource persons will be disbanded. (4) Power of the Grama Sabha will be restored and it

will not be made a political platform. (5) It will be ensured that the benefits of the schemes reaches the target group. (6) List of the benefactors will be eliminated. (7) Benami contractors will be eliminated. (8) The People's Planning accounts will be subjected to timely auditing. (9) A fund will be set up to rehabilitate the poor who are suffering from disease and poverty. (10) A system will be introduced in Grama Panchayats for the storing and marketing of agricultural produce. (11) Taxes in the local bodies will be re-examined. (12) Permanent agency will be set up in Grama Panchayats for environmental protection. (13) Library movements will be strengthened. Schemes will be launched to promote folk arts. (14) Financial aid will be given to the NGO working in villages, women and youth organisation. (15) Educational facilities will be improved, new job opportunities will be generated and more assistance will be given to traditional industries. (16) Improve irrigation, popularise modern farm technology and extend the medicinal plant farming. (17) Ease drinking water problems by tapping local water sources. (18) Open old-age homes. (19) Implement project to improve rural sanitation. Treatment facilities will be streamlined. (20) Garbage disposal plants will be set up.

Influx of Candidates

Unlike the 1995 local body elections there was an influx of candidates, who tested their electoral fortune this time. In toto, there were 56,858 candidates left in the fray for polls, after the last day for withdrawals. In the 13 District Panchayats there were 874 contenders. Malappuram district panchayat where the electoral revision was not held went to the polls only in the second phase.

There were 4850 candidates left in the fray in the Block Panchayats and 45,441 in the Gram Panchayats. In all the four Corporations barring Thrissur there were 1198 contenders. There had been disarray in the UDF camp even as after the date of withdrawals and the PCC chief had to warn rebels to withdraw from the contest or face suspension from the primary membership of the party for six years for indiscipline.

In the LDF, which was also facing the rebels' menace but to a much lesser degree than the UDH. Efforts were made under the directions of the state leadership to sort out issues in Kasaragod and Kannur districts. In Malabar area the Congress seemed reconciled to the pressures of the IUML. Details of candidates are given in Table 5.1.

Table 5.1: Civic Body Divisions in Kerala

Sl. No.	*District*	*Municipal Corpora-tion*	*Municipal Council*	*District Pancha-yat*	*Block Pancha-yat*	*Gram Pancha-yat*
1.	Thiruvananthapuram	458	535	86	446	4667
2.	Kollam	236	194	67	432	3830
3.	Ernakulam	237	732	64	402	4179
4.	Kozhikode	207	246	56	378	3226
5.	Idukki	–	102	58	268	2341
6.	Palakkad	–	461	81	412	3538
7.	Malappuram	–	571	*	328	3714
8.	Pathanamthitta	–	345	58	336	2663
9.	Kottayam	–	437	66	391	3874
10.	Kasaragod	–	207	32	134	1406
11.	Alappuzha	–	729	129	126	4154
12.	Waynad	–	75	34	74	999
13.	Kannur	–	481	61	301	2216
14.	Thrissur	–	–	82	525	4210

* Elections were not held to Malappuram District Panchayat.

MAJOR ELECTORAL ISSUES

The most striking aspect of the local body elections was that, it was not at all the mere number of seats that each political front would capture rather it would be a barometer of sorts to decide the success of their respective strategies adopted in preparation to the next assembly elections to be held in a few months time. In toto, there were three main issues which were debated at length and breadth during the present poll. Primarily the CPM's new political line (tactical political adjustments) permitting local level adjustments with Congress(I) rebels and other UDF partners, particularly the IUML. The second one was the persistent changes raised by the Left election propaganda machine about the BJP-Congress alliance and the last one was the IUML strategy in the current situation and the responses of the Congress to it.

The CPM's much-touted political line of local adjustments worth UDF rebels and coalition partners especially the IUML had fallen by the wayside. The party was forced to remain with local alliances with the IUML in a handle of Panchayats in Malappuram, Kannur and Kasaragod. When compared to the scale of Panchayat elections these local adjustments did not indicate political quakes. The CPM's was a weapon which nearly sliced the UDF, thanks to the factional feuds in the state Congress. At one point of time, it appeared that the IUML would be tethered to the CPM's pen even as reports trickled from the districts about the frantic attempts for local adjustments by the IUML and the CPM. The timely intervention by the IUML supremo, checked the move forwards the CPM. But the party admitted that it had no option but to plough a lonely furrow or cobble a coalition with independents in those Panchayats where the UDF coalition pattern collapsed under the pressure of local imperatives. The CPM tactical line has been adopted mainly to force a political realignment by drawing the IUML out of its long standing association with the UDF. It might have been temporarily thwarted on this score. But what could be of concern to the UDF was that the news had to some extent helped it to shed its stigma *vis-à-vis* the Muslim community. The IUML had already notched up quite few political gains even before the ballot was casted for civic polls. The IUML could able to wrest concessions from both the fronts through deft maneuvers. Morever, the party could project itself as the only moving force in the Muslim politics in Kerala. A close examination of those local alliances outside the UDF show that the IUML had also succeeded in keeping its commitment to the UDF. Its ties outside the UDF fold, wherever it has taken place could not provide any mileage for the LDF because these were forged on the designs and aspirations of the IUML.

There was also a persistent campaign on the part of the LDF especially from the CPM that the Congress and the BJP were hand in glove in the civic body polls would be either proved or disproved conclusively in the poll. The campaign too was unleshed obviously to woo the minority communities by placing upon their fear psychosis of the BJP, which had till recently assumed an aggressive face of Hindutva. The strategy was not at all new because it had been tried out in the previous two parliamentary polls and by elections. In spite of repeated denials by the PCC leadership, the LDF public address systems continued to resonate the allegations. There was no denying the fact that the CPM's political line might have prompted the Congress to make an attempt to consolidate anti-Marxist forces. The effects of the persistent attacks against the Congress could end up giving foothold to the BJP. For the

Congress Party, the civic elections meant a lot. It can feel satisfied that it could hold the horse from bolting. But there are few issues it would sooner have to face up to. The state Congress (I) leadership had to bend backwards to keep the IUML in good humour in several civic bodies. The latter appears to be calling the shots more often than Congressmen would really like. The Congress(I) leadership could sigh in relief that factionalism did not take meaning turn during electioneering.

Other Issues

Besides the issues discussed above the month old electioneering also witnessed high level debate on other issues too. It include, Plus two muddle, Surya Nelli, Kannur power project and the politicization of state police. But it was certainly the people's plan which emerged as the sole and decisive issue at the end of the poll. Being the baby of the LDF, the People's Plan had been its main election plank from the ward go. The Opposition UDF on the other hand, entered the fray pledging to bring in a more vigorous and de-politicised version of People's Plan programme if voted to power. Interestingly, the tone and tenor of the Congress campaign changed halfway through. In the concluding phase, it launched a frontal attack on the LDF Government accusing it of unconstitutionally replacing Rajiv Gandhi's concept of Panchayat Raj with People's Plan. The BJP mainly concentrated on the misrule of Nayanar Government and the laws in the implementation of the People's Plan. A recap of the People's Plan would reveal the trying times the programme had faced, even to the extent of derailment, during the five-year period.

Its survival and emergence as the main poll issue is seen by Plan managers as a positive development for the State in the longer run. Immediately after taking over the reins in 1996, the LDF Government made a significant announcement regarding allocation of 35 to 40 per cent of the State budget to the local bodies. This was followed by a year long campaign to make the people aware of the need to reverse the top-bottom planning process. Setting up of the Sen Committee on devolution of powers wrote as new chapter in the history of the State though many of its recommendations are yet to be implemented. On the political front, unexpected financial and administrative powers bestowed with the local bodies led to a rare unity among the lower level leadership irrespective of political differences. The criterion of population, backwardness and geographical conditions for fund allocation freed the programme from allegations of discrimination on political grounds. However, the misutilization and underutilization of funds by the local bodies during the first two annual plans exposed the inexperience of the elected representatives concerned in handling huge funds. The delay in redeploying staff of various Government departments to the local bodies impeded the institutionalization of the local-level administrative machinery.

Nevertheless, the redeployment had for the first time in the State effected large-scale transfers of the Government staff to the village administration. In the first phase, over 300 employees from department of agriculture, animal husbandry, health, forest, irrigation and public health were redeployed. Redeployment of KSEB staff including lineman and KWA staff could not take place owing to pressure from unions affiliated to the ruling front. During the course of the People's Plan, an unusual understanding was witnessed among the legislators and MPs belonging to both ruling and opposition fronts who feared that decentralization would bring an end to their dominant role in local level development. Though the Opposition members had been alleging over political action of the blame rested on them too. Despite being in the High Level Guidance Committee (HLGC) of the People's Plan, most of the Congress leaders preferred to stay away from its meeting. Even the commitment of the CPM in achieving total decentralization became suspect on various occasions. Fearing erosion of the supremacy of various party branches, a unified and sincere intervention from the State leadership of the CPM was missing. Non-CPM partners in the LDF too attached the People's Plan demanding the scrapping of district, block and State-level experts committees. Even the Opposition had joined the chorus against the panels. People's Plan had been plagued by benami implementation committees propped up by the deadly contractor-politician-bureaucrat nexus at the grassroots level.

Nearly 40 per cent of the committees responsible for implementing the projects are benami, a fact admitted by the Plan managers themselves. The positive side—in terms of achievements of physical targets—is something which cannot be easily ignored.

Construction of 3,06,288 houses, 11,863 km roads, 1,725 bridges, 4,010 culverts, repair of 1,18,019 houses, and setting up of 3000 mini and small enterprises and increase in vegetable production in various parts of the State are among the major achievements of the People's Plans. That all political parties had to commit themselves before the electorate through speeches and manifestoes to bestow the local bodies with more powers has reinforced the view that the People's Plan-model decentralisation has come here to stay.

In short, when we compare the above cited poll issues, People's Plan remained at centre-stage of discussion till the last day, because of the fact that, its impact would be felt in each of the Panchayat depending on the way the programmes have been implemented, because there are UDF ruled Panchayats which have done well or as badly as the LDF ruled Panchayats. Realising this, the LDF even decided to go in for separate election manifesto for each of the local bodies.

POLLING

Elections to the civic bodies were held in two phases on 25 and 27 September, 2000. Over 73 per cent of the voters exercised their franchise in the seven districts during the first phase. In all the seven districts—Kollam, Pathanamthitta, Idukki, Thrissur, Malappuram, Wayanad and Kasaragod—the turnout was enthusiastic. The polling percentage was 70 in Idukki, 70 in Thrissur, 77 in Malappuram, 71 in Wayanad and 74 in Kasaragod.

In the 1995 civic polls, the state had recorded 73.6 per cent polling. In Kollam and Thrissur towns, electronic voting machines were used. There were complaints of malfunctioning of the machines in a few booths resulted in sight holdups in the voting, There were nearly 25,000 candidates in the fray for the three-tier local poll in these seven districts. Though the Election Commission authorities expected some untoward incidents in practically sensitive Kasaragod district, polling went on peacefully barring some minor incidents of impersonation and isolated skirmishes.

During the second phase of the polling over 70 per cent of the voters used their voting right spread over the remaining seven districts. The percentage of polling were:

Thiruvananthapuram - 73, Alappuzha - 70, Kozhikode - 68 and

Kannur - 70. Large scale violence, country bomb explosions and booth capturing marred the elections in Kannur district. Police opened fire at two places in Kannur district to quench the violence. A five year old girl, Ashna lost one of her legs when a bomb hurled allegedly by RSS-BJP workers at Congressmen at Cheruvancheri. Her mother also was injured. At least fifteen others were injured in poll related violence in the district.

Despite tight security, violence erupted in Pamir, Koothuparambu and other areas of the district. In Panoor CPM worker was allegedly attacked by BJP workers. Ballot boxes were taken away from some booths. Activists belonged to almost all major parties were among those injured in Kannur District. A UDF worker was stabbed allegedly by LDF activists at Kadinamkulam in Thiruvananthapuram district. Tension prevailed in the coastal belt of the district Poonthura and Valiyathura. But polling was by and large peaceful in Ernakulam and Kottayam district, barring stray incidents. Detailed district-wise polling percentage is given in Table 5.2.

Table 5.2: District-wise Polling Percentage

Sl. No	*District*	*Polling % in 1995*	*2000*	*Difference*
1.	Thiruvananthapuram	70	66	-4
2.	Kollam	72	70	-2
3.	Pathanamthitta	70	71	+ 1
4.	Alappuzha	72.6	68	-4.4
5.	Kottayam	70.8	73	+2.2
6.	Idukki	70	75	+ 5
7.	Eranakulam	72	73	+ 1
8.	Thrissur	72	70	-2
9.	Palakkad	64	70	+ 6
10.	Malappuram	75	77	+ 2
11.	Kozhikode	70	68	-2
12.	Wayanad	73	71	-2
13.	Kannur	71.8	70	-1.8
14.	Kasaragod	74.5	74	-.5

Note: In 2000 state average was 72.5%. Phase I average was 75% and phase II average was 70%.

VERDICT 2000

Spectacular Show by the UDF and Warning Signs to the LDF

In the local body elections, the UDF had every reason to feel proud of its better show, which was even far beyond its expectations. The poll results should be viewed in context of the fact that it happens to be a dress-rehearsal for the forthcoming assembly elections. The poll results came as a morale booster for each and every constituents of the UDF.

The favourable election results had virtually demolished the CPM created myth about People's Plan Programme, one of the key campaign issues which the LDF and more particularly the CPM had banked on to give it another term. The election results further is that, the people clearly rejected the CPM's style of implementing the people's plan process and shared the general view process about it, expressed even by some of the leading LDF partners like CPI, RSP and NCP. Through this poll, UDF had proved beyond doubt that it could work wonders if it stood united. As cited above the poll outcome had virtually surprised the UDF, because the opposition went into electioneering fearing the money power of the CPM—an unprecedented and unhealthy development in the political development of the state. Further, the poll result also put the seal on the new political line touted by the CPM (popularly blown as the tactical) in its search for a new political planning space. Its election tactic of backing independents and a large number of UDF rebels turned as a non-starter from the beginning. The poll results undoubtedly proves the electorate's disaffection with the opportunistic politics championed by the CPM.

The much debated ties of the CPM with the IMUL, a leading partner of the UDF as many as twenty panchayats in Malappuram district yielded only partial responses. The party had even agreed to the AMEs demands by not contesting on its own symbol. The CPM-IUML ties under the banner of "development councils" had to be satisfied with capturing control of only nine Panchayats. In Alappuzha district, when the UDF had done exceptionally well in the last several elections, the voters handed out different kind of verdict. The LDF was able to more or less retain its hold. In Kollam, the S.N. College issue appears to have had its impact in the urban and semi-urban municipalities. If one were to go the unambiguous results in traditional Left-oriented municipalities like Punalur and Varkala both CPI stronghold, it is clear that the Congress(I) and the UDF benefitted by the problems between CPM and CPI. In Ernakulam, the CPM rebels played a vital role in the industrial belt (Aluva and Kalamassery areas) which ultimately spoiled the prospects of the CPM.

Another significant factor in the poll results was that, the LDF's majority came down considerably in a large number of Panchayats, which the party had retained. The UDF had succeeded in winning more number of seats in the five-layer civic bodies. The UDF constituents together had captured 6,704 constituencies out of 11,799 seats. This was much better than the 1995 results, when the UDF had to concede ruling majorities in many panchayats. However despite winning more panchayat constituencies, the UDF efforts to wrest control had not exactly succeeded. Above all, the CPM-IUML ties which significantly enough was confined only to 20 village Panchayats, provided a hint to the Congress(I), to put an end to its groupism and unwarned tussle between two major groups within the Congress. By forging limited ties with the CPM, it had sent a message that could very well work out a partnership with the Marxism if required.

The voting pattern also demolished the LDF campaign about the Congress-BJP ties though it was true that in some places the BJP got away with one or two seats because of the presense of one or more UDF rebels. The poll results of Eranakulam, Kottayam, Idukki, Thrissur, Malappuram should be an eye-opener for the LDF, which had cried hoarse about the Congress-BJP deal. Local bodies polls are seldom considered to be referendum on the state government mainly because such polls are normally candidate-centred and personality of the people involved in the contest matter more than political issues.

However, one noticeable aspect of the present civic polls was that there came about a definite link between politics at the local and state levels in the form of the People's Plan campaign theme. The campaign's positive impact on Kerala society and it became a local point of the LDF campaign but it was hazardous step. The People's planning process was a success mostly in rural areas, but its beneficial effects were not evident in the urban areas. In the urban areas where the level of popular participation in ward sabhas was abysmally low. The people who were benefited out of the campaign process whole-heartedly accepted it as a new development mantra whereas there was also another section without having any benefit from the campaign. Naturally, they were reluctant towards the people's plan. To some other, the campaign was nothing more than a slogan for the benefit of CPM. Moreover, the corruption charges relating to decentralised planning may well have linked the local bodies poll campaign to other corruption charges such as those regarding selection of consultants for the OECF aided schemes and Kannur versus Ennore power project controversy. While these may not have been decisive factors, they could have added to the anti-incumbancy mood of the electorate, particularly among the middle class.

Anti-incumbency Factors

There were strong indications that people, especially the urbanites were strongly dissatisfied with the government's performance. The swing in favour of the UDF was about seven per cent which cannot be explained fully by the arguments like the Congress-BJP ties as propagated by the CPM. In the rural areas, the candidates were often well-known to the local people. However in the urban areas this was not the case. So the verdict in the urban areas could be considered largely a political vote, based on the performance of political parties, local bodies and the government in power.

It was very clear that the LDF had gone to polls on the assumption that the apparent success of the People's Plan would help it. However, at least some considered the claimed success as debatable. Moreover, the benefits were clouded by corruption and nepotism.

There were also strong contention from various quarters that the monetary benefits often went in favour of party members or party directly. On the Government's side it could not present any image before the voters and even the Chief Minister and his family members too were under the clouds of suspicion. Many crucial Government departments miserably failed to fulfil the aspirations of the people. Industrialisation of the state still remains as a distant dream, despite favourable industrial climate. The youth wings of the LDF which had been vociferous about employment generation were silent after the LDF voted to power. Though information technology promised much, the government could not rise to the occasion. It miserably failed to act quickly and promptly to grab the opportunities.

Further, the state Government was helpless when the prices of key agricultural commodities collapsed. The opposition managed to raise a lot of protest over the Government's initiatives like the consumer card and revenue card. The education sector was not free of controversies. Higher education suffered a lot from overpoliticisation, poor standards of teaching, inadequate facilities and outdated syllabus. The police force acted like instruments in the hands of the politicians rather than agency entrusted to protect the lives and liberties of the people. Apart from the general political trend against the CPM in the state as a whole some other issues also worked against the prospects of the LDF. It include the S.N. College issue, dissidence in the CPM and the widening rift between the CPM and CPI.

The agitation launched by the SFI in S.N. College, Kollam had its concrete impact in the poll outcome. Though it did not make any public appeal, the S.N.D.P. Yogam workers especially its youth wing were actively in the electioneering field round the clock to ensure the defeat of the CPM candidates. In this context, it was also visible that the S.N.D.P. Yogam workers, however did not campaign against the candidates belonged to the other partners of the LDF. The outcome of the elections to panchayat bodies in Kundra Assembly segment in Kollam district alone proves the influence exhibited by the Yogam against the CPM. Katra is the Constituency from where J. Mercy Kutty Amma of the CPM got elected to the Assembly. She incurred the wrath of the Yogam leadership by her active involvement in the SFI agitation which finally turned against the Ezhava community as a Whole. The UDF had won seven out of Eight Grama Panchayats in Kudra, including Thrikkaruva, which was considered as the bastion of the CPM. The UDF won only one Panchayat in Kundara in the 1995 poll.

Moreover, the factional feuds in the CPM got worsened, just before the declaration of the civic polls. There were also CITU media reports which unequally stated that CITU group was active in many parts of the state and during the past several months dissidence was grouping within the official group itself. They all joined together this time and many CPM rebels appeared in various parts of the state who worked relentlessly to ensure the defeat of the CPM candidate. The worsening ties between the CPM and CPI too had played a major role in the defeat of LDF candidates this time. In some districts and areas both the parties contested against each other which made it possible for an easy victory for the UDF. Despite continuing in the LDF both the parties were at loggerheads.

Poor Performance by the BJP

The verdict further reveals that the state BJP could not perform well especially in the rural areas. Out of 12,451 Grama Panchayat constituencies where elections held the party could capture only 215 seats. In the municipalities, the BJP had won 40 seats out of 1569 seats. Thus, the Party had won only 2.54 per cent of the seats in the municipalities, while it could won 17.32 per cent of the seats in the Grama Panchayat constituencies. In this context, it has to be noticed that the overall share of the party in seats in 1995 was only one per cent.

In the Block and District Panchayats, its performance was poorer. It could corner only half a dozen seats. The party had only a very few seats in the District Panchayats. In the municipal areas, many of its victories were due to its secret alliances with some of the partners of the UDF. However, such alliances could not be formed widely in the Panchayats.

For example, its alliances with the Kerala Congress(M), a leading UDF partner, had helped the party to open its account in the Panchayat such as Kuruvilangad in Kottayam district. It could also capture a number of seats in Pathanamthitta district in the same manner. The party had also got benefited from the presence of one or more UDF rebels in some constituencies. In some other places, it had tactical understanding with the LDF constituents regarding support to independents. In Kasaragod district, the BJP gained control of two Panchayats against four last time (1995). It could not extend its ground in the district, though a total of 60 seats were won in various Grama Panchayats. In Kannur district, however it could make inroads, though marginally. Moreover though the number of seats won by the BJP was less than 3 per cent of the total, it had gained importance because of its decisive role in Kochi Corporation, some municipalities and a few panchayats. The new milieu would certainly make it easier for the party to find allies in further elections.

The detailed election results of Grama Panchayat, Block Panchayats, District Panchayats, Municipal Councils and Municipal Corporation are explained in Tables 5.3 to 5.8.

Table 5.3: PRIs in Kerala – 2000

GRAMA PANCHAYATS

Sl. No.	*District*	*No. of Panchayats*	*Women*	*Total Members*	*SC*	*ST*	*SC Women*	*ST Women*
1.	Thiruvananthapuram	78	1096	394	138	7	48	1
2.	Kollam	69	1030	367	140	1	58	-
3.	Pathanamthitta	54	634	237	84	3	25	-
4.	Alappuzha	73	935	339	106	-	26	-
5	Kollayam	74	950	344	88	10	14	3
6.	Idukki	52	625	233	92	33	22	9
7.	Ernakulam	87	1105	405	118	-	29	-
A	Thrissur	92	1221	441	162	1	56	-
9	Palakkad	90	1178	427	196	19	79	6
10.	Malappuram	100	1460	519	131	3	29	-
11.	Kozhikode	77	1090	395	99	1	22	-
12.	Wayanad	25	354	128	12	61	1	23
13.	Kannur	81	1049	382	73	14	5	1
14.	Kasaragod	39	528	190	48	16	8	4
	Total	991	13255	4801	1487	169	422	47

BLOCK PANCHAYAT

Sl. No.	*District*	*No. of Panchayats*	*Total Members*	*Women*	*SC*	*ST*	*SC Women*	*ST Women*
1	Thiruvananthapuram	12	129	48	17	-	5	-
2.	Kollam	13	136	52	18	-	5	-
3.	Pathanamthitta	9	91	36	12	-	3	-
4.	Alappuzha	12	121	46	15	-	3	-
5.	Kottayam	11	110	45	10	1	-	-
6.	Idukki	8	80	52	13	4	3	-
7.	Ernakulam	15	153	80	15	-	-	-
8	Thrissur	17	173	68	21	-	4	-
9.	Palakkad	13	141	55	25	4	11	2
10.	Malappuram	14	165	61	16	-	2	-
11	Kozhikode	12	135	51	14	-	2	-
12.	Wayanad	3	36	13	1	6	-	3
13.	Kannur	9	109	40	7	2	-	-
14.	Kasaragod	4	53	20	4	1	-	-
	Total	52	1638	629	188	18	38	5

DISTRICT PANCHAYATS

Sl. No.	*District*	*Total Members*	*Women*	*SC*	*ST*	*SC Women*	*ST Women*
1.	Thiruvananthapuram	25	9	3	-	1	-
2.	Kollam	24	8	3	-	1	-

(Contd.)

Sl. No.	District	Total Members	Women	SC	ST	SC Women	ST Women
3.	Pathanamthitta	15	5	2	–	1	
4.	Alappuzha	21	7	2	-	1	-
5.	Kottayam	21	7	2	-	1	-
6.	Idukki	15	5	2	1	1	-
7.	Ernakulam	25	9	3	-	1	-
8.	Thrissur	27	9	4	-	2	-
9.	Palakkad	26	9	4	-	2	-
10.	Malappuram	30	10	3	-	1	-
11.	Kozhikode	25	9	2	-	1	-
12.	Wayanad	15	5	1	3	-	1
13	Kannur	23	8	1	-	-	-
14.	Kasaragod	15	5	1	-	-	-
	Total	307	105	33	4	13	1

Table 5.4: Results of Grama Panchayats

District	Total Seats/Poll held	LDF	UDF	Hung
Thiruvananthapuram	78	46	26	6
Kollam	69/66	32	29	5
Pathanamthitta	54/53	18	23	12
Alappuzha	73/72	55	14	3
Kottayam	74/70	19	46	4(1)
Idukki	51/50	12	26	12
Ernakulam	88/82	28	38	16
Thrissur	92/86	33	41	11(2)
Palakkad	90/89	56	28	5
Malappuram	100/81	17	47	4(3)
Kozhikode	77/69	44	19	6
Wayanad	25/21	7	14	0
Kannur	81/79	53	22	4
Kasaragod	39/36	12	13	9(4)

POST-POLL SCENARIO

Though the CPM state Secretariat had described this as BJP-Congress Pact, it was clear that the critics of People's Plan within the Party would ultimately turn their guns against those who had championed for such a developmental programme. As in the case of the literacy movement which was launched by the 1987 LDF Government, the LDF camp especially the CPM was over-enthusiastic to use the people's plan as their Victory mantra.

Table 5.5: Results of Block Panchayats

District	Total Seats/Poll held	LDF	UDF	Hung
Thiruvananthapuram	12	7	3	2
Kollam	13	6	4	3
Pathanamthitta	9	4	4	1
Alappuzha	12	8	2	2
Kottayam	11	4	7	0
Idukki	8	3	5	0
Ernakulam	15/13	2	10	1
Thrissur	17/16	6	7	3
Palakkad	13	7	4	2
Malappuram	14/11	1	10	0
Kozhikode	12	9	1	2
Wayanad	3/2	0	2	0
Kannur	9	8	1	0
Kasaragod	4	1	2	1

Table 5.6: Results of District Panchayats

District	Total Seats/Poll held	LDF	UDF	BJP	OTHERS
Thiruvananthapuram	25	14	11	0	0
Kollam	24/20	14	6	0	0
Pathanamthitta	13	4	9	0	0
Alappuzha	20	15	5	0	0
Kottayam	21/15	7	7	0	1
Idukki	15/14	8	6	0	0
Ernakulam	20	3	17	0	0
Thrissur	27/21	11	10	0	0
Palakkad	26/25	19	6	0	0
Kozhikode	25/16	13	3	0	0
Wayanad	15/11	4	7	0	0
Kannur	23/19	15	3	0	1
Kasaragod	15/10	4	3	1	2

Table 5.7: Results of Municipal Corporations

Name	Seats	LDF	UDF	BJP	Others
Thiruvananthapuram	81	51	23	3	4
Kochi	66	33	31	2	0
Kozhikode	51	32	18	1	0
Kollam	50	24	22	0	4
Thrissur	50	20	28	1	1

However it must be noted that, even the CPM ministers in the present Nayanar ministry, except a few, were not keen to extend a

Table 5.8: Results of Municipal Councils

Name	*Seats*	*LDF*	*UDF*	*BJP*	*Others*
Neyyattinkara	37	21	11	1	4
Nedumangad	31	16	15	0	0
Attingal	25	6	17	0	2
Varkkala	27	12	13	1	1
Punalur	30	14	16	0	0
Paravoor (South)	26	11	14	0	1
Pathanamthitta	26	10	14	0	2
Thiruvalla	33	14	15	4	0
Adoor	22	7	11	1	3
Alappuzha	50	20	21	3	5
Kayamkulam	38	12	21	2	3
Cherthala	29	19	9	0	1
Mavelikkara	23	9	12	0	2
Chenganoor	21	10	9	1	1
Kottayam	37	10	22	1	4
Changnassery	32	16	14	2	0
Vaikom	20	3	15	0	2
Pala	20	9	11	0	0
Thodupuzha	28	10	14	3	1
Aluva	21	6	13	0	2
Perumbavoor	21	11	8	1	1
North Paravoor	20	7	11	0	2
Moovattupuzha	23	11	12	0	0
Angamali	24	8	15	0	1
Kothamangalam	26	12	12	0	2
Thrippunithara	32	20	10	0	2
Kalamassery	33	10	18	0	5
Kunnamkulam	31	14	15	0	2
Irinjalakkuda	22	7	13	0	2
Chalakkudi	29	13	15	0	1
Kodungalloor	24	14	9	1	0
Chavakkad	27	13	12	1	1
Guruvayoor	20	13	7	0	0
Shoranur	27	18	9	0	0
Ottappalam	29	22	6	1	0
Palakkad	50	17	21	7	5
Chittur	24	4	20	0	0
Malappuaram	14	16	0	1	0
Tirur	31	9	20	1	1
Manjerry	39	22	16	0	1
Ponnani	50	25	24	1	0
Perinthalmanna	27	21	6	0	0
Koilandy	38	20	17	1	0
Vadakara	40	25	15	0	0
Kalppatta	21	11	10	0	0
Kannur	38	11	22	0	0
Thalasserv	50	38	12	0	0
Payyannoor	37	31	6	0	0
Koothparamp	23	21	1	1	0
Thaliparamp	35	24	9	1	1
Kanhangad	34	10	18	4	2
Kasaragod	32	2	16	9	5

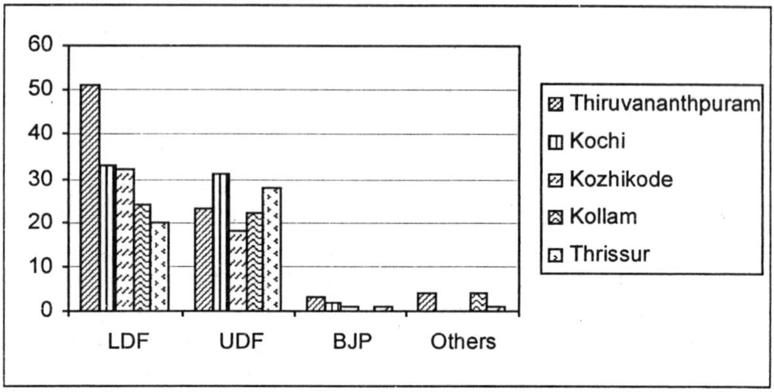

Fig. 5.1: Municipal Corporation Results.

whole-hearted support to the plan programme. Ultimately, the CPM Secretariat's reluctance to accept the setback and also to have an objective analysis of the performance of the LDF government would lead to disastrous consequences in the forthcoming assembly polls.

The state level election results reveals that the LDF could capture 44.87 per cent of grama panchayat wards, while the UDF secured 43.31 per cent of wards. In 1995, the LDF had to close to 60 per cent wards in the grama panchayats. In municipalities also, the UDF performed exceptionally well. Though the LDF was slightly ahead in the rural areas, the civic polls results had given the UDF a favourable atmosphere to surge ahead in the remaining months if the government's performance remains unchanged. It is contextual to note that, the ministers of no other CPM-led government in the past had faced such serious charges of corruption and nepotism as faced by the present ministry led by Nayanar. On many occasions, the remarks and statements made by the Chief Minister had been described as highly insulting and provocative. Moreover, the widespread public criticism against the LDF handling of the Plus Two issue considerably eroded the credibility of the Nayanar ministry.

Though the agitations launched by the UDF against the plus two issue could not attract much public support, the verdict by High Court to cancel the list of plus two schools was a severe blow to the ministry. Further the state education minister's office and several top leaders of the LDF were yet to emerge out of the allegations of serious charges of corruption in sanctioning the plus two schools. Lastly, the intolerance of the CPM and its Kannur model murder politics had also been made as a top level campaign issue by the UDF leadership. The pertinent question before the electorate of the state after the local body polls was that whether the much talked and debated people's plan programme could save the LDF from the severe damage caused by the government and leadership, before the forthcoming assembly polls or not. There ultimately lies the future of LDF in the state politics.

References

C. Gouri Dasan Nair, "Poll Outcome a Warning to LDF", *The Hindu,* 30th September, 2000.

Deepika.

Deshabhimani.

Gilvester Assary, *The New Indian Express,* 24th September, 2000.

Girish Menon, "It's a Morale Booster for the UDF", *The Hindu,* 30th September, 2000.

Girish Menon, "UDF Position Far More Comfortable Now", *The Hindu,* 24th September, 2000.

Janmabhoomi.

M.R. Biju, "LDF's Repeat Performance: Kerala's Local Body Elections", *Economic and Political Weekly,* Vol. XXX, October 14211995.

M.R. Biju, "Panchayat Elections in Kerala", *Kurukshetra,* Vol. XLIV, No. 3, December 1995.

M.R. Biju, *Dynamics of New Panchayati Raj System: Retrospective and Reflections.* Kanishka, New Delhi, 1998.

M.R. Biju, *Parliamentary Democracy and Political Change in India.* Kanishka, New Delhi, 1999.

M.R. Biju, *Politics of Democracy and Decentralisation in India: A Case Study of Kerala,* Atlantic, New Delhi, 1997.

R. Krishna Kumar, The Local Bodies Round, *Frontline,* 29th September 2000.

Roy Mathew, "BJP Performance in Rural Areas", *The Hindu,* 30th September, 2000.

Roy Mathew, "Poll Verdict: A Reflection on Government Performance", *The Hindu,* 2nd October, 2000.

Samakalika Malayalam Weekly, Kochi.

Sree Narayana College Issue: The Sree Narayana College, Kollam named after the great social reformer and saint Sree Narayana Guru is one of the prestigious centres of higher education in South India offering courses up to Doctoral level in all disciplines to more than four thousand students was founded under the aegis of the SNDP Yogam on 17h April, 1947. The institution aims at achieving the high ideals of Sree Narayana Guru who professed the total emancipation of all mankind without any discrimination on caste, creed or religion.

The S.N. College issue started in October 1999, when the Principal issued Compulsory Transfer Certificate to five students who had created trouble in the college. A section of students under SFI started indefinite strike demanding their re-admission. When the agitation turned violent the College Principal filed a writ petition and the High Court of Kerala directed the police officers to see that the law and order situation was maintained and that no damage was caused to college property. The Court also directed that protection should be given to the teachers, non-teaching staff and students of the college and demonstration should not be allowed on the campus.

On 27 October, 1999, SFI students started a relay hunger strike in front of the college, which continued for about three months. On 31st January, 2000 around 10 a.m. hundreds of students along with the expelled students and outsiders carrying SFI, DYFI, CITU flags trespassed into the college campus and conducted demonstration and gheraoed the Principal in his office room up to 12 noon. On the following day, Principal was held hostage by SFI activists from 10 a.m. onwards without permitting him to take food or water or to answer the call of nature. Late in the evening settlement was reached in the presence of the District Collector, the SP and the CPM leaders. As per the settlement out of the four dismissed students would be given permission to write their final examinations in the college without granting them admission and third one would be readmitted and the fourth one's case would be decided by the government to give admission in any college other than S.N. College, Kollam. But after signing the settlement the principal had submitted a letter to the college management which stated "everything with regard to the settlement place without my free will". Meanwhile a statue of Sree Narayana Guru before the SNDP Yogam headquarters very close to the college campus was disfigured by vandals at the midnight of the same day – 1st January 2000. The SNDP Yogam leadership alleged that the statue was defaced by "a group that had participated in the victory march and celebrations" over the S.N. College issue.

Later in his writ petition filed before the High Court, the Principal alleged that the Police Officers who were present on the campus on both these days did not take any action to comply with the High Court order. After examining the entire facts of the case a Division Bench of the Kerala High Court on 12th October, 2000, came down heavily on the Police and ordered for contempt of court against them. The court also directed to post the case for framing charges against the police officials.

The Court found that the Kollam police officials had committed prima facie contempt of court by refusing to implement a court order to provide adequate protection to the teaching and non-teaching staff, students and property of the college. The Court said that the Principal was confined illegally in his room till late in the night. The SP and other police officers contended that they had found the students peacefully sitting in front of the Principal's room. *"We do not understand the meaning of the word peaceful" the judges said. It was the duty of the police to remove the students as soon as they found them sitting in front of the principal's office. It was because of the fact that these persons were allowed to sit in front of the Principal's room that the situation worsened, the court observed. Sometimes, to maintain law and order the police will have to use force. They cannot act like deaf and dumb and as mere onlookers. On behalf of the police it was argued that they were waiting to see whether the problem between the Principal and students would be solved peacefully or not. The Court further opined on it that - 'sorry to state that it was not the lookout of the police to see whether the problem is solved peacefully. or nor! It is true that as far as possible bloodshed should be avoided. But on the mere apprehension that there would be some repercussion, the police should not refrain from taking remedial action. If the version of the respondents are accepted, lawlessness would prevail'.*

Though the police officials had rendered an apology in their affidavits, the Court said that it was not satisfied with the same and that it was of the view that they have to be proceeded against for contempt of court, since there is a prima facie case against them Both these issues finally culminated in an open rift between the CPM and the SNDP Yogam and its repercussions were quite reflected in the Civic Elections, 2000.

The Hindu.
The Kerala Kaumudi.
The Malayala Manorama.
The Mathrubhumi.
The New Indian Express.

6

Local Body Polls, 2005

Tough Time Ahead for the UDF

Article 243E and 243U of the Constitution of India deals with the question of duration of Panchayats and Municipalities and periodicity of elections to the rural and urban local bodies. It says "Every Panchayat/Municipality unless sooner dissolved under any law for the time being in force shall continue for five years from the date appointed its first meeting and no longer". This constitutional provision also prohibits any dissolution of a Panchayat/Municipality during its life by amendment of law. It also provided that an election to constitute a Panchayat/ Municipality shall be completed before the expiry of its duration of five years and in case it is dissolved, the election shall be completed before the expiration of six months from such dissolution. If, however, a dissolved Panchayat/Municipality had a tenure of less than six months left, there is no need for election for such a short period. Thus, conduct of election to the rural and urban local bodies at a five year interval is mandatory.

Elections to the Local body elections in Kerala assumed greater significance because local level democracy is the basic foundation on which the entire democratic edifice rests. The legitimacy of these elections as crucial instruments of a democratic political process at the local level is increasing day by day. Obviously all the social, economic and political factors affecting the states and parliament elections influence the local government elections too.

Against this backdrop, the present study examines the diversified aspects of the recently held local body polls in Kerala. The state of Kerala went for local body polls on 24th and 26th September, 2005, for the 7th time since Independence. The first poll was held in 1953 under the provisions of the then Travancore-Cochin Panchayat Act, 1950. The second election was held in 1963 after the formation of the state in 1956 and after the passing of Kerala Panchayat/Municipality Acts of 1960. It was followed by elections in 1979, 1988, 1995 and 2000.

Pre-poll Scene

The local body elections 2005 had attracted more attention from political parties, media persons, and general public alike due to a number of reasons. Notable among them include:

(a) the local bodies both urban and rural are enjoyed with increased powers and resources, for example, a grama panchayat used to get barely Rs. 1 lakh a year for all its activities before decentralisation, the annual allocation is around Rs. 70 lakh now;
(b) the most important factor deciding the fortunes of both UDF and LDF is likely to be the strategic alliances at the local level between parties belonging even to opposing political views, a constant feature of local body polls in Kerala;
(c) the split in the Congress and the formation of Democratic Indira Congress (Karunakaran) with its compulsion to ally with the LDF in order to teach the parent party a lesson;
(d) the ruling Congress party and the UDF faced the poll with relative harmony this time after parting the ways with Karunakaran Group;
(e) the seat sharing exercise in the LDF camp had witnessed an unprecedented troublesome due to the CPI(M)'s seat adjustments with Karunakaran, against the interest of some of its partners including CPI and RSP;
(f) the UDF on its part faced the electorate with the absence of two former constituents - Kerala Congress faction led by T.M. Jacob and RSP splinter group led by A.V. Thamarakshan;
(g) The LDF faced the electorate with more optimism mainly because in all the elections held in the state since the UDF came to power in 2001, the left had scored thumping victory including the Lok Sabha polls in May 2004 in which the LDF won 18 out of 20 seats.

Table 6.1: Total No. of Voters in Kerala – 2005

Sl. No.	District	Male	Woman
1	Thiruvananthapuram	1186137	1237849
2	Kollam	1019598	947614
3	Pathanamthitta	507192	458583
4	Alappuzha	891955	789653
5	Kottayam	764624	729351
6	Idukki	449225	448206
7	Eranakulam	1302365	1226649
8	Thrissur	1277999	1136603
9	Palghat	953258	890039
10	Malappuram	1171861	1139233
11	Kozhikode	1143417	954763
12	Wayanad	305076	270463
13	Kannur	857442	789913
14	Kasaragod	437598	418774
	Total	12267747	11437693

Polling

Elections were held in two phases. Eight southern districts—Thiruvananthapuram, Kollam, Alappuzha, Kottayam, Kollam, Pathanamthitta, Idukki, Ernakulam and Thrissur went to the poll on 24th September and the remaining districts - Malappuram, Kozhikode, Wayanad, Kannur and Kasaragod went to the poll on 26th September. 59.94 percentage polling was recorded in the first phase whereas 61.75 per cent voting was recorded in the final phase. Minor scuffles between party volunteers, scores of complaints related to bogus voting and a few charges of booth capturing were reported from the northern districts. The highest polling was recorded in Idukki district - 64.64 per cent. Thiruvananthapuram district came at the bottom with 52.87 per cent. The district-wise details from 1995 onwards are given in Table 6.2.

Voter's Apathy

The two vital aspects of the local body election appeared to be voter apathy and confusions aroused from the anomalies in the preparation of voter's list. Voter apathy had been striking in urban areas particularly in the southern parts of the state. Even if the

Table 6.2: Number of Polling Stations

		No. of Polling Stations		
Sl. No.	*District*	*No. of Rural Polling Station*	*No. of Urban Polling station*	*Total No. of Polling Stations*
1	Thiruvananthapuram	2722	607	3329
2	Kollam	2419	298	2717
3	Pathanamthitta	1482	102	1584
4	Alappuzha	2224	228	2452
5	Kottayam	2283	124	2407
6	Idukki	1434	32	1466
7	Ernakulam	2799	734	3533
8	Thrissur	3065	374	3439
9	Palakkad	2891	190	3081
10	Malappuram	3678	198	3876
11	Kozhikode	2769	492	3261
12	Wayanad	861	25	886
13	Kannur	2556	263	2819
14	Kasaragod	1278	82	1360
	Total	32461	3749	36210

overall figure is taken polling is likely to be lower by four or five percentage from that in 2000, when 66.5 per cent of the voters cast their votes. The major reason for the fall in polling percentage was due to the reason that the campaign that stressed little on local level development and more on political issues having no connection with the problems of grassroots. With the LDF, led by the CPI(M) deciding to go in for local level tie-ups with DIG (K), the whole political debate got entangled in emergency and there was very little discussion on which way the state's efforts at democratic decentralisation should be taken.

The coming together of political antagonists also might have left the voters cold. The reported anomalies in the delimitation of wards and preparation of voter's list also appeared to have played a major part in pouring cold water over voter's enthusiasm. There have been reports of candidates themselves not been able to cast their votes and several persons left without voting as their names figured in lists pertaining to far-off booths. In urban areas, the voters appeared to have chosen not to go through the ordeal of checking their names in several lists in several booths so that they could exercise their franchise.

Only the diehard voters were prepared to go from booth to

booth, based on helpful tips provided by political party workers and booth agents to cast their votes. The confusion over distribution of postal ballots to state employees deployed on poll duty has only confounded the situation, if one were to go by reports of skirmishes pouring in from various district headquarters.

Table 6.3: Polling Percentage from 1995 to 2005

District	Polling % in 1995	Polling % in 2000	Polling % in 2005
1. Thiruvannthapuram	70	66	52.87
2. Kollam	72	70	59 50
3. Pathanamthitta	70	71	62
4. Kottayam	70.8	73	64.34
5. Idukki	70	75	64.64
6. Alappuzha	72.6	68	62.08
7. Ernakulam	72	73	56.09
8. Thrissur	72	70	58.76
9. Palakkad	64	70	61
10. Malappuram	75	77	63.03
11. Kozhikode	70	68	62.25
12. Wayanad	73	71	61
13. Kannur	71.8	70	63
14. Kasaragod	74.5	74	60

Table 6.4: Grama Panchayat—Election Results—2005

District	LDF	UDF	Hung
Thiruvananthapuram	75.64	16.66	7.69
Kollam	85.91	7.44	7.04
Pathanamthitta	40.74	38.88	20.37
Alappuzha	78.08	16.43	5.47
Kottayam	46.66	26.66	26.66
Idukki	67.30	17.30	5.38
Ernakulam	60.22	13.63	26.13
Thrissur	81.52	4.53	13.04
Palakkad	73.62	19.78	6.59
Malappuram	14.70	71.56	8.82
Kozhikode	84	8	8
Kannoor	78.58	17.5	3.75
Kasaragod	43.58	33.33	10.25
Total	65.03	22.44	11.52

Table 6.5: Block Panchayat—Election Results—2005

District	*LDF*	*UDF*	*BJP*	*Hung*
Thiruvananthapuram	83.33	16.66	0	0
Kollam	100	0	0	0
Pathanamthitta	33.33	33.33	0	33.33
Alappuzha	100			
Kottayam	36.36	45.45		18.18
Idukki	50	12.5		37.5
Ernakulam	73.33	13.33		13.33
Thrissur	88.23	5.88		5.88
Palakkad	92.30	7.69		
Malappuram	714	92.85		
Kozhikkodu	100			
Kannoor	100			
Kasaragode	100			50
Total	72.36	19.07		8.55

Table 6.6: District Panchayat—Election Results—2005

District	*LDF*	*UDF*	*BJP*	*Hung*
Thiruvananthapuram	71.42	25	0	3.57
Kollam	92.59	3.7		3.7
Pathanamthitta	52.94	41.17		5.88
Alappuzha	82.60	17.39		
Kottayam	43.47	52.17		4.34
Idukki	87.5	12.5		0
Ernakulam	60.71	28.57		17.64
Thrissur	76.66	16.66		6.6
Palakkad	96.55	3.44		0
Malappuram	21.87	78.12		
Kozhikkodu	89.28	7.14		3.57
Kannoor	92	8	0	
Kasaragode	50	43.75	6.25	
Total	69.82	26.62	0.29	3.25

The Verdict

The CPI(M) led LDF has registered a landslide victory on the local body polls, LDF candidates won all the five city Corporations, 725 out of 999 Grama Panchayats, 122 out of 152 Block Panchayats, 33 out of 52 municipalities and 12 out of 14 District Panchayats.

In a state where switching loyalty to political fronts every five years is almost a genetic trait, the LDF's sweeping victory comes as no surprise. The distinctive left turn by the electorate with the LDF by capturing both urban and rural local bodies alike, will not only leave the ruling DDF red in the face but will cast a shadow over the assembly elections due early 2006. But to call this a copy of the great march of the left (May 2004) which saw the conquering of 19 of 20 Lok Sabha constituencies in the State, would be farfetched because that issues dominated the campaigning.

The LDF aided by tactical adjustments with DIG (K) gave the UDF a comprehensive drubbing. The UDF could acquit itself somewhat tolerably only in Pathanamthitta, Kottayam and Malappuram districts. The surprise gainer is the BJP which emerged as the largest single party in Palakkad Municipality, came seemed in 18 wards in Thiruvananthapuram corporation and opened its account in several municipalities. The UDF-BJP tie-up apparently proved more beneficial to the BJP than the UDF. On the other hand, the adjustments between the LDF and the DIG (K) proved useful and the DIC(K) to turn the election into a show of strength.

The UDF has failed to break the LDF's winning streak that started with the previous Lok Sabha polls. The sweep of the LDF victory even in the traditional UDF strongholds in the local bodies elections clearly show that the ruling coalition has not succeeded in correcting its equations with social forces that have come to play a vital yet silent role in Kerala Politics. The only consolation that the UDF can have from the election results is that the expected post-election political realignment on account of new local level adjustments forged by the DIC(K) and the CPI(M), LDF might not come about soon. The DIC(K)-LDF ties have also done considerable damage to the UDF, setting the stage for the BJP to make important gains. Right from the beginning, the general feeling was that a political alignment was due on account of the split in the Congress. The UDF partners have by and large managed to hedge their positions in areas of their influence, the same cannot be said in the case of the Congress, the Congress had to suffer in several areas.

Besides, the Congress had to carry a lot of baggage in terms of accommodating several local level leaders belonging to the Karunakaran faction which preferred to stick to the Congress depriving it of an opportunity to select winning candidates.

People's Verdict—An Eye Watch

In the poll the LDF has made a spectacular progress both in the percentage of votes and share of seats. The Front has scored 9 per cent votes and 22 per cent seats more than the UDF.

Even if the contribution of the PIC(K) is not counted, the LDF has scored 5 per cent votes and 18 per cent of seats more than the UDF. The LDF candidates have secured an average of 420 votes compared to 340 of the UDF vote share of the LDF and UDF came as 51 per cent and 31 per cent respectively.

The voting pattern of the rural local bodies further reveals the sharpness and depth of the verdict. The LDF has performed exemplary well in the intermediate and district level letters compared to the village panchayat level. In the higher levels, the influence of caste, peer groups, kinship, personality factor of the candidate, family links etc. will play a crucial or determining factor at the bottom level compared to the higher tiers. Naturally party and political consideration will give way to other factors. In the case of district level panchayats, most of the candidates were district level political leaders of each party and naturally people will give prime significance to his/her party connections than other parameters.

The electoral statistics further reveals that the difference of seats between both the Fronts were 21 per cent, 33 per cent and 47 per cent respectively in the GPS, BPs and DPs. The district-wise poll results further reveals that the LDF has secured over 50 per cent of votes in all districts of the state except Malappuram, Kasaragod and Pathanamthitta. The election results has also shown that the CPI(M) has ranked top in the case of mass support. The party has contested in 55 per cent seats and won 31 per cent votes and 40 per cent seats. The party has scored an average of 471 votes per constituency throughout the state. Thus, percentage of victory for the party came to 72 per cent. But the party could not make much progress in minority belts including Pathanamthitta, Kottayam, Ernakulam, Malappuram districts out of the 31 per cent of votes won by the party 3 per cent was from the support of independents sponsored by the party. On the other hand, the Congress party has contested in 70 per cent of the seats but its share of votes came down to 29 per cent and average vote per constituency came to 347.

Percentage of success was 32 per cent. But the IUML has more or less retained its strength in the northern Kerala. It has contested in 14 per cent of seats and its vote share came to 7 per cent. But it has depicted a success rate of 62 per cent, with an average vote share of 453 per constituency. The DIC(K) had fielded candidates only in 16 per cent of the seats and scored 5 per cent of votes and 4 per cent of seats. The party could show its strength in Kottayam, Idukki, Ernakulam, Thrissur, Kozhikode and Wayanad districts. In the poll, the BJP had made much progress. It has not only increased the number of seats but its share of votes too in Pathanamthitta, Kasaragod, Thrissur and Trivandrum districts. The Kerala Congress (Mani) has also done well in its areas of influence such as Palai, where it won 14 out of 17 seats it contested under the UDF banner (see Tables 6.7 and 6.8).

Karunakaran Factor

When the campaign for the local body polls was on the whole debate was centred on the LDF's tie-up with the DIC(K) and the way the CPI(M) was doing business with K. Karunakaran, the perpetrator of all the dark deeds of emerging. Although the LDF's tactical adjustments with the DIC(K) was supposed to be limited to those wards where the LDF could not on its own defeat the combined might of the UDF and the BJP the two sides found it convenient to extend it to almost the entire state. This deduct happen when heartburn and there were many in the CPI(M) and the LDF who found it hard to go campaigning hand in hand with their former bitter enemies. But as the result show, the experiment has been proved by and large fruitful. Now, that the LDF has crossed the first hurdle, it could well hope to retain the DIC(K) as an informal ally as long as it suits the two sides or till the political equations at the state level undergo another shift. The UDF and the media's focus on the emergency angle might also prove because the UDF may not be able to play the same trump when the assembly polls come. It should also be noted that though the LDF and the DIC(K) are informal allies, the former is not dependent on the DIC(K) for running any of the five corporations or municipalities. The DIC(K)'s main gain in the election was its success in seeing the UDF particularly the Congress worsted in the poll.

Table 6.7: Municipal Council-Election Results—2005

District	*Municipal Council*	*Total Seats*	*LDF*	*CPM*	*CPI*	*DIC*	*RSP*	*JD*	*KC (J)*	*KC (S)*	*LdF (Ind)*	*NCP*	*Cong (S)*	*UDF*	*INC*	*KC (M)*	*UDF Ind*	*CMP*	*IUML*	*JSS*	*BJP*	*Independent*	*Others*
1	2	3	4	5	6	7	8	9	10	11	12		13	14	15	16	17	18	19	20	21	22	23
TVPM	Nevyattinkara	41	21	17	3	1								19	18	1					1		
	Varkala	30	16	15	1	2	1							4	4								
	Attingal	28	176	14	1	2	1							4	4						1		1
	Nedumangad	36	27	20	7	3								5	5								CPM Reb-1
Kollam	Punalar	32	26	17	7	2	1				1		1	6	6								
	Paravur	29	19	14	3		1				1			9	9						1		1
PTA	Tirivalla	36	11	4	1	4		1		1			1	17	9	7	1				3		3
	PTA	29	12	8					2	1				12	12						3		
	Adoor	25	10	4	3	1					2			13	12	1							
ALPY	Chengannur	24	7	2		1			1	1	3		1	13	8	3	1				1		Ind 2
	Mevilikkara	25	6	5	1				1					15	14	1			3	2	1	2	Ind. 2 (Reb. of CPM & INC)
	Alappuzha	50	27	15	8	4								19	13	1				2			PDP-1
	Cherthala	32	21	16	5									10	9	1			6			2	CPM Rep.-1
	Kyamkulam	41	18	12	4	2								21	14	1							
KTYM	Kottayam	38	16	12	2									19	19							1	
	Pala	23	9	1	4	2					2			14		14						1	
	Vaikom	23	15	7	4	3			1					7								1	
	Changanassery	34	17	12		3			3					17	7	4					6		
Idukki	Thodupuzha	32	11			2			5					18	12	1			4			1	
Ernakulam	Angamali	27	12	7		3					3			13	11	1	1					1	CPM Reb. -1
	Kalamesseri	39	14	12		1	2				3			21	16				5			3	DIC(K) Inc.1
	Perumbavoor	24	11	7	2	1								10	9				1		1	1	

(Contd.)

1	2	3	4	5	6	7	8	9	10	11	12		13	14	15	16	17	18	19	20	21	22	23
	Kothamanglam	28	18	2	4	1			4				1	10	9				1				POP-1
	Trippunithara	37	25	22	2					1				9	7	2					2	1	
	Paravoor	26	17	8	5	4								9	9								
	Aluva	23	13	13										9	9							1	
	Moovattupuzha	25	20	12	5				3					5	3				2				
Thrissur	Guruvayoor	22	15	7	3	2			1					5	4						2		
	Kunnamkulam	34	21	20	1						1			7	5		1				2	1	CPM Reb. -1
	Chalakkudy	33	17	5	1	2		1						12	11		1					4	
	Chavakkadu	29	22	17	3	2					8			7	11			1					
	Kodungalloor	27	13	5	8	1								9	4				1		3		BJP Ind. 1
	Inngalakuda	25	9	6	1	2								14	13	1						1	UDF Reb.-1
Palakkad	Palakkad	50	16	15	1	1								16	11				5		17		
	Ottapalam	33	22	21	1									4	4	3			3		4		
	Shornur	30	20	20										8	8						1		CPM Reb.-1
	Chittoor	26	9	9	1							1		14	14							2	
Kozhikodu	Kollandi	41	35	27		5		1				1		4	1				3		2		INL-1
	Vadakara	44	29	20	13			3					1	15	5				10				INL.-2
Malappuram	Malappuram	37	10	10		1								26	3				23				
	Menlen	47	16	15	1									30	5				25				INL-1 League Reb. 1
	Perinthalmanna	31	18	15										12	4		4		4				
	Poonani	48	30	29				1			3			17	9		1		1		1		
	Tirur	35	14	10	2	1		1				1		17	4				13				INL-2 League Reb. 1
Wayanad	Kalpatta	25	15	9	1	2		3						10	5				5				
Kannur	Kannur	39	14	10	1			1						25	13				12				INL-2
	Kuthuparambu	25	24	18	3			1			1			0									INL.-1

(Contd.)

1	2	3	4	5	6	7	8	9	10	11	12		13	14	15	16	17	18	19	20	21	22	23
	Thaliparambu	41	23								1			16	3				13				
	Payyannur	41	32	27	2	1		1		1				9	6				3				
	Thalasseri	50	32	26	2	1		1						15	5				10				INL-2
Kasaragod	Kasaragod	35	5	2	1									17					17		1		INL-2. BJP Reb. 12
	Kanhagad	40	10	12		3		1						20	4		1		9		2		INL-2
																					3		
																					11		
																					4		

Table 6.8: Municipal Corporations—Resul^ts 2005

TVPM	*Total*	*LDF*			*UDF*			*Others*
	86	73		(84.88%)	10		(11.62%)	BJP-1
		CPI (M)	46	(53.48%)	Congress	8	(9.30%)	
		DIC (K)	8	(9.3%)	IUML	2	(2.32%)	
		KC (Sec)	1	(1.16%)				
		KC (S)	1	(1.16%)				
		CP1(M) Ind	1	(1.16)			-	
		RSP	1	(1.16)				
Kollam	52		37	(71.15%)			10 (19.23%)	DIC I
		CPI (M)	21	(40.38%)	Cong(S)	8	(15.38)	CPM Rebel 1
		CPI	12	(23.07)	CMP	1	(1.92)	PDP-1
		RSP	3	(5.76)	RSP(M)	1	(1.92)	Ind-1
		CPI(M) Ind	1	(1.92)				
KZDU	55		47	(85.45)		7	(12.72)	BJP-1
		CPI (M)	30	(54.54)	Cong.	3	(5.54)	
		DIC(K)	8	(14.54)	IUML	4	(7.27)	
		Janatha Dal	4	(7.27)				
		NCP	1	(1.8)				
		CPI	2	(3.6)				
		INL	1	(1.8)				
		CPM (Reb)	1	(1.8)				
Kochi	71		42	(59.15)		23	(32.39)	
		CPI(M)	34	(4.84)	Cong	20	(28.16)	DIC(K) -4
		CPI	3	(4.22)	IUML	2	(2.8)	BJP-1
		Janatha Dal	2	(2.81)	KC(M)	1	(2.8)	Ind-1
		KC(J)	1	(1.4)				
		Con (S)	1	(1.4)				
		RSP	1	(1.4)				
Trissur	52		34	(65.38)		17	(32.69)	Ind -1
		CPI (M)	23	(44.23	Cong	17	(32.69)	
		CPI	4	(7.69)				
		Janatha Dal	2	(3.84)				
		KC(J)	2	(3.84)				
		DIC (K)	4	(7.69)				

Congress Escaped from a Total Rout

As far as the DIC(K) is concerned, it can also claim that it has succeeded in its goal of defeating the "Oommen Congress" but the sweep of LDF victory does not give it the flexibility to force any dramatic change in the political landscape. On the other hand, the only consolation for the UDF and for the Congress is that it has succeeded in prevailing a total washout from the state politics. The ruling coalition might have lost out in terms of capturing power in the local bodies across the board, but has been able to notch up a presentable percentage of votes at least in the urban bodies. The sudden flurry of political activity since Ramesh Chennithala took over as PCC chief and the working relationship between him and the chief minister appear to have helped the Congress in preventing a total rout.

Impressive Performance of the BJP

The much talked electoral pact that the UDF had made with BJP has more or less proved to be beneficial for the BJP. The party was eagerly waiting to spread its wings in Kerala to gain from the weakness of both the fronts. The party though with only a minority of seats, became a deciding factor in about 60 local bodies that produced hung result. The party is set to rule four or five panchayats and tumed as the biggest party in nearly 10 panchayats. It also won double the number of seats it did in 2000. Its most impressive victories have been in Palakkad, Kasaragod, Thrissur and Pathanamthitta districts.

In Palakkad municipality it won 17 seats to become the largest single party in a 50 member council. The LDF has clearly established control over more than 60 per cent of the local bodies despite all the brave talk of the UDF leaders, they would certainly be worried about the implicated of this runaway victory of the LDF even after the Oommen Chandy Government had positioned itself as the champion of development and demonized the LDF for being anti-development. The results would also be evaluated in terms of the relative gains made by the various UDF partners and depending on this the inner coalition equations could also change.

The poll results cannot be read as a vote against the Chandy government, but it would certainly force it to a rethink in terms of forging strategies that would help it to retain its traditional bases and correct serial equations. Further, the possibility of the Congress leadership taking a hard look at the local body poll outcome and thinking up ways to win back the break away faction cannot also be rule out for the simple reason that politics is the art of the possible.

Comparison with Lok Sabha Polls—2004

A comparative study of the voting trends in the Lok Sabha Polls of 2004 with Local body polls 2005 shows a favourable trend in favour of the UDF. The United Front has improved from 38.45 per cent in the Lok Sabha Election, when it lost all but one of the 20 constituencies in the state to 40.38 per cent in the Local body polls - an increase of 1.3 per cent. The UDF has made this remarkable show despite the split in the Congress and departure of the Kerala Congress (Jacob), RSP faction led by A.V. Thamarakshan and the formation of DIC(K) that went to the battle with an electoral understanding with the LDF, but its support came down to 42.26 per cent. The electoral statistics further reveals that the LDF had won 46.23 per cent of the polled votes in the Lok Sabha polls of 2004. The DIC(K) with which the LDF had made an electoral understanding in 12 out of 14 districts got 4.45 per cent of the votes. Thus, even if the votes of the DIC(K) are taken into consideration, the pro-LDF base has not expanded much in the state. It has gone up only from 46.23 per cent to 46.71 per cent, a slight increase of 0.48 per cent (see Tables 6.9 to 6.12).

Table 6.9: Civic Poll Results 2005 and 2000 – Front-wise Percentage

Political Party (Front)	*Seats*	*Votes*	*Vote Average*	*Percentage success*
LDF	11.066 (55%)	8490528 (50%)	420	51
UDF	6653 (33%)	6937544 (41%)	340	33
BJP	368 (2%)	964133 (6%)	48	5

Table 6.10: Civic Poll Results 2005 and 2000 – Party-wise Percentage

Left Front	*% of Victory*	*United Front*	*% of victory*	*Others*	*% of victory*
CPM	72	Congress	32	BJP	5
CPI	55	IUML	62	Indp.	12
JD(S)	51	KC(M)	36		
KC(J)	48	JSS	17		
NCP	47	CMP	6		
RSP	33	KC(B)	8		
Other parties	20				
DIC	25				
Total	51	Total	33		

Table 6.11: District-wise Percentage of Votes—2005

District	*LDF*	*UDF*	*CPM*	*CPI*	*DIC*	*CONG*	*IUML*	*BJP*
Trivandrum	51	39	33	7	5	36	1	8
Kollam	53	39	28	15	3	32	0.3	4
Pathanamthitta	44	44	19	8	3	38	-	10
Alappuzha	49	41	29	11	1	32	2	5
Kottayam	43	47	21	11	7	25	0.1	2
Idukki	53	44	23	12	7	34	0.3	1
Ernakulam	47	44	22	6	7	39	2	3
Trichur	49	39	25	11	8	32	3	9
Palakkad	54	39	32	8	1	38	5	5
Malappuram	42	50	20	5	1	15	35	4
Kozhikodu	54	37	29	5	9	22	11	7
Wayanadu	48	46	25	3	11	29	14	4
Kannur	58	33	44	6	4	22	7	5
Kazarkodu	43	34	30	2	5	17	15	16
Total	50	41	31	8	5	29	7	6

Table 6.12: Civic Polls Results 2005 and 2000—A Comparative Appraisal

Local	*LDF/DIC*			*UDF*		*Difference*	*BJP*			*Hung*		*Total*
	2005	*2000*	*Variation*	*2005*	*2000*		*2005*	*2000*	*Diff*	*2005*	*2000*	
GPs	649 (65%)	436 (47%)	+18	224 (23%)	374 (40%)	-150	55%	3.3%	—	115 (12%)	114 (12%)	993 (927)
BPs	110 (72%)	68 (47%)	+25	29 (19%)		-34	—	—	—	13 (9%)	14 (10%)	152 (145)
DPs	11 (75%)	9 (64%)	+2	2 (14%)	4 (29%)	-2	—	—	—	1 (7%)	NIL	14 (4)
Municipal Councils	33 (63)	19 (37)	+ 14	13 (25)	23 (44)	-10	—	—	—	10 (19%)	NIL	52 (52)
Municipal Corporations	5 (100)	2 (40%)	+3	NIL	1 (20%)	+ 1	—	—	—	2 (40%)		5 (5)
Total	808 (66)	534 (47)	+274	268 (22)	465 (41)	-197	5 (04)	3 (0.26)		135 (11%)	140 (12%)	1216 (1142)

The National Democratic Alliance (NDA) which had contested in all the Lok Sabha constituencies in the State in 2001, had secured 12.12 per cent of the votes and won one seat (P.C. Thomas, Muvattupuzha). P.C. Thomas' entry into the LDF through a merger of his party with Kerala Congress (Joseph), the NDA has come to mean just the BJP here. The BJP polled 5.79 per cent of the votes in the local body elections. The drop by 6.33 from 12.12 per cent in 2004 to 5.79 per cent in 2005 has mainly because the party had fielded candidates barely in half the number of the constituencies. Independents and others got 3.20 per cent of the votes in the 2004 elections whereas in 2005 with more independents in the fray, their share went up to 7.12 per cent. In this context, it has to be further noted that this high per cent include the share of those independents supported by the LDF and the UDF.

Community Outfits and their Support

Various community organisations working in the state showed their affinity and enmity after giving a break to their so-called apolitical images or equal-distance stand for the time being. Right from the SNDP Yogam, the NSS, The Latin Christian, Jamat Islami, NDF, Dheevara Sabha etc. have given open or secretive calls to their followers to choose right candidate. The SNDP Yogam leads the way by issuing a three point circular or priority list to its members in choosing the candidates which is more or less a direct exhortation it to favour the UDF. "Give priority to Ezhava candidates; when two Ezhava candidates are in the fray give priority to those who love the community and when to non-Ezhava candidates are in the fray give priority to those who have an affinity to the community."

The NSS has also given clear indication to its followers in favour of the UDF despite its proclaimed equidistant policy. But the Latin Catholic church has not come out in open this time in favour of any particular front. Almost similar was the case of the Jacobite and Orthodox factions of the Christian Community. Though the UDF has somehow managed to ensure the support of the Orthodox faction despite certain inner rumblings, it has lost a close ally in the Jacobite faction owing to the recent attack on priests and parishioners at a Jacobite church in Aluva. Further, various Muslim organisations have come out with their own advise to their followers on the candidates they should favour. Jama-At-Islami has given clear indication in favour of the LDF. They have come out with open criticism on the development agenda of the

Community outfits and their support

Pro-UDF	Pro-LDF
SNDP Yogam NSS Dheevara Sabha Orthodox Christian	Latin Catholics Jacobites Jama-At-Islami Kanthapuram Sunni NDF

UDF and described it as 'Pro-rich'. Similarly Sunni faction has given clear signals to its followers to vote in favour of the LDF whereas the NDF has adopted a strategy supporting the LDF.

Claims of the Left Front—Post-Poll Scenario

The poll review report adopted by the Left Front claimed that it had secured 49 per cent of the total votes polled, up from 46 per cent in the 2004 Lok Sabha polls. The report further claimed that LDF had scored 15.33 lakh votes more than the votes it had secured in the 2004 Lok Sabha elections. The UDF's tally of votes also rose during the period by 11 lakh, but this was more than accounted for by the sharp fall in BJP's share of votes, from 12 per cent of the total votes polled in 2004 to a little above 5 per cent. In numerical terms the fall came to 8.81 lakh votes. The ruling front's performance in the local body elections was dismal when compared with that in the 2001 Assembly elections as its vote share had fallen by 8.38 lakh from 2001 tally. Further, the tolal number of votes polled in 2005 polls was 1.72 crore as compared to 1.50 crores in the 2004 Lok Sabha elections and 1.57 to 2004 and 14.73 lakh votes as compared to the 2001 assembly polls.

Representation of Women in the PRIs of Kerala—2005

The LDF had secured 71 per cent of the additional votes polled in 2005 and registered an unprecedented victory in the polls gaining control of 725 Grama Panchayats, 122 Block Panchayats, 33 Municipalities and 12 District Panchayats and all the five Municipal Corporations. It further showed that the LDF was capable of securing a massive victory even when a higher number of votes were polled and there was no urban-rural divide when it came to its supremacy in the three-tier local bodies. Moreover, the IUML had lost control of several local bodies in Malappuram, Kozhikode and Kannur Districts including Kuttichira Grama Panchayat which had always returned League veterans (Table 6.13).

Table 6.13: Representation of Women in PRIs—2005

	Total Number of members	*Seats reserved for women*	*Actual number of women*	*Percentage*
Grama Panchayats	16,139	5,380	6,125	38
Block Panchayats	2,004	668	725	36.2
District Panchayats	339	113	124	36.6

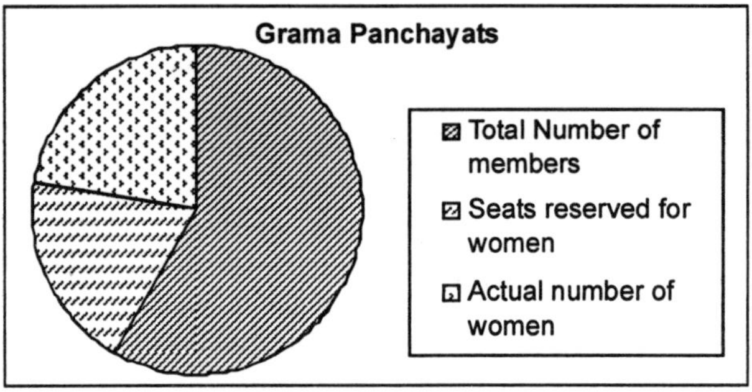

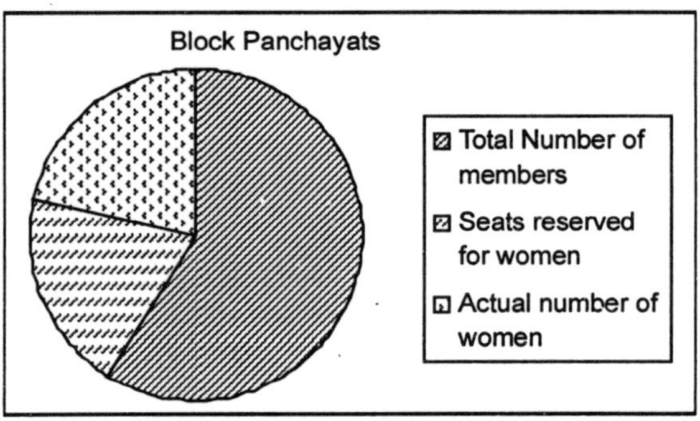

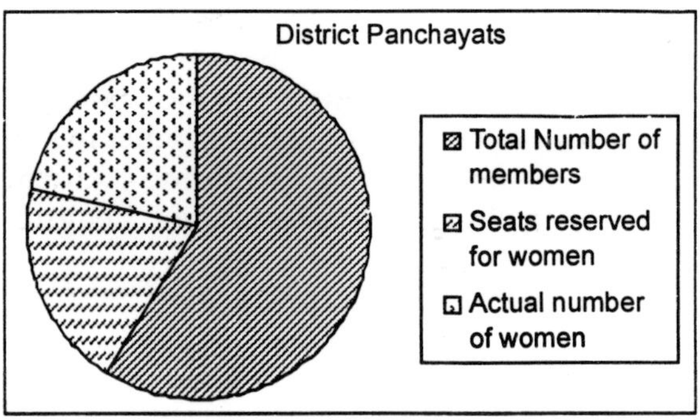

District-wise votes secured by both the fronts are clearly shown in Tables 6.14 to 6.27.

Table 6.14: Civic Polls 2005 in Kerala: District-wise Votes Secured by Fronts—Kasaragod

Total Votes Polled: 639907

District Name	*Front*	*Votes Secured*	*Percentage*
Kasaragod	LDF	243337	38.03
	UDF	204997	32.04
	Independent	80591	12.59
	BJP	78936	12.34
	DIC(K)	29921	4.68
	Others	2125	0.33

District-wise Votes Secured by Political Parties - Kasaragod

Total Votes Polled: 653614

Name of the District	*Party Name*	*Votes Secured*	*Percentage*
Kasaragod	CPI(M)	194602	29.80
	INC	112990	17.30
	BJP	106377	16.30
	ML	97901	15.00
	DIC(K)	34059	5.20
	INL	23817	3.60
	LDF (IND)	23556	3.60
	Independent	21326	3.30
	KC(J)	17940	2.70
	CPI	10648	1.60
	CMP	8779	1.30
	JD(S)	880	0.10
	SP	642	0.10
	KC(M)	97	0.00

Table 6.15: Civic Polls 2005 in Kerala: District-wise Votes Secured by Fronts—Kannur

Total Votes Polled: 1320844

District Name	*Front*	*Votes Secured*	*Percentage*
Kannur	LDF	710328	53.78
	UDF	452359	34.25
	Independent	84602	6.41
	DIC(K)	46820	3.54
	BJP	25855	1.96
	Others	880	0.07

District-wise Votes Secured by Political Parties—Kannur
Total Votes Polled: 1357637

Name of the District	Party Name	Votes Secured	Percentage
Kannur	CPI(M)	599098	44.10
	INC	298584	22.00
	ML CPI	97999	7.20
	BJP	74177	5.50
	DIC(K)	65757	4.80
	JD(S)	50057	3.70
	CMP	43046	3.20
	INL	30202	2.20
	Independent	29643	2.20
	KC(M)	27656	2.00
	KC(J)	21088	1.60
	NCP	18997	1.40
	KC(S)	378	0.10
	Congress(s)	370	0.00
		85	0.00

Table 6.16: Civic Polls 2005 in Kerala: District-wise Votes Secured by Fronts—Kozhikode

Total Votes Polled: 1598644

District Name	Front	Votes Secured	Percentage
Kozhikode	LDF	679494	42.50
	UDF	546481	34.18
	Independent	175330	10.97
	DIC(K)	119429	7.47
	BJP	77610	4.85
	Others	300	0.02

District-wise Votes Secured by Political Parties—Kozhikode
Total Votes Polled: 1590917

Name of the District	Party Name	Votes Secured	Percentage
Kozhikode	CPI(M)	457936	28.80
	INC	352193	22.10
	ML	168381	10.60
	DIC(K)	135251	8.50
	JD(S)	129977	8.20
	BJP	117173	7.40
	CPI	84360	5.30
	CMP	27432	1.70

(Contd.)

Name of the District	*Party Name*	*Votes Secured*	*Percentage*
	Independent	26823	1.70
	NCP	25783	1.60
	LDF (IND)	22399	1.40
	KC(M)	17647	1.10
	JSS INL	17099	1.10
	Congress (S)	5338	0.30
	BSP	1539	0.10
	RJD	1006	0.10
	KC(S)	393	0.00
	KC(J)	132	0.00

Table 6.17: Civic Polls 2005 in Kerala. District-wise Votes Secured by Fronts—Wayanad

Total Votes Polled: 405833

District Name	*Front*	*Votes Secured*	*Percentage*
Wayanad	UDF	144814	35.68
	LDF	138449	34.11
	Independent	81413	20.06
	DIC(K)	30350	7.48
	BJP	10567	2.60
	Others	240	0.06

District-wise Votes Secured by Political Parties—Wayanad

Total Votes Polled: 409016

Name of the District	*Party Name*	*Votes Secured*	*Percentage*
Wayanad	INC	116436	28.50
	CPI(M)	102145	25.00
	ML	57582	14.10
	DIC(K)	45768	11.20
	JD(S)	25924	6.30
	BJP	14837	3.60
	Independent	11874	2.90
	LDF(IND)	11465	2.80
	KC(M)	11445	2.80
	CPI	10617	2.60
	KC(B)	921	0.20
	CMP	2	0.00

Table 6.18: Civic Polls 2005 in Kerala: District-wise Votes Secured by Fronts—Malappuram

Total Votes Polled: 1808898

District Name	Front	Votes Secured	Percentage
Malappuram	UDF	746818	41.29
	Independent	623327	34.46
	LDF	387894	21.44
	BJP	36688	2.03
	DIC(K)	13201	0.73
	Others	644	0.04

District-wise Votes Secured by Political Parties—Malappuram

Total Votes Polled: 1797599

Name of the District	Party Name	Votes Secured	Percentage
Malappuram	ML	627104	34.90
	CPI(M)	356780	19.90
	INC	274077	15.30
	LDF (IND)	208923	11.60
	CPI	94921	5.30
	Independent	81484	4.50
	BJP	66607	3.70
	NCP	26485	1.50
	KC(J)	23616	1.30
	DIC(K)	19747	1.10
	JD(S)	15615	0.90
	JSS	1551	0.10
	PDF	339	0.00
	KC(M)	323	0.00
	Congress(S)	27	0

Table 6.19: Civic Polls 2005 in Kerala: District-wise Votes Secured by Fronts—Palakkad

Total Votes Polled: 1375701

District Name	Front	Votes Secured	Percentage
Palakkad	LDF	682119	49.58
	UDF	452791	32.91
	Independent	122569	8.91
	BJP	59717	4.34
	DIC(K)	39314	2.86
	Others	19191	1.39

District-wise Votes Secured by Political Parties—Palakkad
Total Votes Polled: 1375681

Name of the District	*Party Name*	*Votes Secured*	*Percentage*
Palakkad	CPI(M)	521820	37.90
	INC	433267	31.50
	CPI	108370	7.90
	ML	69003	5.00
	BJP	68681	5.00
	JD(S)	51241	3.70
	LDF (IND)	40944	3.00
	Independent	32370	2.40
	CMP	14554	1.10
	KC(B)	14348	1.00
	DIC(K)	10921	0.80
	BSP	3419	0.30
	Congress(S)	2545	0.20
	KC(S)	1557	0.10
	JSS	1149	0.10
	SHIV SENA	700	0.10
	KC(J)	392	0.00
	RSP(B)	351	0.00
	RSP	26	0.00
	INL	13	0.00
	RJD	10	0.00

Table 6.20: Civic Polls 2005 in Kerala: District-wise Votes Secured by Fronts—Thrissur

Total Votes Polled: 1655770

District Name	*Front*	*Votes Secured*	*Percentage*
Thrissur	LDF	639286	38.61
	UDF	566025	34.19
	Independent	249844	15.09
	DIC(K)	119343	7.21
	BJP	73628	4.45
	Others	7644	0.46

District-wise Votes Secured by Political Parties—Thrissur
Total Votes Polled: 1655493

Name of the District	Party Name	Votes Secured	Percentage
Thrissur	INC	532073	32.10
	CPI(M)	416816	25.20
	CPI	173994	10.50
	BJP	153550	9.30
	DIC(K)	128329	7.80
	Independent	53844	3.30
	JD(S)	46228	2.80
	ML	45574	2.80
	KC(M)	38880	2.40
	KC(J)	22844	1.40
	NCP	17751	1.10
	JSS	12989	0.80
	CMP	11506	0.70
	RSP	366	0.00
	JD(U)	343	0.00
	Congress(S)	176	0.00
	SP	132	0.00
	BSP	54	0.00
	RJD	30	0.00
	KC(S)	14	0.00

Table 6.21: Civic Polls 2005 in Kerala: District-wise Votes Secured by Fronts—Ernakulam

Total Votes Polled: 1679757

District Name	Front	Votes Secured	Percentage
Eranakulam	UDF	600798	35.77
	LDF	542284	32.28
	Independent	396061	23.58
	DIC(K)	105523	6.28
	BJP	34070	2.03
	Others	1021	0.06

District-wise Votes Secured by Political Parties—Ernakulam
Total Votes Polled: 1663101

Name of the District	Party Name	Votes Secured	Percentage
Ernakulam	INC	644892	38.80
	CPI(M)	367493	22.10
	DIC(K)	113910	6.90
	LDF (IND)	108319	6.50
	CPI	97260	5.90
	Independent	94072	5.70

(Contd.)

Name of the District	Party Name	Votes Secured	Percentage
	BJP	54284	3.30
	KC(M)	51050	3.10
	ML	35399	2.10
	KC(S)	25296	1.50
	Congress(S)	24722	1.50
	KC(J)	23472	1.40
	NCP	14992	0.90
	JD(S)	3259	0.20
	RSP	2122	0.10
	UDF (IND)	1310	0.10
	BSP	897	0.10

Table 6.22: Civic Polls 2005 in Kerala: District-wise Votes Secured by Fronts—Alappuzha

Total Votes Polled: 1232257

District Name	Front	Votes Secured	Percentage
Alappuzha	LDF	493836	40.08
	UDF	441062	35.79
	Independent	218208	17.71
	BJP	43314	3.52
	DIC(K)	28581	2.32
	Others	7256	0.59

District-wise Votes Secured by Political Parties—Alappuzha

Total Votes Polled: 1227523

Name of the District	Party Name	Votes Secured	Percentage
Alappuzha	INC	396431	32.30
	CPI(M)	351730	28.70
	CPI	130580	10.60
	Independent	58663	4.80
	BJP	57269	4.70
	JSS	49440	4.00
	KC(M)	41113	3.40
	KC(J)	24887	2.00
	JD(S)	22137	1.80
	ML	21115	1.70
	RSP	20833	1.70
	KC(S)	20587	1.70
	LDF (IND)	19992	1.60
	DIC(K)	8032	0.70
	PDP	2219	0.20
	BSP	1197	0.10
	NCP	920	0.10
	RSP(B)	343	0.00
	CMP	18	0.00
	INL	17	0.00

Table 6.23: Civic Polls 2005 in Kerala: District-wise Votes Secured by Fronts—Idukki

Total Votes Polled: 612412

District Name	*Front*	*Votes Secured*	*Percentage*
Idukki	UDF	225606	36.84
	LDF	214075	34.96
	Independent	133939	21.87
	DIC(K)	32988	5.39
	BJP	5360	0.88
	Others	444	0.07

District-wise Votes Secured by Political Parties—Idukki

Total Votes Polled: 627105

Name of the District	*Party Name*	*Votes Secured*	*Percentage*
Idukki	INC	211308	33.70
	CPI(M)	145084	23.10
	CPI	72431	11.60
	KC(J)	70647	11.30
	KC(M)	47552	7.60
	DIC(K)	42767	6.80
	Independent	18454	2.90
	JSS	12734	2.00
	BJP	4007	0.60
	ML	1583	0.30
	BSP	538	0.10

Table 6.24: Civic Polls 2005 in Kerala: District-wise Votes Secured by Fronts—Kottayam

Total Votes Polled: 1061633

District Name	*Front*	*Votes Secured*	*Percentage*
Kottayam	UDF	404275	38.08
	LDF	335025	31.56
	Independent	256221	24.13
	DIC(K)	32260	3.04
	BJP	20609	1.94
	Others	13098	1.23

District-wise Votes Secured by Political Parties—Kottayam
Total Votes Polled: 1053760

Name of the District	Party Name	Votes Secured	Percentage
Kottayam	INC	258381	24.50
	KC(M)	218713	20.80
	CPI(M)	208863	19.80
	CPI	114270	10.80
	DIC(K)	76075	7.20
	KC(J)	62851	6.00
	Independent	34392	3.30
	BJP	23144	2.20
	KC(S)	20910	2.00
	LDF (IND)	20404	1.90
	UDF (IND)	11379	1.10
	BSP	2736	0.30
	ML	682	0.10
	NCD	590	0.10
	JD(S)	145	0.00
	CMP	80	0.00
	RSP	68	0.00
	SP	68	0.00
	KC(B)	5	0.00
	Sivasena	4	0.00

Table 6.25: Civic Polls 2005 in Kerala: District-wise Votes Secured by Fronts—Pathanamthitta

Total Votes Polled: 666643

District Name	Front	Votes Secured	Percentage
Pathanamthitta	UDF	242986	36.45
	LDF	198931	29.84
	Independent	176411	26.46
	BJP	43040	6.46
	Others	2917	0.44
	DIC(K)	2358	0.35

District-wise Votes Secured by Political Parties—Pathanamthitta
Total Votes Polled: 664257

Name of the District	Party Name	Votes Secured	Percentage
Pathanamthitta	INC	250092	37.70
	CPI(M)	128933	19.40
	BJP	63939	9.60
	LDF (IND)	61020	9.20
	CPI	53081	8.00
	KC(M)	38400	5.80

(Cond.)

Name of the District	Party Name	Votes Secured	Percentage
	DIC(K)	20296	3.10
	Independent	16817	2.50
	KC(J)	14322	2.20
	JD(S)	11903	1.80
	BSP	3631	0.60
	KC(S)	80	0.00
	CMP	742	0.10
	RSP	432	0.10
	JSS	376	0.10
	NCP	206	0.00
	ML	67	0.00

Table 6.26: Civic Polls 2005 in Kerala: District-wise Votes Secured by Fronts—Kollam

Total Votes Polled: 1352376

District Name	Front	Votes Secured	Percentage
Kollam	LDF	572694	42.35
	UDF	448506	33.16
	Independent	186586	13.80
	DIC(K)	71172	5.26
	BJP	48601	3.59
	Others	24817	1.84

District-wise Votes Secured by Political Parties—Kollam

Total Votes Polled: 1340958

Name of the District	Party Name	Votes Secured	Percentage
Kollam	INC	424892	31.70
	CPI(M)	377985	28.20
	CPI	205295	15.30
	RSP	68406	5.10
	Independent	55706	4.20
	BJP	48552	3.60
	DIC(K)	39788	3.00
	CMP	31662	2.40
	JSS	29002	2.20
	KC(B)	27703	2.10
	KC(J)	18963	1.40
	ML	4557	0.30
	RSP(B)	3540	0.30
	KC(M)	2122	0.20
	NCP	1017	0.10
	BSP	794	0.10
	PSP	511	0.00
	JD (S)	427	0.00

Table 6.27: Civic Polls 2005 in Kerala: District-wise Votes Secured by Fronts—Thiruvananthapuram

Total Votes Polled: 1541124

District Name	*Front*	*Votes Secured*	*Percentage*
Thiruvananthapuram	LDF	653557	42.41
	UDF	528653	34.30
	Independent	153532	9.96
	BJP	116296	7.55
	DIC(K)	78923	5.12
	Others	10163	0.66

District-wise Votes Secured by Political Parties—Thiruvananthapuram

Total Votes Polled: 1567575

Name of the District	*Party Name*	*Votes Secured*	*Percentage*
Thiruvananthapuram	INC	563024	35.90
	CPI(M)	521353	33.30
	BJP	119956	7.70
	CPI	104231	6.70
	DIC(K)	68254	4.40
	JD(S)	52136	3.30
	Independent	44571	2.80
	RSP	22676	1.50
	ML	20184	1.30
	CMP	18261	1.20
	KC(S)	10358	0.70
	KC(M)	9344	0.60
	KC(J)	5423	0.40
	NCP	1899	0.10
	Sivasena	1505	0.10
	Congress(S)	1247	0.10
	JSS	1069	0.10
	INL	1060	0.10
	BSP	448	0.00
	RSP(B)	422	0.00
	PSP	78	0.00
	KC(B)	76	0.00

Postscript

Before conclude, it is contextual to note that a performance review of the local-self Governing Institutions in Kerala during the past decade has revealed that despite registering notable achievements in local development, the civic bodies still have a long way to go in emerging as effective local governments to creatively carry out their constitutional and administrative responsibilities. The review noted that majority of the elected representatives do not have a vision on decentralization of powers, the rights and responsibilities of members, presidents, secretaries and standing committees, the primary goals of local governance, office administration and the responsibilities of the staff who come under their purview. Many members lack imagination for preparing projects for the entire panchayats and are concerned only with improving facilities in their wards. Being unaware of the formalities they are unable to conduct meetings. They are also incapable of formulating projects and exploring the possibilities of working in a complimentary manner. Such lapses often reflect in the functioning of civic bodies and lead to corruption.

References

Frontline.

M.R. Biju, "LDF's Repeat Performance: Kerala's Local Body Elections", *Economic & Political Weekly*, Vol. XXX, Nos. 418 42, October 14-21, 1995.

M.R. Biju, "Local Body Polls in Kerala: Warning Signal for the Left", *Mainstream*, Vol. XXXIX, No. 18, April 21, 2001.

M.R. Biju, *Decentralisation: The Indian Experience*, National, Jaipur, 2006.

M.R. Biju, *Dynamics of New Panchayati Raj System: Reflections and Retrospections*, Kanishka, 1998.

M.R. Biju, *Parliamentary Democracy and Political Change in India*, Kanishka, New Delhi, 1999.

M.R. Biju, *Politics of Democracy and Decentralisation in India*, Atlantic, New Delhi, 1997.

The Hindu, Thiruvananthapuram.

The New Indian Express, Thiruvananthapuram.

The Week.

7

Local Body Polls, 2010

UDF Smashes LDF Fortresses

The local body elections 2010 had attracted more attention from political parties, media persons, and general public alike due to a number of reasons. Notable among these include:

(1) The local bodies both urban and rural are enjoyed with increased powers and resources, for example, a grama panchayat used to get barely Rs. 1 lakh a year for all its activities before decentralisation, the annual allocation is around Rs. 70 lakhs now;
(2) The most important factor deciding the fortunes of both UDF and LDF is likely to be the strategic alliances at the local level between parties belonging to even opposing political views and visions, a constant feature of local body polls in Kerala.
(3) For the LDF the civic polls 2010 was a means to examine whether - the welfare, popular measures of V.S. Government namely viz., Rice for Rs. 2/-, EMS Housing Scheme, Asraya Project and a lot more for the welfare of the downtrodden, will produce positive outcome or not.
(4) The LDF also had tried to examine whether their well-oiled political and organisational machinery throughout the state will give gains to the front.
(5) The LDF had an edge over the selection of better women candidates through their organisational network and developmental initiatives like Kudumbashree. Through the poll the party made an enquiry on the future prospects of this mechanism.

(6) The poll was also considered as a referendum on the issues like interference of the church in politics, alleged attempt of LDF for the consolidation of Hindu majority votes.
(7) The UDF on the other hand considered the poll to expose their political strength and mass base with new constituents like Socialist Janatha (Democratic) and Kerala Congress (Joseph).
(8) The UDF also tried to explore anti-incumbency factors by exposing the internal troubles within the leading partner of the LDF, personal rivalries between the Chief Minister and party secretary, charges of corruption, nexus with lottery and land mafia etc.
(9) Compared to earlier polls, the internal troubles and differences within the UDF camp was resolved well in advance particularly with JSS, CMP and Kerala Congress.
(10) The poll was also treated as a means to validate the strength of SJD in Malabar and Kerala Congress(M) in the Central Travancore. The Kerala Congress(M) was seeking a twin result—a vote against the LDF and reassertion of its claim of being a larger player in the region. Either way, political leaders believe that the results will have a long-standing impact on the State's politics as it moves towards the Assembly elections early next year.

POLLS IN TWO STAGES

Elections to the Local body polls in the state were held in two stages. First stage was on 23 October and the second stage was on 25th. Over 75.72 per cent of the voters exercised their franchise during the first stage held in seven districts viz., Thiruvananthapuram, Kollam, Pathanamthitta, Kozhikode, Wayanad, Kannur and Kasaragod. Barring stray incidents of violence and booth capturing in Kannur district the polling passed off peacefully. According to electoral statistics, Wayanad recorded the highest polling 79.78 per cent and Thiruvananthapuram the lowest 69.27 per cent. The voter turnout in Kollam was 73.58 per cent, Pathanamthitta 70.54 per cent, Alappuzha 77.75 per cent, Kozhikode 76.99 per cent and Kannur 79.48 per cent.

The voter turnout in the second phase held on 25th October was pegged at 75 per cent. According to the official figures of the

State Election Commission (SEC) Alappuzha registered the highest polling 77.75 per cent, followed by Malappuram 75.6 per cent, Kottayam 75.64 per cent, Ernakulam and Palakkad 75 per cent and Thrissur and Idukki 73 per cent.

During the first phase of the poll barring few incidents of violence and booth capturing in Kannur, the polling passed off peacefully as referred earlier. Based on the Collector's report, the SEC has ordered for repolling in five places. A marked indifference on the part of the voters in urban centres seemed to have upset the candidates and their campaign managers initially. The polling in the Thiruvananthapuram city limits remained below 10 per cent till 9 am. It gradually picked up to reach 36 per cent by 2 pm, and 52.5 per cent by 4.30 pm. Meanwhile, the state average increased from 45 per cent at 2 pm to 64 per cent by 4 pm. The polling rate was by and large consistent in Kozhikode, Kannur and Wayanad. Kollam also recorded an impressive turnout of 46 per cent by 2 pm and 65 per cent by 4.30 pm.

During the second phase of the poll, violent incidents were reported from Alappuzha and Kannur where repolling was held at seven booths in five places, marred the election. A sub-inspector from special branch was hacked when he tried to tackle a person, reportedly a CPI(M) activist, who entered a booth at Ambalappuzha in Alappuzha district with a sword. The police officer sustained serious injuries. Three CPM and two BJP activists were reported to have suffered injuries in a clash that followed. Skirmishes were reported from polling booths at Kainakari in Alappuzha district. Ballot papers in a booth at Bharanikavu in the same district had to be replaced on detecting a mix up in the names of candidates.

The repolling in Kannur district was marred by complaints of intimidation of voters and clashes near the booths in Pattuvam and Thillankeri grama panchayats. This was despite a heavy deployment of the Kerala and Karnataka police. The booths recorded impressive turnouts, Mattool 74.5 per cent, Pattuvam 73, Irikkur 79, Thillankeri 63 and Payyannur 80.47 per cent. The United Democratic Front (UDF) boycotted the repolling in two booths in the district alleging that the poll authorities failed to ensure free and fair polling. The UDF accused the CPI(M) of intimidating voters. A hartal called by the BJP in the district in protest against the attack on the vehicle of a Rashtriya Swayamsevak Sangh functionary at Kelanpeedika, near Iritty, on Sunday was near-total. Three police personnel, including a Deputy Superintendent of Police, were injured in a bomb attack reportedly by BJP-RSS workers at Iritty following a protest march. The police opened fire in the air.

When polling drew to a close in the evening, queues were seen in Malappuram district, which witnessed heavy polling. As many as 254 booths in the district were identified as sensitive and 50 vulnerable, but no untoward incident was reported. Ernakulam district registered an impressive turnout. The rival fronts claimed that the higher turnout will work to their advantage. The State Election Commission has ordered repelling at Booth No. 4 in Ward 20 of Kochi Corporation on Tuesday. This was following a snag in the electronic voting machine.

Incidents of minor violence were reported from Palakkad, which witnessed a 10 per cent increase in the polling compared to the 2005 elections. Owing to a dispute over ballot papers, polling was held up for nearly 30 minutes at Ward 5 in Thrikkaderi grama panchayat. Following a minor scuffle, the police scared away CPI(M) and Janakeeya Vikasana Munnani workers at the Akkipadam booth in Kumaramputhur grama panchayat. Minor incidents were reported from the Thiruvzhamkunnu and Attappady tribal belts.

Table 7.1: Voting Percentage in the Local Body Polls

District	*2010*	*2005*
Thiruvananthapuram	69.27	52.87
Kollam	73.58	59.50
Pathanamthitta	70.54	62.00
Alappuzha	77.75	62.80
Kottayam	75.64	64.34
Idukki	73.00	64.64
Ernakulam	75.00	56.90
Thrissur	73.00	58.76
Palakkad	75.00	61.00
Malappuram	75.60	63.73
Kozhikode	76.99	62.25
Wayanad	79.78	61.00
Kannur	79.48	63.00
Kasaragod	77.68	60.00

POST-POLL SPECULATIONS

The polling percentage in the local body elections held in 2005 was 62.71 and it has gone up to 79.78 per cent in 2010. The total electorate in 2005 was 2.93 crore and it came down to 2.27 crore in 2010. This would mean that though the total number of electorate had come down in 2010, the polling percentage had gone up. It was the massive deletion of names from the voters' list which resulted in the decline of total number of voters. However, it is interesting to note that in the 2009 Lok Sabha elections, the total number of electorate in the State was 2.18 crore and the polling percentage was 73.33.

So, when the polling percentage was 62.71 in 2005, the LDF swept the local body polls. When the polling percentage was 73.33 per cent in 2009, the UDF swept the Lok Sabha polls in the State. Who will have an edge when the polling percentage reached at 79.78 becomes the million dollar question. It is evident that there has been an increase of 12.8 per cent in the polling percentage this time. But this cannot be claimed to be advantageous to any particular party. This proves the fact that neutral votes have polled more this time and it would be a vital factor in determining the winners. A marginal swing of neutral votes would determine who will have the edge this time.

The high percentage of voting in the current local body elections signals the success of political parties in mobilising voters to polling booths. Given the average of 75 per cent voting in the two stages of elections, it is safe to assume that the issues that came up during the campaign, local as well as state-wide, have polarised the voters to come out in large numbers to vote.

The United Democratic Front (UDF) and the Left Democratic Front (LDF) leaderships, in their post-election analyses, have made tall claims about the outcome being in their favour on the basis of the higher percentage of polling. The focus of political parties is on the results of the district panchayats, municipalities and corporations, which will provide a ready-made yardstick to gauge their performance. The fact that the percentage of votes polled will be later reckoned for recognition by the election authorities gives a competitive edge to the outcome.

While the secret was firmly locked in the ballot boxes and EVMs till counting day, it was becoming clear that the results would throw up answers to two issues: popularity or unpopularity of the LDF government, and the validation of redrawing of communal equations since the 2009 Lok Sabha elections.

Senior leaders observed that the voting would reflect the changed equations—the erosion in the LDF with the departure of the Socialist Janata (Democratic) and the merger of the Kerala Congress (J) with the Kerala Congress(M). A major poll issue was the "interference" of the Church in politics, with the LDF accusing the UDF of appeasing the Catholic Church, and the UDF leaders retorted that the LDF was trying to consolidate the Hindu majority votes. Sources said that the result would validate this process triggered off in the Lok Sabha elections. There is also a sub-script to the results for the UDF. The results would validate the strength of the SJD in Malabar and the Kerala Congress(M) in Central Travancore. The Kerala Congress(M) will be seeking a twin result—a vote against the LDF and the reassertion of its claim of being a larger player in the region. Either way, political leaders believe that the results will have a long-standing impact on the State's politics as it moves towards the Assembly elections early next year.

PEOPLE'S VERDICT, 2010

The people's verdict in the 2010 polls clearly shows that, for the first time the UDF has stormed grassroot citadels that were hitherto monopolised by the Left. UDF's muscular showing has decimated the myth that grama panchayats and block panchayats are the bastions of cadre-based political parties. The Congress, finally, has bridged the urban-rural divide. The Congress war cry, which was generally considered suited only for the Assembly and the Lok Sabha polls, percolated right down through the three tiers of the Panchayati Raj system. Taking even the Congress leadership by surprise, the party has put up an unprecedented performance in the local body polls almost sweeping the entire Central Travancore and even some of the Marxist bastions in the southern districts.

If the UDF outplayed the CPM-led LDF in Kochi and Thrissur Corporations, it shocked the Marxist party in Thiruvananthapuram. The UDF has secured an absolute lead in the grama panchayats, block panchayats, municipalities and district panchayats. Among the block panchayats, the UDF is leading in 79 while the LDF could secure lead only in 60. The grama panchayats, perhaps, threw up the biggest surprise. The UDF is leading in 510 panchayats while the LDF has lead only in 362. Among the municipalities, the UDF is leading in 39 and the LDF is leading only in 18. Among the district panchayats, the UDF is leading in eight and the LDF only in five. This is the first time that the UDF has secured such a massive lead in all the sectors irrespective of the rural and urban areas of the state. Kollam, Alappuzha, Palakkad and Kannur are the only districts where the CPM-led LDF could put up a good show. In all the other districts, the UDF has given a tough fight for the CPM. In the districts of Thiruvananthapuram, Pathanamthitta, Idukki, Kottayam, Ernakulam, Thrissur, Malappuram, and Wayanad, the Congress-led UDF has dominated the show.

FACTORS WORKED FOR UDF IN CENTRAL TRAVANCORE

In addition to the widespread resentment among the voters against the LDF dispensation, the massive mandate in favour of the UDF in the local bodies polls in Central Travancore underscores the sway of a host of other factors, especially the role of the Church in determining the final outcome in a decisive way. It is also notable that the Christian consolidation in favour of the UDF candidates had not led to a corresponding wave among the majority communities and favouring the opposite political camp. One of the salient features in the run-up to the current polls in the Christian-dominated areas in the region was that the interference of the Church leadership was on a low-key pattern in the eyes of common society, but piercing for the faithful.

The strategy has apparently worked out very well without creating bad blood among the majority communities and eventually helping the UDF in a big way. The Church was systematic in roping in every vote upon which it can have a say, going by the fact that all those associated with it and residing in far-flung areas outside the district were directed to reach their native places and cast their votes. The phenomenon was visible everywhere on the polling day.

Despite the reservations expressed by some quarters within the UDF, the poll results reveal that the unification of the Kerala Congress factions led by K.M. Mani and P.J. Joseph has created an added political muscle for the regional party in its strongholds.

Conversely, the UDF bandwagon in Central Travancore will never be the same again since the notable aspect will have to be addressed collectively by the front in any poll in the region in future. It could even give the much-needed breather for a beleaguered Joseph politically, probably before the Assembly polls slated for early next year. The landslide victory of the UDF in Kottayam district has also brought out the role of a few prominent local CPM leaders into question.

It was well-known that over and above the cadre-based character and collectivity of the CPM, the final stamping on the candidature of many in the LDF banner was according to the wishes of such leaders, against whose style of functioning the people nurtured a deep grudge. The worst in the people's mandate against the Left was in Vaikom belt, considered to be one of a few strongholds and which was rated to give some relief for them amid the UDF sweep. The ruling LDF could manage just one-third of the total 26 seats in Vaikom municipality, indicating that the CPI, which had outstanding political issues with the major coalition partner, had pulled the rug from under the feet of the CPM, eventually immersing the front together. That even a highly politically-conscious voter could take decisions on the basis of grassroot realities and will not get carried away with mere political considerations is also borne from the verdict.

The Church had played a crucial role in a few pockets in Vaikom also to hand out impressive gains for the UDF. The role of women voters against the backdrop of a large number of women candidates in the fray with scope of lot of them poised to take the reins of many local bodies, which was one of the factors which led to a huge poll percentage, is also believed to have aided the big sweep for the UDF across the district and adjoining ones. The trend among the voters in favour of the UDF was also noted with both urban centres and rural pockets working in unison to turn the tide.

UDF CONQUERED TERRITORY THAT HAS HITHERTO ELUDED

The United Democratic Front (UDF) has every reason to feel proud about its electoral performance given its record in the previous elections to the panchayats and the civic bodies. The victory has been even across the three tiers of panchayats, which many perceive as a vote against the Left Democratic Front's rule at the State and the local levels.

The victory, by and large, maintains a pro-UDF trend witnessed during the Lok Sabha elections in 2009 and the subsequent Assembly by-elections. Kollam district is, perhaps, the only exception with the Opposition front way behind. The UDF went into the elections with reservations about delimitation of wards and the voters' list and apprehensions about bogus voting. But the results show that all these have been misplaced. Similarly, its misgivings about its chances with 50 per cent of the seats reserved for women appear to have been baseless, more so when the coalition appears to be the major beneficiary of this reform. Though the counting of votes in Kozhikode district will be held only on Sunday, the UDF has gained by the political shifts that took place in a year with the entry of the Socialist Janata (Democratic) into its fold and the merger of the Kerala Congress(J) with the Kerala Congress(M).

In Wayanad, the Socialist Janata (Democratic) has contributed much to its victory, but a clear picture will emerge only when votes are counted in Kozhikode. The election results in Kottayam, Idukki, Ernakulam and Thrissur indicate that the UDF has benefited from the consolidation of the Catholic community behind it. In Malappuram, parts of Kannur and Kasaragod, the UDF has benefited from the consolidation of Muslim votes. The most significant aspect of the elections is the inroads that the UDF has been able to make into the grama panchayats, cornering nearly 55 per cent of them.

IMPRESSIVE PERFORMANCE OF THE BJP

Early preparations and united work have paid off for the Bharatiya Janata Party (BJP) in the elections to local self-government institutions in the State, though marginally. The party had started its preparations ahead of the ruling and Opposition fronts and had managed to choose relatively better candidates this time than in the last elections. Not many social or political factors could be reckoned as the reasons for the party's improved performance in the polls. But party sources say that it could tap its social base better this time.

The people's disenchantment with the ruling front and the

development agenda put forward by the party would have contributed marginally to the party's performance. However, the impact of local factors and local development issues is more significant. The biggest break for the party this time is in the Thiruvananthapuram Corporation where it could recover lost ground. The party had experienced a heavy erosion in its support base in the by-election to the Lok Sabha from the Thiruvananthapuram constituency just a month after the elections to local bodies in 2005. The BJP's campaign had been undermined from within, following dissentions in the party. Five years since then, the party could make a concerted effort and translate its support base into six seats in the city Corporation. An Independent representing the Dheevra Sabha and supported by the party has also won the polls. The BJP had only one seat in the outgoing Corporation council.

However, the party's performance is poorer in Kasaragod district and Palakkad municipality where it has a political base. In Kasaragod district, the BJP had its presidents in six grama panchayats, and five of the panchayats were under its control. This time, it has to be satisfied with majority in two panchayats and possible control of two other panchayats with support of Independents. In the district panchayat, its tally has come down from two to one. In Palakkad municipality, its seats have dropped from 17 in 2005 to 15.

At the same time, the party could expand its reach to other parts of the State. It has fielded candidates for 9,922 out of 21,456 seats and could win in new areas. In the grama panchayats, it has won about 450 seats, compared to 236 in 2005. This figure excludes Independents supported by the party, which exceed 50. It may go up further when the results from Kozhikode district are added up after the counting on October 31. Its score in the block panchayats at the moment is the same as last time, seven. In municipalities, the party has expanded its representation. It has won 79 seats in 28 municipalities against 71 in 23 municipalities in the last elections. Besides, 11 Independents supported by the BJP in different municipalities have got elected.

The BJP has improved upon its tally compared to the previous local body polls. The party has got significant representation in Thiruvananthapuram Corporation — six seats, two in Kochi, one in Thrissur and 76 seats in various municipalities, the highest of

15 in Palakkad municipality. The party candidates finished runners-up in eight wards in Thiruvananthapuram Corporation. The party will play a crucial role in deciding the rulers in four municipalities. The SDPI has also opened its account fray securing one seat each in Kannur and Thodupuzha municipalities. A distinct feature of the local body elections this time is that 50 per cent of the over 21,000 seats are reserved for women in the multi-tier local self-government bodies.

The UDF wrested the Kochi Corporation from the LDF after three decades, winning 46 out of the 74 seats. The LDF won 23 wards and the BJP 2 and Independent 3. The UDF also emerged victorious in the Thrissur Corporation, winning 44 out of the 55 seats. Here, the LDF got six seats, the BJP one and Independents four seats. The LDF has retained the Thiruvananthapuram Corporation winning 51 out of the 100 seats, leaving 41 to the UDF, six to the BJP and two to Independents. The LDF won the Kollam Corporation for a third successive term bagging 34 out of the 55 seats. The UDF got 18 seats and others, three seats.

THE SDPI FACTOR

An unexpected SDPI (Socialist Democratic Party of India) factor, which managed to garner a considerable number of votes, has raised an alarm bell forcing the Indian Union Muslim League (IUML) and the People's Democratic Party (PDF) to deliberate on the circumstances that led to a large scale flow of Muslim votes from their base to the SDPI. Though the IUML had strongly opposed the SDPI right from its inception, it never considered it as a threat to its vote base in the block panchayats and grama panchayats in Ernakulam district.

Nevertheless, the IUML had cashed in on the opportunity, resulting from the attack on Thodupuzha Newman's College teacher T.J. Joseph by alleged SDPI activists, to lacerate the SDPI as a 'communal organisation with bad credentials'. However, the results of the local body polls has come as a shocker to both the IUML and the PDF as the SDPI has managed to attract quiet a number of Muslim votes contesting alone against the IUML and the PDF. While SDPI candidate Prof. Anas, an accused in the lecturer attack case, won the Vanchinad division of the Vazhakkulam block panchayat by garnering 3,992 votes, the PDF candidate could manage only 223 votes. The SDPI made considerable inroads into the vote base of the IUML and in most of the divisions, the PDP was pushed to fifth and sixth positions. The blocks where the PDP was relegated to lower positions included Malleppalli (SDPI-111. PDP-66), Cheravalloor (SDPI-573, PDP-76) and Koteepeedikka (SDPI-57, PDP-40).

The SDPI, which had fielded candidates in all the seats where the IUML had contested, was able to gain some votes but not enough to defeat the League candidates. At Kunjunnikkara in Aluva where the SDPI and the League had clashed head on, the former was able to get 379 votes, which was same as that garnered by the League candidate. The other major panchayats where the SDPI garnered votes pitting against the League included Eramam South (IUML-658, SDPI-331), Kadavuppadam (IUML-629, SDPI-201), Edayyappuram West (IUML-366, SDPI-182) and Mulavoor North (IUML-489, SDPI-112).

THE LDF RETAINED KOZHIKODE

The LDF had escaped without any grievous hurt in the civic election in Kozhikode district. The poll results were announced on 31st October. With its 39 councillors, the CPI (M) alone secured simple majority in the 75 member Kozhikode Corporation Council and had the support of two members representing its ally, the Nationalist Congress Party (NCP). The Congress led UDF won 34 seats. The LDF has retained power in the Vadakara municipality 27 out of the total 47 seats. The UDF bagged 17 seats. Three independent candidates, including a Congress rebel also got elected. In the Koyilandy municipality, the LDF secured 27 out of the 44 seats. The UDF won 14 seats eight more than what it had in the previous council. The BJP secured three seats.

Front-wise and District-wise Picture

Compared to the previous local body polls held in 2005, the UDF got 15.65 lakh more votes this time. The United Front has received 46.09 per cent of the total votes polled in the state. Out of 1,83,26,367 votes polled, the UDF captured 84,47,977 votes. In the year 2005, the UDF got 68,82,314 votes out of total 1,69,84,236 i.e. 40.52 per cent. In 2010, the UDF has received 6,84,482 more votes than the LDF. In total, the LDF has received a total 77,63,495 votes in 2010. In 2005, the LDF had won the electoral support of 45.32 per cent voters and in 2010, it had reduced to 42.36 per cent. Compared to the previous poll, there was an increase of 13,42,131 voters in 2010. It shows that majority of the new voters extended their faith and confidence in the UDF. Compared to the UDF and LDF, the position of the BJP has increased drastically. In 2005, the party got 9,64,133 votes and in 2010 it had gone up to 11,47,297 i.e., an increase of 1,83,164 votes. The LDF had suffered bitter experiences from Malappuram, Ernakulam and Kottayam districts. In these district UDF has increased or strengthened its mass base by capturing over 4 lakh, 1.5 lakh and 1.25 lakh votes respectively. Table 7.1 further reveals the mass base of various political combinations in the state politics – front-wise, district-wise and percentage-wise.

Table 7.1: District-wise and Front-wise Poll Details

District	*Total votes polled*	*UDF*	*LDF*	*BJP*	*Others*
Thiruvananthapuram	16,82,099	7,11,869 (42.32%)	7,20,286 (42.82%)	1,34,039 (7.96%)	1,15,905 (6.89%)
Kollam	14,34,817	6,26,318 (43.65%)	6,88,545 (47.98%)	67,095 (4.67%)	52,859 (3.68%)
Pathanamthitta	6,78,132	3,12,327 (46.05%)	2,74,565 (40.48%)	56,417 (8.31%)	34,823 (5.13%)
Alappuzha	12,58,095	5,63,417 (44.78%)	5,71,612 (45.43%)	68,424 (5.43%)	54,642 (4.34%)
Kottayam	11,26,151	5,61,723 (49.87%)	4,35,016 (38.62%)	49,211 (4.36%)	80,201 (7.12%)
Idukki	6,43,231	3,42,078 (53.18%)	2,58,413 (40.17%)	19,617 (3.04%)	23,126 (3.59%)
Ernakulam	18,42,321	8,96,072 (44.29%)	7,54,313 (40.94%)	89,037 (4.39%)	1,02,899 (5.58%)
Thrissur	17,98,343	8,20,412 (45.62%)	7,61,114 (42.32%)	1,26,337 (7.02%)	90,480 (5.03%)
Palakkad	15,54,728	6,81,317 (43.82%)	6,92,017 (44.51%)	98,616 (6.34%)	82,778 (5.32%)
Malappuram	20,79,413	11,08,349 (53.30%)	6,99,973 (33.66%)	1,08,514 (5.21%)	1,62,577 (7.81%)
Kozhikode	17,34,212	7,82,047 (45.09%)	7,49,428 (43.21%)	1,21,642 (7.01%)	81,095 (4.19%)
Wayanad	4,34,912	2,15,414 (49.53%)	1,74,983 (40.23%)	24,213 (5.56%)	20,302 (4.66%)
Kannur	13,78,964	5,49,217 (38.82%)	7,24,016 (52.50%)	71,418 (5.17%)	34,313 (2.48%)
Kasaragod	6,80,949	2,77,417 (40.72%)	25,921 (38.06%)	1,12,712 (16.55%)	31,609 (4.64%)
Total	**1,83,26,367**	**84,47,977 (46.09%)**	**77,63,495 (42.36%)**	**11,47,297 (6.26%)**	**9,67,598 (5.27%)**

WARD-WISE PICTURE

The ward-wise evaluation of the poll shows that the Congress has made a spectacular performance in the Poll, compared with 2005 poll. The party has captured 3161 more wards this time. It is an exemplary performance shown by the Congress party in the recent past in the state politics. In 2005 Poll, the Congress party came victorious only in 4454 wards. In 2010 it has gone up to 7615.

The second leading partner of the UDF, Muslim League performed well this time. In 2005, the League had established elected Electoral control in 1919 wards. In 2010 it has gone up to 2235. The other leading UDF partner, Kerala Congress (M) too performed well. In 2005, KC(M) had 411 wards. It has gone to 818 in 2010. The Socialist Janata Dal, who left LDF and joined hands with UDF, just before the poll won in 174 wards. The INL captured control in 45 wards. In toto, the UDF has won on 11200 wards whereas the LDF confined in 8527 wards and BJP in 480 wards.

Compared to the Congress, the CPM has suffered heavy losses. The party has lost 1055 wards, compared to 2005 poll. In 2005 poll, the CPM has captured 8056 wards. It had decreased to 7001 in 2010. Its partner, CPI too suffered humiliating defeat. In 2005, CPI has won 1392 wards. In 2010 it came down to 1017. The seat share of RSP, another partner in the LDF came down to 70 from 77.

Tables 7.2 to 7.5 illustrate the details regarding front-wise ward-wise and party wise performance.

Table 7.2: Ward-wise Performance

Party	*Grama Panchayat*	*Block*	*District*	*Municipality*	*Corporation*
UDF	8501	1230	194	1097	178
LDF	6607	828	134	803	155
BJP	384	7	1	79	9
Others	1183	30	3	202	17

UDF Established Control Over 90 Assembly Segments

Another remarkable feature of the Poll was that the UDF had established a clear lead over LDF in 90 assembly segments. As per as vote share is concerned, the UDF has captured only 40.52 per cent votes in the 2005 poll. It has gone up to 46 in 2010. Compared to the UDF, the LDF had won 49 per cent votes in 2005.

Table 7.3: Performance of the UDF

Party	*GP*	*Block*	*Dist.*	*Mun.*	*Corpn.*
Congress	5729	873	123	746	144
Muslin League	1717	220	35	248	15
KC(M)	643	95	21	55	4
Socialist Janata	127	19	8	11	9
KC(B)	31	4	2	0	0
KC(J)	30	9	1	2	0
INL	32	4	3	7	0
JSS	27	1	0	2	2
CMP	18	5	1	7	3
KRSP(B)	12	0	0	0	1
UDF (Independent)	135	0	0	19	0

Table 7.4: Performance of LDF

Party	*GP*	*Block*	*Dist.*	*Mun.*	*Corpn.*
CPI(M)	5431	680	106	661	123
CPI	778	122	24	77	16
RSP	51	5	4	2	9
NCP	34	8	0	2	2
JD(S)	14	3	0	2	0
KC (Thomas)	14	3	0	2	0
Con (S)	6	0	0	4	1
LDF (Indep)	279	7	0	51	4

Table 7.5: People's Verdict 2010—At a Glance

	Total	*UDF*	*%*	*LDF*	*%*	*BJP*	*Others*
Grama Panchayats	978	565	57.77	348	35.58	2	63
Block Panchayats	152	92	60.52	60	39.47	0	0
District Panchayats	14	8	57.14	6	42.85	0	0
Muncipalities	57	40	70.17	17	29.82	0	0
Corporations	5	2	40.00	3	60	0	0

It has decreased to 42 per cent in 2010. In 2005, the LDF got a total votes of 84,90,258. It came down to 77,67,888 in 2010. The front had lost over 4 lakh votes. The only solace for the LDF is that, it has made a slight better performance compared to the 2009 parliament poll. In total, the front has increased its vote share of about one per cent. In the 2006 assembly poll, the LDF captured 48.63 per cent votes. The BJP has captured 5.68 per cent votes in 2005. The party has made a slight improvements this time

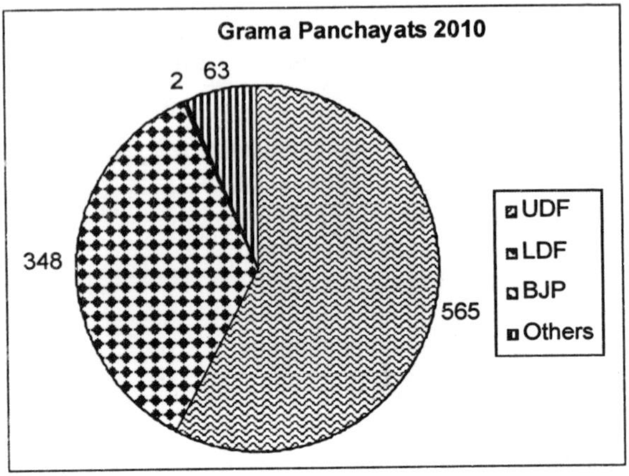
Grama Panchayats 2010
2
63
348
565
UDF
LDF
BJP
Others

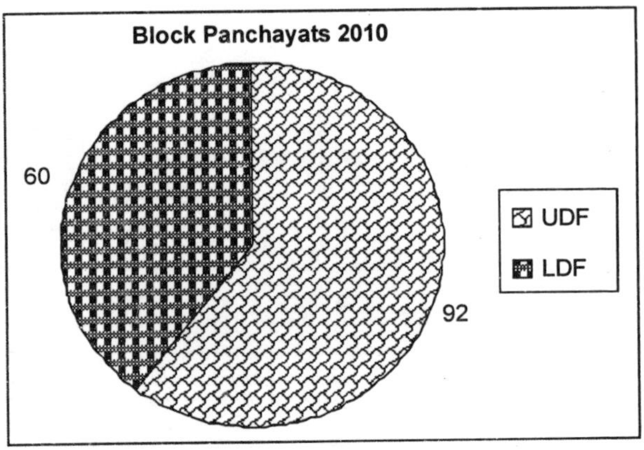
Block Panchayats 2010
60
92
UDF
LDF

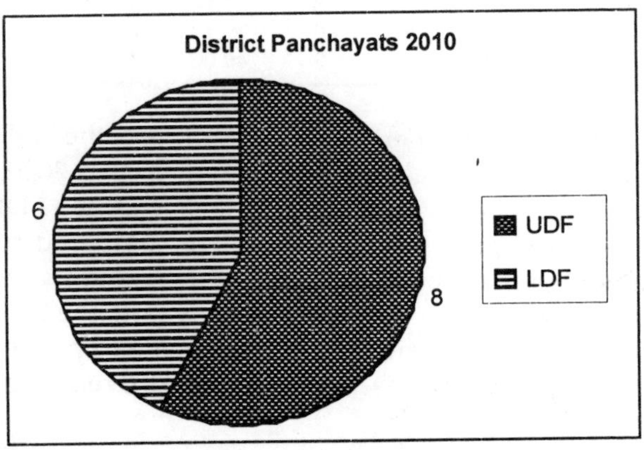
District Panchayats 2010
6
8
UDF
LDF

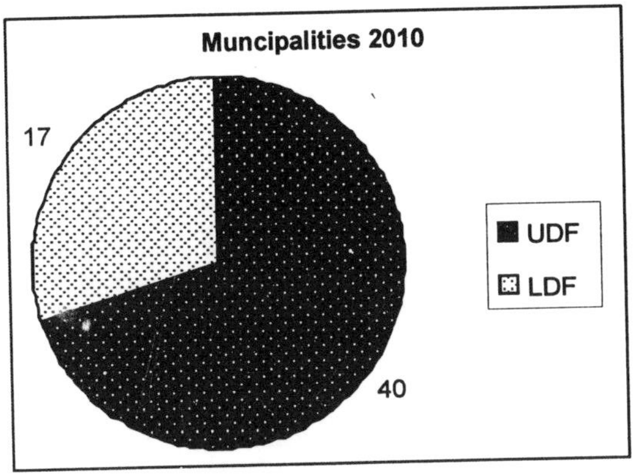

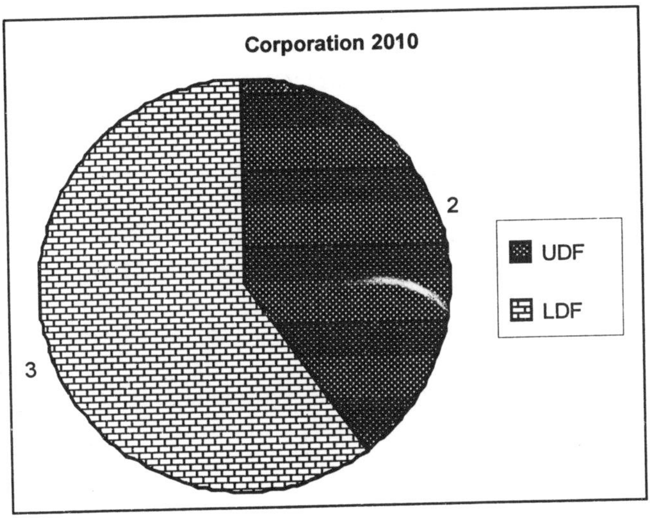

Post-Poll Claims by the CPM Leadership

The CPM state Secretary in his post-poll review claimed that the UDF has secured 84,55,193 votes, whereas the LDF has garnered 77,67,888 votes. In the percentage-wise too the difference between the two fronts was 3.69 per cent. According to him, while the UDF has won 46.01 per cent of votes and the LDF got 42.32 per cent votes. He further stated that, the LDF had contested the 2010 polls without several of the allies who were with it—[KC (J), INL. JDS] - during the 2005 local body polls and 2009 Lok Sabha polls.

According to the party secretary, in 2005, the LDF has secured 49.22 per cent of votes. Since the alliance had got only 42.32 per cent votes in 2010. It would mean that, the LDF had suffered a loss of 6.9 per cent votes. The allies and outside-backers of 2005 has secured 9.18 per cent votes. Democratic Indira Congress (Karunakaran) (DICK)—had 4.67 per cent; Janata Dal (Secular) had 2.30 per cent, Kerala Congress (Joseph) had 1.79 per cent and Indian National League 0.35 per cent. He also added that, "If it were an automatic subtraction of their share, the percentage this time would have been only 40.04 per cent."

The actual percentage on the contrary, showed a 2.2 per cent increase in the vote share of the LDF. In 2000 local body polls, the LDF had got 42.64 per cent votes which would mean that the erosion into 1000 time was only 0.32 per cent as he claimed. Further, the LDF's total share of votes has also gone up as compared to 2009 Lok Sabha elections. In the Lok Shaba Polls, the LDF had captured only 38.40 per cent vote share against 40.23 per cent in 2005 and 41.47 per cent in 2000. The actual increase from 2009 in terms of votes came to 10.64 lakh from 67,47,438 to 77,81,671.

WHAT WENT WRONG FOR THE LDF?

(1) Anti-incumbency Factors

The poll outcome, showing a clear advantage for the Opposition United Democratic Front (UDF) in both urban and rural local bodies, indicate that the Opposition was successful in whipping up a wave in its favour across the State and that the poll strategy of the Communist Party of India-Marxist (CPI-M) had little in it to carry the ruling front to safety, and worse, had a lot in it to harm its cause. Given the nature of the verdict, it will be hard to rule out a strong anti-incumbency mood among the electorate across the State.

The UDF's success in unleashing a focussed campaign over State-level issues, such as the lottery scam, may be one of the major reasons for this, but there will be others such as the inability of the CPI (M) to put its own house in order and the way it virtually drove out parties with local-level clout out of the alliance. On issues such as the lottery scam, the government was seen to be pulling in opposite directions with Chief Minister V.S. Achuthanandan being seen as proactive even as the rest of the government and the alliance seemed far from decisive in their response to the whole issue. The State government's argument that the onus of controlling the other-State lottery mafia rested with the Centre fell flat with each new development.

(2) Welfare Measures Failed to Catch Votes

The UDF has already bagged 544 grama panchayats, 89 block panchayats, 39 municipalities, eight district panchayats and two municipal corporations. The trend would very likely be the same when the votes polled in the 75 or so grama panchayats and other local and civic bodies in Kozhikode district too are counted. The UDF could not have scored so emphatic a victory if the LDF campaign managers were right, which means that welfare pay outs and benefits did not create a politically educated category but only an easily swayed, largely consumerist mass.

(3) Row with Church

The strong showing by the UDF in the central districts suggest that the CPI(M) bid to take on the Church was counterproductive. It did not win the LDF the votes of the majority community and resulted only in hardening of Christian votes. The crushing defeat that the LDF suffered in the Thrissur Corporation and the loss of the Kochi Corporation, which it had been controlling for the past three decades, could be the direct fallout of this. It could even be the case that the real beneficiary of the anti-Church campaign of the CPI(M) was the Bharatiya Janata Party (BJP), which has put in a noteworthy showing in some of these districts.

Chief Minister V.S. Achuthanandan and CPI(M) State Secretary Pinarayi Vijayan have described the setback temporary, but CPI State Secretary Veliyam Bhargavan has, in his initial response to the poll outcome, admitted that an anti-incumbency mood might also have influenced the outcome to a certain extent. When the UDF routed the LDF in the 2009 Lok Sabha elections, the Opposition had led in 100 Assembly segments. This time, it should be a matter of relief for the LDF that the number of constituencies where the UDF has sway will be less than that figure, when the counting of votes in Kozhikode is completed.

(4) Communal Votes

The LDF leadership is, however, right on one point that there was a massive consolidation of communal votes across the State. If it was a consolidation of Christian votes in the former Central Travancore, in the north and in many pockets across Kerala, it was consolidation of Muslim votes. It was, in many ways, a backlash that the LDF did not deserve as a government, but could not avoid as a political formation. And, in that sense, it is tough to see the outcome as a verdict on the performance of the LDF government. The reason why and how the Christian consolidation came about is complex, but the way the CPI(M) strategy of taking on the Church contributed to it is there for everyone to see. The whole debate over mixing religion and polities, an old theme used to its full potential by none other than E.M.S. Namboodiripad, obviously did not win it any new friends. Coming as it did on the heels of the incidents at CMS College, Kottayam, it also further alienated the Church of South India (CSI), though not acutely in the coastal belt of south Kerala.

Only the Latin Catholic community appears to have taken a relatively neutral position in the whole debate. In the case of the Muslim community too, the CPI(M) appears to have failed to look closely at the nuances of the developments within the community and its organisational representations, the beneficiary being the Bharatiya Janata Party. In the event, the debate did not remain what it should have been and the LDF paid a heavy price for it as it did not have the means or ability to reach out to the other side of the political divide with cogent arguments.

However, though figures to prove anything are yet to come by, the Kudumbasree initiative appears to have done some good for the LDF, particularly in grama panchayats. But, even here, there could be some surprise in store. Preliminary indications are that the Congress also might have benefited from the participation of Kudumbasree activists in the elections. Only the final figures would tell the whole story. Equally interesting would be the way women have, if at all, performed in general wards. All the relevant figures could be pointers to the way women's politics evolves in the new political situation at the grassroots and the UDF's responsibility is much greater here than it ever was.

At a purely organisational level the CPI(M) and other LDF constituents would also have to see how their inability to put up a joint fight in many places contributed to their collective failure; Kottayam, where the CPI(M) and CPI were openly at each other's throat, being an example. And, within the CPI(M), though factionalism as a pan-Kerala, centrally driven, phenomenon has been snuffed out to a very large extent, much appears to have come unhinged at the time of the elections on account of various local factors. All this just means that the LDF collectively and its constituents individually have their tasks cut out.

Concluding Observations

As cited earlier, it can be stated that in the 2010 polls for the first time, the UDF has stormed grassroot citadels that were hitherto monopolised by the Left. UDF's muscular showing has decimated the myth that grama panchayats and block panchayats are the bastions of cadre-based political parties. The Congress, finally, has bridged the urban-rural divide. The Congress war cry, which was generally considered suited only for the Assembly and the Lok Sabha polls, percolated right down through the three-tiers of the Panchayati Raj system. Taking even the Congress leadership by surprise, the party has put up an unprecedented performance in the local body polls almost sweeping the entire Central Travancore and even some of the Marxist bastions in the southern districts.

The UDF captured absolute control over corporations in Kochi and Thrissur. Similarly, the UDF captured absolute control over grama panchayats, block panchayats and district panchayats throughout the state. In block panchayats, the UDF got 89 and the LDF captured 49. The grama panchayats, perhaps, threw up the biggest surprise. The UDF got control in 525 while the LDF got 301. The BJP had established control over 2 and others in 75. Among the municipalities, the UDF got 34 and LDF got 12. In 11 municipalities none got absolute majority. Among the district panchayats, the UDF got 8 and LDF got 5. This is the First time that the UDF has secured such a massive lead in all the sectors irrespective of the rural and urban areas of the state. Kollam,

Alappuzha, Palakkad and Kannur are the only districts where the CPM-led LDF could put up a good show. In all the other districts, the UDF has given a tough fight for the CPM. In the districts of Thiruvananthapuram, Pathanamthitta, Idukki, Kottayam, Ernakulam, Thrissur, Malappuram, and Wayanad, the Congress-led UDF has dominated the show.

If a mandate is a slice of social psychology, then the Left in the state has failed to read the mind of its people. The miscalculation that development agenda would eclipse all political controversies have poorly failed. The deliberate attempt to showcase development and steer public mind from politics and communal factors only brought them to the fore-front.

Long before the UDF zeroed in on its candidates or even thought of the word campaign, the LDF was taking the development activities undertaken by local bodies to the far and wide of the state. Its grassroot machinery had jumped into the election scene much before others had even given it a thought. Seminars, exhibitions, Kudumbasree melas—every possible idea was utilised. Rice for Rs. 2/-, EMS Housing scheme, Asraya project and a lot more for the welfare of the poor was projected. But all went in vain.

The ballot has shown that it is a misconception of the Left that half the voting population are beneficiaries of their various welfare schemes. If the beneficiaries form a mere 20-30 per cent, it is to be assumed that the rest of 60-70 per cent decided the fate of the Left this time. For the latter, it is not rice or house that matters. But improvement of living conditions, roads, undisrupted water supply and better facilities. Even the behaviour of politicians in public sphere matters for this group.

The Left often forgets that it can be a centralised and closed party but it cannot impose its character on the people. The party needs to converse with the upper levels of society just the way they communicate with the grassroot. Before conclude, the LDF particularly the CPI(M) needs to politically educate its grassroot cadres and not feed them on development activities which have gained acceptance. Tables from 7.6 to 7.12 further illustrate the details.

Table 7.6: List of Candidates in Civic Polls, 2010 in Kerala

District	*Grama Panchayat*	*Block*	*District*	*Municipality*	*Corp.*	*Total*
Thiruvananthapuram	4689	500	115	489	642	6435
Kollam	4163	460	106	332	276	5337
Pathanamthitta	2712	350	77	351	-	3490
Alappuzha	3866	499	84	697	-	5146
Kottayam	3941	458	98	536	-	5033
Idukki	2518	324	58	116	-	3016
Ernakulam	4425	579	122	1213	378	6717
Thrissur	5092	701	127	799	251	6970
Palakkad	4800	540	125	589	-	6054
Malappuram	6251	763	145	919	-	8078
Kozhikode	4408	552	123	276	410	5769
Wayanad	1407	197	78	88	-	1770
Kannur	3336	411	95	603	-	4445
Kasaragod	2009	338	69	329	-	2745

Table 7.7: Civic Polls 2010 in Kerala—Detailed Results

Corporation
Total - 5 UDF – 2 LDF – 3 BJP – 0

Table 7.8: District Panchayats

District	*Total*	*UDF*	*LDF*	*Hung*	*Others*
Thiruvananthapuram	26	14	12	0	0
Kollam	26	8	18	0	0
Pathanamthitta	17	9	8	0	0
Alappuzha	23	19	4	0	0
Kottayam	23	19	4	0	0
Idukki	16	16	0	0	0
Eranakulam	26	22	3	0	1
Thrissur	29	17	12	0	0
Palakkad	29	11	18	0	0
Malappuram	32	30	2	0	0
Wayanad	16	13	2	0	1
Kannur	26	6	20	0	0
Kasaragod	16	6	9	1	1
Kozhikode	27	12	15	0	0

Table 7.9: Block Panchayats

District	Total	UDF	LDF	Hung	Others
Thiruvananthapuram	11	6	4	1	0
Kollam	11	3	8	0	0
Pathanamthitta	8	7	0	1	0
Alappuzha	12	7	5	0	0
Kottayam	11	10	1	0	0
Idukki	8	8	0	0	0
Eranakulam	14	13	1	0	0
Thrissur	16	9	7	0	0
Palakkad	13	5	8	0	0
Malappuram	15	14	1	0	0
Wayanad	4	4	0	0	0
Kannur	11	0	11	0	0
Kasaragod	6	3	3	0	0
Kozhikode	12	4	8	0	0

Table 7.10: Grama Panchayats

District	Total	UDF	LDF	Hung	Others
Thiruvananthapuram	73	36	25	12	0
Kollam	70	24	37	9	0
Pathanamthitta	54	36	14	4	0
Alappuzha	73	32	37	4	0
Kottayam	73	58	10	5	0
Idukki	53	41	10	2	0
Eranakulam	84	66	6	12	0
Thrissur	88	45	33	10	0
Palakkad	91	36	51	4	0
Malappuram	100	88	8	4	0
Wayanad	25	21	3	1	0
Kannur	81	27	54	0	0
Kasaragod	38	15	13	8	2 (BJP)
Kozhikode	75	34	40	0	1

Table 7.11: Municipalities—District-wise

District	Total	UDF	LDF	Hung	Others
Thiruvananthapuram	4	1	1	2	0
Kollam	3	1	1	1	0
Pathanamthitta	3	2	0	1	0
Alappuzha	5	2	0	3	0
Kottayam	4	3	0	1	0
Idukki	1	1	0	0	0
Eranakulam	11	10	1	0	0
Thrissur	6	2	4	0	0
Palakkad	2	0	2	0	0

(Contd.)

Table 7.11: (*Contd.*)

District	*Total*	*UDF*	*LDF*	*Hung*	*Others*
Malappuram	7	6	0	1	0
Wayanad	1	1	0	0	0
Kannur	5	1	4	0	0
Kasaragod	3	2	1	0	0
Kozhikode	2	0	2	0	0

Table 7.12: Tally of Municipalities—Municipality-wise

Muncipality	*Total*	*UDF*	*LDF*	*BJP*	*Others*
Thiruvananthapuram					
Niyyatinkara	44	20	20	0	4
Nedmangad	39	16	18	2	3
Attingal	31	13	17	1	0
Varkala	33	18	11	1	3
Kollam					
Karunagappally	35	21	14	0	0
Paravur	32	15	16	1	0
Punalloor	35	11	24	0	0
Pathanamthitta					
Adoor	28	17	9	0	2
Pathanamthitta	32	17	10	2	3
Thiruvalla	39	17	5	0	0
Alappuzha					
Alappuzha	52	25	26	0	1
Cherthala	35	18	10	0	7
Kayamkulam	44	21	16	2	5
Mavelikkara	28	13	8	2	5
Chegannur	27	14	10	1	2
Idukki					
Thodupuzha	35	22	6	4	3
Kottayam					
Kottayam	52	27	18	3	4
Pala	26	18	1	0	7
Vaikom	26	17	8	0	1
Changanassery	37	14	12	0	11
Eranakulam					
Eloor	31	14	13	3	1
Maradu	33	22	10	0	1
Thripunithura	49	25	22	1	1
Aluva	25	22	2	0	1
Angamaly	30	15	13	0	2

(*Contd.*)

Table 7.12: (*Contd.*)

Muncipality	*Total*	*UDF*	*LDF*	*BJP*	*Others*
North Paravur	29	14	13	0	2
Kalamassery	42	22	17	0	3
Perumbavoor	27	15	9	1	2
Thrikakkara	43	28	13	0	2
Kothamangalam	31	23	8	0	0
Muvathupuzha	28	10	14	0	4
Thrissur					
Guruvayur	43	17	25	1	0
Chavakkad	32	11	21	0	0
Kunnmangalam	37	14	15	2	6
Chalakkudy	36	23	4	0	9
Irinjalakuda	41	28	9	1	3
Kodungalloor	44	11	26	5	2
Palakkad					
Palakkad	52	23	9	15	5
Chottur	29	26	3	0	0
Ottappalam	36	11	15	4	6
Shoranur	33	8	13	3	9
Malappuram					
Malappuram	40	30	8	0	2
Manjeri	50	38	8	0	4
Perinthalmanna	34	17	16	0	1
Tirur	38	28	7	0	3
Ponnai	51	25	22	1	3
Kottakkal	32	24	5	2	1
Nilambur	33	21	8	0	4
Wayanad					
Kalpetta	28	20	7	0	10
Kannur					
Kannur	42	33	8	0	1
Thalassery	52	14	35	2	1
Koothuparamba	28	4	24	0	0
Taliparamba	44	13	31	0	0
Payyannur	44	16	28	0	0
Kasaragod					
Kasaragod	38	24	2	11	1
Kanhangad	43	22	16	5	0
Neelaswaram	32	10	20	0	2
Kozhikode					
Koilandi	44	14	27	3	0
Vadakara	47	17	27	0	3

References

The Hindu, Thiruvananthapuram.
The Kerala Kaumudi, Kollam.
The Kerala Sabdam, Kollam.
The Malayala Manorama, Kollam.
The Mathrubhumi, Kollam.
The New Indian Express, Thiruvananthapuram.

8

Local Body Polls, 2015

Impressive Performance by the Left and the BJP

In one of its biggest electoral comebacks in recent times, a united LDF sidestepped major political hurdles with sound on-ground strategies, though it could not encash completely on the abundant factors. After it suffered a major setback in 2010, the CPM-led Left front has returned to local bodies across the state, thanks to a 'reverse Aruvikkara effect', coupled with other factors. On the one hand, talks of the SNDP-BJP alliance right at the beginning of the polls had set off the Left campaign. The 'Aruvikkara factor' worked in the LDFs favour this time. If the BJP making inroads into the Left vote bank turned out to be prime reason for CPM losing in Aruvikkara, this time around the UDF was at the receiving end. The anti-incumbency factor against Oommen Chandy government, specifically Vigilance court verdict against Finance Minister K.M. Mani in the bar scam, was also crucial.

Also, the blistering effect of V.S. Achuthanandan on its opponents too cannot be ignored in LDF win. Biting the dust more than once in the past decade, the CPM, this time, was wise enough not to ruffle any feathers at least in public. With the leadership leaning on the veteran comrade to sail through, the wily politician with his layman connect could easily convert the popular upsurge against both the UDF and BJP into votes for the Left. While there was a substantial flow of Hindu votes to BJP following the SNDP-BJP alliance, the reverse flow to the Left camp originating from an unprecedented and solid minority consolidation—formulated through a perceived threat from Sangh Parivar—was more than able to make up for it. Beef row and its ripples, along with CPM's timely intervention in taking up these issues added to the Left campaign. CPI politburo member Pinarayi Vijayan was at the forefront in bringing the beef controversy among the middle-class in a state with a substantial minority population.

EMERGENCE OF THE BJP AS A KEY PLAYER IN STATE POLITICS

The remarkable outcome of 2015 Civic polls was that though the CPI (M)-led Left Democratic Front (LDF) has made a dramatic return to dominance at the grassroots in Kerala in a keenly contested local bodies' election, which have also pushed the Bharatiya Janata Party (BJP) to the front as a claimant to the State's bi-polar political space. In a clear reversal of political fortunes as compared to the 2010 elections, the Opposition alliance has been able to gain control of close to 551 of the 941 grama panchayats, 90 of the 152 block panchayats, 43 of the 87 municipalities, besides an upper hand in four out of the six Corporations in the State. The LDF could win only 365 grama panchayats in 2010. Going by the latest count, it could be the ruling United Democratic Front (UDF) that finally ends up with a similar tally.

Although overshadowed by the LDF's return to prominence in grassroots governance, the BJP has put in an eye-catching performance by winning 14 grama panchayats by the last count, coming second in the Thiruvananthapuram Corporation, emerging the single largest party in the Palakkad municipal council and, generally, increasing its tally of grama panchayat wards from 384 in 2010 to 930 plus this time. It has pushed the UDF to the third position in the capital city, opened its account in the Kollam Corporation, and emerged a crucial presence in several municipalities. However, its tie-up with SNDP Yogam general secretary Vellappally Natesan to build a broad Hindutva plank does not appear to have had the desired effect, the alliance failing to make any significant impact in Kollam, Kottayam and Alappuzha.

The impressive outing that the BJP had in the poll may appear to be enough of an indication that the party may be poised to elbow its way into serious reckoning between the two coalitions in the State's traditionally bipolar polity. From 480 wards that it has won in 2010, the BJP has been able to make a quantum jump bagging around 1,300 seats this time. The party's much taunted electoral tie-up with the SNDP Yogam did not fire to the expected extent. It had optimistically targeted anywhere between 4,000 and 5,000 seats before the campaign began. However, the groundwork done by its parent body, RSS has yielded rich dividends in urban areas across the State including the Thiruvananthapuram and Kozhikode Corporations and the Palakkad municipality.

The BJP has been able to increase its vote share of 12 per cent which it got in the Lok Sabha elections to over 18 per cent. But its State leaders failed to effectively gamble with a newly-cobbled formation of Hindu organizations, unlike the Left parties that had upped the ante against the BJP by wooing minorities, especially the Muslim community. But the party can heave a sigh of relief that from its tally of just three grama panchayats confined to Kasaragod district, it will now rule in at least 20 local bodies all the way from Kasaragod to Thrissur, Pathanamthitta and Thiruvananthapuram. Besides, the BJP had made deep inroads into the traditional pocket-boroughs of both the LDF and UDF. This is though its strategy of harvesting anti-CPI(M) and anti-Congress votes of the Hindu sections, drawn up by its Central leadership, met with only limited success. The party has been able to moderately increase its vote share among the Nair and the Ezhava/Thiyya communities. Had it not been confronted by the issues such as beef ban, the police raid in Kerala House and the intra-party squabbles, the BJP's rating would have gone much higher, feel observers. Now the party is gearing up for organizational polls this month and the process will be completed in December. The Central leadership is expected to effect some major changes in the State unit, with the RSS having a major say on it. But it is yet to be seen whether the party's social engineering methodology, which was deftly employed to consolidate and micro-manage castes in the State, can yield it much in Assembly polls barely six months away.

SUCCESS OF BJP THROUGH RSS STRATEGY

The notable increase in the Bharatiya Janata Party's (BJP) tally in local bodies from 473 to 1,244 is being seen as an outcome of the Rashtriya Swayamsevak Sangh's (RSS) strategy to keep its majority community vote base intact, while striking a strategic alliance with the Sree Narayana Dharma Paripalana (SNDP) Yogam. The RSS was insistent on winning the confidence of community organisations such as the Nair Service Society (NSS) and the Kerala Brahmana Sabha in all districts.

The Sangh had also briefed the BJP leadership that it was not ready for any compromise on a three-fold increase in the number of seats. The strategy to win the confidence of influential community organisations in each locality, mainly in candidate selection, seems to have yielded its results too. The BJP would be decisive in determining the ruling party in Kasaragod district panchayat and also a number of urban and rural local governments. Since the rival fronts have resolved not to seek its support, the party may abstain from voting and the largest party would be invited to form the committees as in Thiruvananthapuram Corporation. The success of the Sangh poll strategy seems to have helped to wrest seats in some of the United Democratic Front (UDF) and the Left Democratic Front (LDF) strongholds. Notable among them are the seven seats it won in Kozhikode Corporation and also its accomplishment in registering presence in the Tirur, Parappangadi, Kannur, Thalassery, and Iritty urban local governments.

Except in Chavakkad, the BJP has made its presence felt in all municipalities and become a formidable force in Kodungalloor, where it got 16 members elected. The party's performance in four municipalities in Alappuzha and five in Kottayam district, have virtually come as a surprise to the UDF. It is learnt that the theory that its strategic alliance with the SNDP Yogam would become ominous in winning the votes of forward communities has been proved wrong. When the party drew a blank in Cherthala, a place where the Yogam leadership claims to wield considerable clout, its performance in the urban local governments in Kottayam, Idukki and Alappuzha district shows that its forward caste vote bank is still intact. This has also prompted the Sangh to devise new strategies for the Assembly elections, sources said.

SNDP-BJP ALLIANCE TO NEW HEIGHTS

The electoral understanding between the Bharatiya Janata Party (BJP) and the Sree Narayana Dharma Paripalana (SNDP) Yogam may come up for a thorough review in the backdrop of the local bodies poll results. The impressive performance of the party in the capital as well as its traditional strongholds across the State, is being attributed to the well-oiled efforts of the Rashtriya Swayamsevak Sangh (RSS), which had taken over the party campaign machinery right from the start. While the BJP has made a notable surge in its strongholds – mainly Thiruvananthapuram Corporation and Palakkad municipality – and also defeated some important leaders of the Left Democratic Front (LDF) and the United Democratic Front (UDF), the Yogam leadership could not achieve any major gains even in the seven southern districts, where it had boasted of doing much.

The BJP's showing in Thiruvananthapuram Corporation, its success in opening its account in the district panchayat and consolidating its position in three panchayats, besides making a formidable presence in the rural areas of the district, are all sought to be credited to the systematic functioning of the RSS election machinery. The same applies to Kollam Corporation where the party got two members elected to the council. The party had deputed a senior leader to co-ordinate the candidate selection and campaigning in the southern districts and that has brought palpable gains to the party too. Party sources stated that the lackluster performance of the Yogam-BJP alliance in the seven districts and also in Kozhikode, where the alliance was initially launched, would come up for scrutiny. The claims of the Yogam leadership stood disproved and a preliminary review has found that the party could still bank on only its traditional support base, mainly the voters from the Nair and other forward communities. The results have also given the BJP leadership the elbow room to take a firm stance on its alliance with the Yogam in future.

UNITY AMONG THE LEFT

After remaining in the doldrums for much of the past four years, the Opposition Left Democratic Front (LDF) appears to have successes in doing the right things on the ground and in the sphere of ideas to emerge on top in the local bodies elections. At the level of thrust and parries, the LDF was able to hold its own, thanks to the many issues that cropped in the course of the fortnight-long campaign. The alliance had started out with visible trepidation over the emerging tie-up between the BJP and SNDP Yogam general secretary Vellappally Natesan. But, soon the LDF leaders, particularly Leader of the Opposition V.S. Achuthanandan, began going all out against Vellappally Natesan, breaching the immunity that he used to enjoy as a community leader. That raised serious questions about the credibility of the BJP-Vellappally alliance, which is probably borne out by the poll outcome in Kollam, Alappuzha and, to some extent in Kottayam, which are considered areas of Vellappally Natesan's influence.

BEEF CONTROVERSY AND VIGILANCE COURT VERDICT

The LDF's biggest offensive in the idea sphere came over the 'beef controversy'. The polling trends in non-Muslim League influence areas show that the beef row, coupled with the anti-minority sentiment sought to be spread by the BJP and the Sangh Parivar in different parts of the country helped the LDF to position itself as the best bet for the minorities. This is very likely to have resulted in a movement of Muslim votes away from the Congress and the UDF. If the strong stand on majoritarian politics helped it to win the hearts of the secular sections besides the minorities, the LDF could use the last-minute Vigilance Court verdict in the bar bribery case to address the larger population which has been living through one corruption charge after another against the UDF.

The LDF was a house united by a singular purpose of regaining the ground lost in 2010 and taking on the BJP-Vellappally alliance and that has helped the Front to take on the UDF. In effect, the LDF is now a two-party alliance, comprising the CPI(M) and the CPI, the others being too inconsequential to bring in any substantial electoral dividend. Of the two, it is the CPI(M) which bears the burden of carrying the front's battles forward. Thus, the unity that the leaders of the CPI(M) could achieve on poll eve was as crucial as anything else to the impressive victory that the LDF fashioned.

OVEROPTIMISM IN THE UDF CAMP WENT WRONG

The results have greatly upset the United Democratic Front's (UDF) calculations, even if there is nothing to indicate that it suffered a big drubbing. The UDF was overoptimistic about a fair victory that would have given it a psychological edge in the Assembly elections, even if it certainly could not repeat the 2010 verdict which had given it control over 70 per cent of the state's local bodies. At best, the UDF leadership can now console itself that the results have reaffirmed the relevance of bipolar politics that the State is known for. And that was how senior leaders, including Chief Minister Oommen Chandy sought to explain away the UDF's turn out. Even after the announcement of poll results, the Chief Minister reiterated that "The UDF's vote base is intact." Clearly, it was its usual banes of poor candidate selection, rebel menace, the Congress factional tussles and lack of unity between coalition partners have all accounted for polling down the UDF. But there are certain trends that emerged in this election that might make the ruling coalition partners more uncomfortable.

All through the campaign, the UDF leaders had maintained that the LDF was most likely to face erosion of its votes owing to the electoral understanding between the BJP and the SNDP. But it would appear that the erosion took place more from the UDF camp, which was relegated to the third place in Thiruvananthapuram. The BJP's emergence as the largest party in Palakkad municipality also cannot be seen lightly. The major partners in the UDF coalition – Indian Union Muslim League (IUML) and the Kerala Congress (M) – can claim to have retained their bases in Malappuram and Kottayam respectively, but the RSP had suffered a blow in Kollam, with its Left-leaning vote base abandoning it. The Congress party itself appears to be the major loser in the election. It could not curb the rebel menace and in several places the rebels went on to win, as in Kannur and Kasaragod. In Kannur Congress rebel P.K. Rajesh will decide who will rule the Corporation. The victory of rebel candidates has gone on to prove that the party leadership has failed to gauge the pulse of the respective local areas. In Thrissur, rabid factionalism proved to be costly for the Congress party.

The UDF will have to reconsider whether it should bring back the rebels and wrest control. Similarly, even if it sounds unthinkable, it would also have to take a call on whether it should have ties with the LDF to keep the BJP from wresting the advantage in hung local bodies. The Congress party is unlikely to witness any major outbursts, though factions might push for more space with the Assembly elections in mind. Details are shown in Tables 8.1 to 8.5.

Table 8.1: Number of Polling Stations in 2015

District	*No. of Polling Stations*		
	Urban	*Rural*	*Total*
Thiruvananthapuram	792	2463	3255
Kollam	377	2360	2737
Pathanamthitta	132	1326	1458
Alappuzha	268	1984	2252
Kottayam	253	2078	2331
Idukki	69	1384	1453
Ernakulam	748	2356	3104
Thrissur	482	2816	3298
Palakkad	284	2689	2973
Malappuram	480	3431	3911
Kozhikode	670	2297	2967
Wayanad	99	748	847
Kannur	440	1994	2434
Kasaragod	119	1284	1403
Total	**5213**	**29210**	**34423**

Table 8.2: Polling Percentage—2015

District	*Panchayat*	*Municipality*	*Corporation*	*District Aver.*
Thiruvananthapuram	76.22	76.47	62.9	71.9
Kollam	77.42	77.34	69.9	74.9
Pathanamthitta	72.89	72.14	0	72.5
Alappuzha	81.38	77.95	0	79.7
Kottayam	78.79	77.77	0	78.3
Idukki	78.07	81.26	0	79.7
Ernakulam	84.60	81.38	69.62	78.5
Thrissur	78.78	78.95	71.88	76.5
Palakkad	80.93	76.77	0	78.9
Malappuram	79.97	79.44	0	79.7
Kozhikode	83.06	82.48	74.7	80.1
Wayanad	82.42	80.63	0	81.5
Kannur	81.83	80.16	74.75	78.9
Kasaragod	78.69	76.49	0	77.6
State Average	**79.65**	**78.51**	**70.62**	**77.76**

SEVERE BLOW TO THE STATE CONGRESS

The civil polls results are personally a severe setback to the Chief Minister, who had set an agenda that it will be a referendum on

Table 8.3: Analysis of Polling percentages of General Elections

	1995	2000	2005	2010	2015
No. of Candidates	58,702	60,307	64,159	70,915	75,549
No. of Polling Stations	28,282	28,274	36,210	37,233	34,423
No. of Voters	2,05,08,855	2,25,04,328	2,37,05,440	2,40,12,535	2,51,08,536
No. of Votes Polled	1,50,74,169	1,48,73,110	1,69,84,236	1,83,26,367	1,95,24,397
Percentage of Polling	**735**	**66.09**	**70.35**	**76.32**	**77.76**

Table 8.4: Reservation of Wards

LSGI	Total Wards	SC			ST			Woman Gents	Total Women
		Women	Gents	Total	Women	Gents	Total		
Grama Panchayat	15962	748	966	1714	103	139	242	7409	8260
Block Panchayat	2076	76	146	222	11	20	31	1015	1102
District Panchayat	331	16	16	32	02	04	06	150	168
Municipality	3122	117	110	227	07	08	15	1198	1538
Corporation	414	15	12	27	00	00	00	194	209
Total	**21905**	**972**	**1250**	**2222**	**123**	**171**	**294**	**9932**	**11277**

Table 8.5: Reservation of Seats for President, Chairman and Mayor

LSGI	Total Wards	SC			ST			Woman Gents	Total Women
		Women	Gents	Total	Women	Gents	Total		
Grama Panchayat	941	46	46	92	08	08	16	417	471
Block Panchayat	152	08	07	15	02	01	03	67	76
District Panchayat	14	00	01	01	00	00	00	07	07
Municipality	87	00	03	00	00	01	00	44	00
Corporation	06	00	00	00	00	00	00	03	00
Total	**1200**	**54**	**'57**	**108**	**10**	**10**	**19**	**538**	**554**

his government and a mandate for the continuance of the UDF government in Kerala. Since, it is bag of mixed results for UDF with a reversal of fortunes in the Gram, Block Panchayats and face saving results in the district Panchayats, Municipalities and Corporations. The Chief Minister can bank on excuses. It is unlikely that there will be any immediate challenge to his leadership, but political firework will definitely flare up in the UDF camp. Contrary to the calculations of UDF, it was not the LDF which had suffered owing to the BJP-SNDP tie-up in the most of the areas where the latter have put a notable performance, but the ruling front itself. A shift in votes from the Nair community in favour of

BJP had also turned costly. Moreover, the UDF leadership unlike Left had spared the SNDP Yogam leadership while attacking the BJP. Despite the claims and reassuring posters of the UDF and the Congress leadership, the morale of party activists was low while countering allegations of corruption aired by the opposition against the UDF government, including Bar scam. Another main factor attributed to the comparatively poor show of the UDF is the organizational weakness of leading partner Congress in the districts and grassroots level. That UDF had no systematic mechanism like the CPM to monitor and guide the functioning of local bodies under its control is also believed to have created divisions at the local level, when it was controlling around 68 per cent of the local bodies.

IUML'S STRAINED RELATIONS WITH THE CONGRESS

IUML leadership is in a troubled mood as the outcome of the local body elections in Malappuram district, considered to be the stronghold of the party, has indicated declining strength of the party. Though the UDF had managed to win 61 grama panchayats, 13 block panchayats, lone district panchayat and nine municipalities, IUML's two senior leaders have openly admitted to party's poor performance in the elections after losing three main municipalities—Perinthalmana, Ponnani and Tirur to the LDF and failing to maintain a considerable number of wards which the BJP and the rebels of Congress, IUML, SDPI and Welfare Party under the banner Janakiya Munnani managed to win. In municipalities like Kondotty, Parapanangadi, Kottakkal and Nilambur, Independent candidates under Janakiya Munnani fared well. They managed to win 17, 18, 8 and 8 seats respectively.

The BJP, for the first time in the election history of the state, had managed to win 38 wards from 12 municipalities and 94 grama panchayats in the district. Senior IUML leader and Industries Minister P.K. Kunjalikutty also said that it was a major setback for the party in the recent times. "We know the issues. But this won't affect the party", he told reporters. The fight between the Congress and the IUML was one of the major reasons for the poor show and it was well capitalised by the LDF. Though the IUML leadership declined that the party had no backdoor alliance with the CPM, rumours were *rife mat* in certain panchayats. IUML workers worked in favour of the CPM candidate to defeat the official UDF candidate. While the UDF won 2,315 wards in 94 grama panchayats, the LDF won 595 wards and the independents of Janakiya Munnani 237 wards. "The rise of Janakiya Munnani affected the IUML's prospects in many wards in the district. Apart from this, there has been an erosion of Congress votes in favour of the LDF", said IUML leaders.

Even the Sunni Yuvajana Sangham (SYS) was not happy with the IUML and there was a strain in the relationship between the two. SYS, which is the feeder organisation of Samastha Kerala Jam-Tyyathul Ulema, the Sunni scholars' forum, is the traditional vote bank of the IUML

RESULTS NOT ROSY FOR THE RMP

The 2015 civil poll results were not at all happy for the Revolutionary Marxist Party (RMP) which failed to get expected seats, while contesting against the CPM-led LDF in Vadakara Municipality, Onchiyam, Azhiyoor, Chorode and Eramala Grama Panchayaths. The results have in fact forced the RMP leadership to chalk out a plan on strengthening their political activities. The RMP leaders discussed the option of supporting the UDF in Onchiyam, where the Party had won six seats and the UDF captured four seats out of Seventeen. The RMP leadership was of the firm opinion that the alliance if worked out will definitely spoil the chances of LDF which had won Seven seats. Surprisingly, the UDF had increased its tally which in a way confirms their secret pact with the RMP. In Azhiyoor and Chorode the RMP could capture only two seats. But in Eramala it had got three seats. Though the Party had fielded three candidates in Vadakara Municipality only a single candidate came victorious. In the 2010 polls the Party had failed to win a single seat in Vadakara Municipality. But it captured two seats (out of eighteen) in Azhiyoor, one seat in Chorode (out of twenty one) and three seats in Eramala (out of nineteen).

THE SUCCESS OF MUNNAR WOMEN'S COLLECTIVE

Penkal Otrumai, the collective of women plantation workers whose agitation in Munnar shunning all political parties had caught the State's imagination, tasted success at its maiden electoral outing.

Gomathy Augustine, one of the collective's leaders, was elected from the Nallathanni division to the Devikulam block panchayat. They also bagged two seats in the Munnar grama panchayat. The collective had contested from 13 wards of the Munnar grama panchayat, 16 of the Devikulam grama panchayat, six divisions of the block panchayat and one division of the district panchayat. Unable to match the financial muscle of political parties in the fray, the collective had done a very low profile campaign, mostly confined to distributing pamphlets highlighting their agonies and exploitation, and the media reports on their agitation. The women workers who led the agitation were upbeat that they could have at least three of them in the civic bodies. "It is a reflection of people's support for our cause. We had no money to do the campaigning, but we are happy", said Mahalakshmi of old Munnar. Related details are provided from Tables 8.6 to 8.12.

Table 8.6: How Kerala Voted—2015

Party Alliance	*Grama Panchayat*	*Block Panchayat*	*District Panchayat*	*Municipal Councils*	*Municipal Corporation*
LDF	551	90	7	45	2
UDF	362	61	7	40	2
BJP	14	0	0	1	0
Others	14	1	0	0	2 (Hung)
Total	**941**	**152**	**14**	**87**	**6**

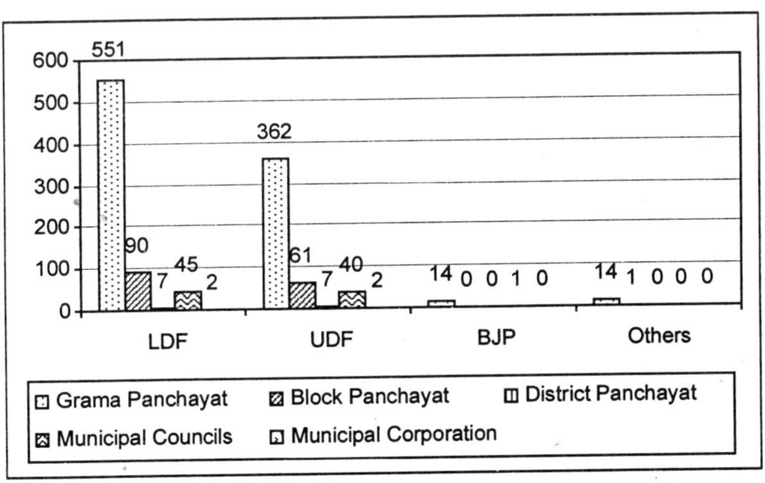

Table 8.7: Total No. of Voters in 2015—District-wise

District	*Voters*	*Male*	*Female*
Thiruvananthapuram	26,02,589	12,25,840	13,76,749
Kollam	20,23,749	9,57,614	10,66,135
Kottayam	15,03,581	7,38,425	7,65,156
Pathanamthitta	10,01,325	4,68,807	5,32,518
Alappuzha	16,40,898	7,76,774	8,64,124
Idukki	8,49,184	4,21,703	4,27,481
Ernakulam	23,79,087	11,67,670	12,11,417
Thrissur	24,36,213	11,56,007	12,80,206
Palakkad	21,31,322	10,33,371	10,97,951
Malappuram	29,05,103	14,24,744	14,80,329
Kozhikode	22,76,217	10,94,341	11,81,876
Wayanad	5,73,513	2,82,201	2,91,312
Kannur	18,34,051	8,50,414	9,83,637
Kasaragod	9,51,703	4,60,431	4,91,272

LDF IN 2010 AND 2015

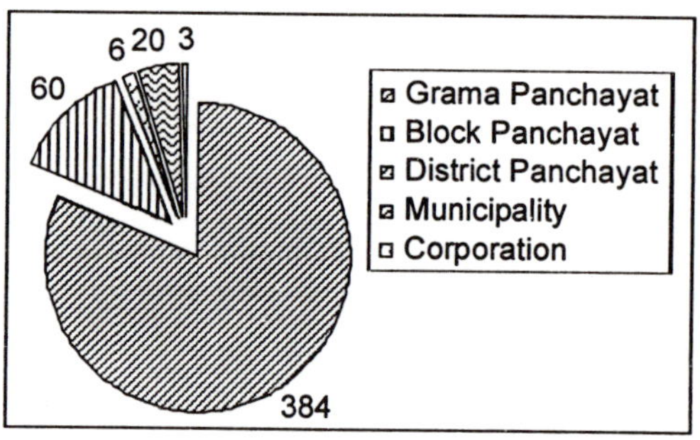

UDF IN 2010 AND 2015

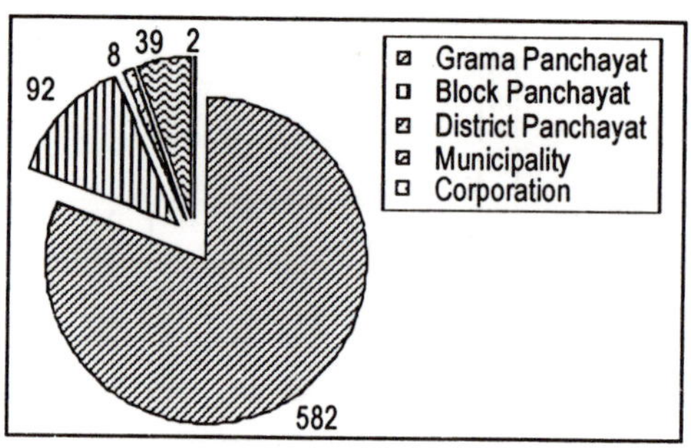

Table 8.8: Results in Detail—Party-wise Left Democratic Front

LDF	*Grama Panchayat*	*Block*	*District*	*Municipal Council*	*Corporation*
CPI(M)	5903	854	134	934	163
CPI	934	178	37	102	24
Janata Dal(S)	60	9	3	8	2
NCP	31	16	3	6	3
Congress(S)	5	0	0	6	2
Kerala Congress(B)	15	1	0	3	0
Kerala Congress (Secular)	23	4	1	4	0
CMP(A)	2	1	0	2	0
NSC	2	2	0	8	0
LDF Independent	641	21	0	180	1
INL	9	2	0	10	1
Total	**7625**	**1088**	**178**	**1263**	**196**

Table 8.9: United Democratic Front

UDF	*Grama Panchayat*	*Block*	*District*	*Municipal Council*	*Corporation*
Congress	4221	608	92	756	109
IUML	1420	206	37	437	20
KC(M)	456	75	12	85	2
RSP	37	4	1	6	6
JDU	65	13	4	12	3
UDF Independent	93	4	0	15	1
KC(Jacob)	23	5	0	5	0
CMP(John)	6	2	0	3	1
JSS(R)	3	0	0	0	1
Total	**6324**	**917**	**146**	**1319**	**143**

Table 8.10: Bharatiya Janata Party

BJP	*Grama Panchayat*	*Block*	*District*	*Municipal Council*	*Corporation*
BJP	905	21	3	225	51
BJP independent	26	0	0	10	0
Kerala Congress (PCT)	2	0	0	1	0
Total	**933**	**21**	**3**	**236**	**51**

Table 8.11: Others

Others	*Grama Panchayat*	*Block*	*District*	*Municipal Council*	*Corporation*
Independent	1021	52	4	245	22
SDPI	32	0	0	7	1
PDP	5	0	0	3	0
WPI	7	0	0	0	0
AIADMK	6	0	0	0	0
JSS	3	1	0	0	0
CPI(ML)	1	0	0	1	1
MCPI(U)	0	0	0	3	0
BSP	2	0	0	0	0
RSP(M)	1	0	0	0	0

RESULTS IN DETAIL

Results in Municipal Corporations – BJP's Stunning Victory

The elections to the six City Corporations have thrown up a mixed result, with the performance of the Bharatiya Janata Party proving to be a stunner. The BJP dashed the hopes of the two rival fronts, the Left Democratic Front and the United Democratic Front in Thiruvananthapuram, denying the former a distinct majority to rule and pushing the latter to the third position in the 100-member council. The Left Democratic Front registered a creditable victory in Kollam and Kozhikode, while the UDF maintained its course in Kochi by winning 38 wards in the 74-member city Corporation. In Kannur, the LDF and the UDF were tied at 27 each in the 55-member newly formed City Corporation. The chances of the UDF assuming power revolved around the position that the rebel Congress candidate P.K. Ragesh, who defeated the official candidate. In Thrissur, which was considered a UDF bastion, the LDF emerged the surprise winner, taking advantage of the factional feuds in the Congress. The fate of Thiruvananthapuram, Thrissur and Kannur City Corporations now revolves around whether the Congress will amend its rather strict guidelines not to have any ties outside the UDF framework. In Thrissur and Thiruvananthapuram, it would have to decide whether it would support the LDF dispensation. In Kannur it would have to decide whether it wants to seek the support of its rebel after having taken strong position against him when he decided to contest disregarding the KPCC's directive.

Table 8.12: Municipal Corporation

Municipal Corporation	*Total*	*LDF*	*UDF*	*BJP*	*Others*
Thiruvananthapuram	100	42	21	34	3
Kollam	55	36	16	2	1
Kochi	74	30	38	2	4
Thrissur	55	25	21	6	3
Kozhikode	75	48	20	7	0
Kannur	55	27	27	0	1

While the leadership of the two rival fronts mull over the next course of action, the BJP is sitting pretty in Thiruvananthapuram with 34 members. Many of these wards were won in a tightly fought triangular contest. In Kozhikode, it made a breakthrough by winning six wards. In Thrissur also it has won six wards. The BJP's performance in the corporation shows that the party has kept its mandate of preparing the ground for the Assembly elections, particularly in Thiruvananthapuram where it has apparently consolidated on its vote percentages registered in a series of elections since 2011.

Results in Municipal Councils – Impressive Performance of the Left

The opposition Left Democratic Front (LDF) has made an impressive comeback in urban areas in the State winning 44 of the 87 municipalities, up from just 17 that it had won in 2010. Ruling United Democratic Front (UDF) has had to satisfy itself with 41 municipalities, though it has been able to win 1,318 municipal wards, more than the 1,263 wards that the LDF has gained control of. The Bharatiya Janata Party (BJP) has put in its best performance in Palakkad where it has emerged as the largest single party three short of majority. Across the State, the party has gained control of 236 municipal wards and could turn out to be a crucial player in some of the municipalities later.

While the LDF has won majority of municipalities in Thiruvananthapuram, Kollam, Thrissur, Kozhikode and Kasaragod districts, the UDF has gained the upper hand in Kottayam, Alappuzha, Ernakulam, Malappuram and Wayanad districts. In Pathanamthitta, Idukki, Palakkad and Kannur districts the two alliances have gained equal number of municipalities. If the LDF and UDF had shared the four municipalities in Thiruvananthapuram in 2010, the LDF has swept all four this time. In Kollam, the LDF has won all four, including the newly created Kottarakara, wresting two that the UDF had won in 2010. In Pathanamthitta, while the LDF has won Adoor and Pandalam, the UDF has gained control of Tiruvalla and Pathanamthitta. In Alappuzha, the UDF has won Alappuzha, Chengannur, Cherthala and Harippad and the LDF Kayamkulam and Mavelikara. In Kottayam, the UDF has won four out of six, leaving two to the LDF. In Idukki, the two alliances have shared one each.

In Ernakulam as well, the LDF has been able to improve its tally to 5 out of 13, even as the UDF has gained control of 8 municipalities, one less than that in 2010. In Thrissur, the UDF has put up an impressive show winning 5 municipalities against two by the LDF. In Palakkad, the two alliances have shared three municipalities each while the BJP has emerged on top in Palakkad, The IJDF's best performance is in Malappuram, where it has won 9 out of 12 municipalities, the remaining 3 have gone to the LDF. In Kozhikode, the number of municipalities has gone up from two in 2010 to seven this time. Of these, Feroke, Koyilandy, Mukkom, Ramanattukara and Vadakara municipalities have been won by the LDF and the newly formed Koduvally and Payyoli by the UDF. In Wayanad, two out of the three—Kalpetta and Suithan Bathery—have been won by the UDF and Mananthavady by the LDF. In Kannur, the two alliances have shared the eight municipalities. In Kasaragod, the LDF has won two and UDF one municipality. Among others, the Socialist Democratic Party of India (SDPI) has put up a good show in Eerattupetta, winning four seats and the Welfare Party, the political arm of the Jamaat-e-Islami, has won nine municipal wards.

Results in District Panchayats – Wake-up call to both fronts

It is quite possible that there is a parallel between the district panchayats election in 2010 and the just-concluded poll from the point of view of them being barometers to gauge the general sentiment of the electorate ahead of the Assembly polls. The election in October 2010 almost foretold the outcome of the Assembly elections that was due to happen a few months hence. The UDF which was in the Opposition in the Assembly at the time, secured eight district panchayats while the ruling LDF romped home with six. While the Left front suffered a bad jolt in all other local body segments State-wide, the district panchayats poll result ruled out any anti-incumbency at work against the V.S. Achuthanandan government.

The Assembly polls in 2011 proved this beyond doubt when the UDF just about scraped through to wrest power by a slender majority of four seats. The district panchayats are evenly shared between both coalitions this time around, which indicates that the months in the run up to the Assembly polls next year would be critical for both fronts lest it should be a hung verdict. On the face of it, there are no big surprises as both fronts have held their fortresses with the WE gaining a slight edge in terms of number of wards in its kitty — 178 of the total 331 across the State. The UDF got 146. Independents, including a Kerala Congress (anti-merger group) candidate backed by the LDF, won four seats while the BJP sprang a mild surprise with three seats—two in Kasaragod and a seat in Thiruvananthapuram.

Not completely unexpectedly; the BJP combine retained the Edaneer ward in Kasaragod besides wresting Puthige from the CPI(M). In Thiruvananthapuram, it opened account in the district panchayat by wresting Venganoor from the SJD. The party came a close second in at least three wards in Kasaragod. However, given the high-voltage campaigning it carried out, the outcome should disappoint the cadres. In Palakkad where the combine emerged as the single largest formation failed to make any waves in the district panchayat, as the LDF scooped out 27 of the 30 wards. For the Kerala Congress(M), the district panchayat results must be really heartening as it won nine wards across Pathanamthitta, Alappuzha, Kottayam and Idukki districts in Central Kerala. The bar bribery case, it seems, has only marginally dented its vote bank. The beleaguered former chief whip of the UDF, P.C. George, MLA, saved his face as the Kerala Congress (Secular) secured the Poonjar ward from the KC(M). While parties like the SDPI made marginal impact, they could not secure a berth in any district panchayat. For the major fronts, however, the verdict is a wake-up call. Despite stepping on the gas, the LDF was not able to put tip a stellar performance. For the LDF, which was resting on the laurels of three bypoll wins, it would mean that the coalition's mass base has begun to erode.

Entangled in Coalition Politics of the UDF

The Oommen Chandy-led UDF Government seems to be heading

the UPA way by defending the indefensible, citing compulsions of coalition politics and if a course correction is not done, its fate in next year's assembly polls will be no different. Despite a barrage of correction allegations bar fear bribery scam against Finance Minister K.M. Mani and High Court slamming the Vigilance Director's intervention in preparation of the final report, the Chief Minister has been brazen and irreverent to the snowballing public opinion against his government. Coalition politics reared its ugly head again recently when Jacob Thomas was removed as chief of State Fire and Rescue Services, coming under Muslim Leagues' portfolio of urban affairs. Thomas had locked horns with the powerful builder's lobby over safety standards at high rises and shopping malls and attempted to strictly implement safety regulations for high-rises.

Chandy's constant refrain "where's the proof?" every time allegations surface be it from liquor baron Biju Ramesh or former Fire Chief Jacob Thomas, will have its limits. The heavy blow suffered in the 'semi-final' local body polls is an eye opener for Chandy who will be well aware that discontent will be brewing among the Congress cadre at the grassroots level. The extended rope given to allies has become longer and longer. Both Muslim League and Kerala Congress(M) have paid the price and suffered heavy losses from its own backyards. It remains to be seen how Chandy, a shrewd politician, reins in the allies and regains the people's trust in the next 5-6 months before the finals—the Assembly election.

Vote Variation between the LDF and the UDF—24,408

In the Civic Polls 2015, the difference of votes between the LDF and the UDF was 24,408. The LDF scored 74,01,160 (37.36%) and the UDF bagged 75,76,752 (37.23%) votes. The BJP made a spectacular progress compared to 2010 polls. BJP secured 26,31,271 (13.28%) votes. In Grama Panchayat, the LDF secured 59,38,258 votes and the UDF scored 58,73,409 votes and the BJP got 19,90,073 votes, independents and others secured 18,26,959 votes. In Municipal corporations and the Municipal councils, LDF secured 14,62,902 and UDF scored 15,03,343, BJP scored 6,41,198 and others got 5,74,194 votes. Another striking feature of the result was that vote share of the LDF depicted a diminishing graph compared to the part three civic polls, whereas the vote share of the UDF though it went up in 2010 polls but it came down in 2015. Further the BJP in the 2010 polls secured 11,47,297 votes compared to 26,31,271 this time. Moreover, compared to 2010 polls, LDF and UDF lost 3.5 lakh and 10 lakh votes respectively. For more statistics see the Tables 8.13 – 8.21.

Table 8.13: Front-wise, and Party-wise Vote Share from 2005 to 2015 Polls

Year	*LDF*	*UDF*	*BJP*
2005	7697251 (45.32%)	6882314 (40.52%)	964133 (5.68%)
2010	7763495 (42.36%)	8447977 (46.09%)	1147297 (6.26%)
2015	7401160 (37.36%)	7376752 (37.23%)	2631271 (13.28%)

Table 8.14: Front-wise, and Party-wise Vote Share in the 2015 Polls Panchayat/LDF

Party	*Total Votes*	*Percentage*
CPM	4300712	27.52
LDF(IND)	756006	4.84
CPI	722351	4.62
JDS	54761	0.35
NCP	43571	0.28
INL	20646	0.13
KCS	14689	0.09
KCB	12364	0.08
Congress(S)	5310	0.03
CMP(A)	4824	0.03
NSC	2728	0.02
Forward Block	296	—
Total	**5938258**	**38**

Table 8.15: Panchayat/UDF

Party	*Total Votes*	*Percentage*
Congress	4114676	26.33
IUML	1126103	7.21
KCM	315708	2.02
Independent	152028	0.97
JDU	78677	0.50
RSP	53023	0.34
CMP(John)	12135	0.08
KCJ	18069	0.12
JSS(G)	2990	0.02
Total	**5873409**	**37.58**

Table 8.16: Panchayat/BJP Front

Party	Total Votes	Percentage
BJP	1903590	12.18
Independent	80828	0.52
KC(PCT)	5178	0.03
RSP(BOL)	400	–
LJP	77	–
Total	**1990073**	**12.73**

Table 8.17: Panchayat/Others

Party	Total Votes	Percentage
Independents	1650439	10.56
SDPI	93969	0.60
Welfare Party	41314	0.26
Aam Admi	9426	0.06
AIADMK	2659	0.02
BSP	6277	0.04
CPIML	1997	0.01
JSS	2016	0.01
MCPI (U)	2120	0.01
PDP	12883	0.08
Siva Sena	1941	0.01
RSPM	1604	0.01
Trinamool	79	–
AISAK	62	–
DPSP	57	–
PNP	42	–
RPI	33	–
KVC	23	–
AKTP	16	–
Total	**1826959**	**11.69**

Table 8.18: Front-wise, and Party-wise Vote Share in the 2015 Polls Municipal Councils/Corporations—LDF

Party	Total Votes	Percentage
CPM	1052294	25.16
CPI	169030	4.04
Independents	150822	3.61
JDS	21355	0.51
NCP	19525	0.47
INL	16820	0.40
Congress(S)	14954	0.36
NSC	5751	0.14
CMP(A)	4867	0.12
KCB	3155	0.08
KC(S)	2972	0.07
Forward Blocks	1357	0.03
Total	**1462902**	**34.98**

Table 8.19: Municipal Councils/Corporations—UDF

Party	*Total Votes*	*Percentage*
Congress	1004703	24.03
IUML	351236	8.40
KCM	52727	1.26
JDU	29051	0.69
RSP	26399	0.63
Independent	22544	0.54
CMP(John)	10020	0.24
KCJ	5323	0.13
JSS(R)	1340	0.03
Total	**1503343**	**35.95**

Table 8.20: Municipal Councils/Corporations—BJP Front

Party	*Total Votes*	*Percentage*
BJP	624300	14.93
Independent	14554	0.35
KC (PCT)	1506	0.04
RSP (BOL)	655	0.02
LJP	183	
Total	**641198**	**15.33**

Table 8.21: Municipal Councils/Corporations—Others

Party	*Total Votes*	*Percentage*
Independents	5047727	12.07
SDPI	33601	0.80
Welfare Party	15731	0.38
AAM Admi	6667	0.16
PDP	5572	0.13
BSP	769	0.02
CPIML	2104	0.05
JSS	1514	0.04
MCPI(U)	1557	0.04
Siva Sena	627	0.01
PNP	233	0.01
RLSP	44	–
RPI(A)	11	–
RSP(M)	855	0.02
SP	48	–
AISAK	27	–
Trinamool	56	–
KJP	14	–
KVC	7	–
Total	**574194**	**13.73**

CONCLUDING OBSERVATIONS

The 2015 Civil Polls in Kerala was generally described as a semi-final for the assembly polls 2016, In the poll, the CPI(M) led recorded a resounding victory in three-tier panchayat polls gaining close to 58 per cent of local bodies. The UDF on the other hand which won about 65 per cent local bodies in 2010 suffered a severe setback while the BJP had a historic performance, doubling its tally and vote share, and becoming the runners-up in Thiruvananthapuram Municipal Corporation. Out of the six city corporations, the LDF retained two—Kollam and Kozhikode become the single largest front in Thiruvananthapuram and snatched power from the UDF in Thrissur, though could not gain majority. The UDF retained Kochi while the newly-formed Kannur has both fronts winning equal seats. The capital city corporation had the biggest surprise—an unexpected BJP upsurge. The saffron party gained 34 seats pushing the UDF to the third position. Out of the total 86 municipalities which went to the polls, the LDF gained majority in 44. While 41 went to the UDF. The BJP has emerged the single largest party in Palakkad. In 7 municipalities no front will be able to claim power without the support of BJP or fringe elements.

In the district panchayats, the LDF and the UDF shared seven each – thereby the left front improving its tally of six in 2010. The LDF won 178 district panchayats division, the UDF 146 and BJP 3. Out of the 15962 Grama Panchayat wards, 7601 wards went to the LDF. The UDF gained 6295 while the BJP got 931. At the block panchayat level too, it was LDF upsurge with 1052 block panchayat wards going to the LDF, 879 to the UDF and BJP got 21. In a major come back to Kerala's electoral politics, LDF cashed in on the anti-incumbency factor against the present UDF government while unleashing a scathing campaign against its corrupt practices, particularly the bar bribery scam against the finance minister K.M. Mani. On the other hand, the poll results also turned as a writing on the wall for the UDF for which its winning streak has come to an end. A study performance by UDF ever since assumed office has come to an end, making it clear that its journey forward won't be smooth. The BJP had a creditable performance in several municipalities and grama panchayats thereby once again proving that it has come of age, compared to the 2010 tally of 520 seats, it improved its tally to 1244 seats. The BJP could stage a creditable performance in Pathanamthitta, Alappuzha, Thrissur and Kozhikode.

Dress rehearsals are important in theatre, for they tell all those on stage and behind the curtains where things have gone wrong and what failed to click with the audience. The electoral 'semi-final' that Kerala has just been witness to also has many lessons and warnings for the key players in State politics. As Chief Minister Oommen Chandy himself put it, the outcome of the local government elections is a clear warning to the ruling UDF leadership, particularly for the Congress. The Congress strategy of looking away when corruption charges piled up before its doors and its carefully nurtured insouciance as the BJP and SNOP Yogam general secretary Vellappalli Natesan forged an alliance, primarily with the objective of undercutting the CPI(M) in its strongholds, and its inability to present a united front before the electorate have all cost it dear. The Congress would have to first tackle the inner turbulence that is likely to erupt and then look at how best it can keep the flock together. With Assembly elections just about six months away, the proverbial writing on the wall should be loud and clear.

For the CPI(M) and the Opposition LDF, the message is about continued cohesion among the CPI(M) leaders, particularly Leader of the Opposition V.S. Achuthanandan and CPJ(M) Polit Bureau member Pinarayi Vijayan. That they are not exactly on the same page on the question of alliance in the Assembly elections and beyond was clear from the body language of both as political Kerala discussed the issue, triggered by an off-the-cuff remark from CPI leader C. Divakaran. The CPI(M) leaders had fanned out to the far corners of the State on their own and, whether his detractors would like or not, Mr. Achuthanandan was the pivot of the LDF campaign. The CPI(M) would have to decide how to place him in its scheme of things when the Assembly elections come. On the plus side, it can feel gratified that it could achieve such a big success with just the CPI by its side.

For the BJP, a critical look at how its tie-up with SNDP Yogam general secretary Vellappally Natesan had actually fared, perhaps internally, may have to precede anything else. But that looks unlikely given the fact that it was an alliance forced upon the State leadership from above. Any such review would depend on what happens elsewhere, say Bihar. True, the party was able to attract a share of the Nair votes, like in Thiruvananthapuram Corporation, despite the tie-up with Natesan, but that is small solace when viewed against the larger canvas of Assembly polls. That the party's rise is being seen with trepidation by the minorities should also make its leadership think about bringing in some significant nuances into its words and deeds in Kerala.

Moreover, the UDF refrain, led by Chief Minister Oommen Chandy - as much about it being a referendum on the government as that it is fighting the polls as a 'united' front - has misfired, going by saturdays results. In retrospect, any dissent from within if allowed about bar bribery case would have been received positively by the voting public. That was not to be. Result: a real whipping at the grassroots level—grama, block, district, municipality, corporation. For the CPM, faced with the spectre of erosion in its core constituency vote bank, with SNDP supremo Vellappally Natesan threatening to pull the rug from under its feet by openly aligning with the BJP, it is a great escape. The victory is all the more sweet for the comrades as the erosion of Hindu votes and the polarisation thereof has evidently come at the cost of the UDF.

Further, upper class Hindu vote aggregation, cutting across caste lines, has definitely become a reality, as is borne by the Thiruvananthapuram corporation results. Political Kerala, having taken for granted the agglomeration of Muslim, Christian and a section of Hindu votes primarily in favour of the UDF and to a lesser degree and by a different combination for the LDF, has woken up to reality that a bulk of Hindus did vote for the BJP. That too, shorn of the need for any intermediaries. Surely, neither the UDF nor the LDF can any longer wish away the BJP as an undeniable political reality in Kerala. Poised mid-way between the Aruvikkara by-poll and the 2016 Assembly elections, the LDF has all the reasons to believe it is on a winning wicket. Enough time for the UDF to go back to the planning board and rework strategy. Perhaps it won't hurt to do the morally right thing regarding basic issues like corruption. For the BJP to proclaim with self-confidence it is a state-level force, a maiden entry to the Kerala Assembly is a must. For now, the verdict is lucid, clear. The UDF has decisively lost the semi-finals to the LDF, and to some extent, to the BJP. There is hard work ahead for all three though, ahead of the Assembly polls, 2016.

References

Anil S., "Kerala Rolls", *The New Sunday Express*, 8th November, 2015.

Biju E. Paul, "SNDP-BJP Coalition Fall Flat on Its Back in the Polls", *The New Sunday Express*, 8th November, 2015.

C. Gouridasan Nair, "A Semi-Final Full of Messages", *The Hindu*, 8 November, 2015.

Deccan Chronicle, Kochi.

Gireesh Menon, "Its Mixed Results in Corporations", *The Hindu*, 8 November, 2015.

Kala Kaumudi Weekly, Thiruvananthapuram.

Kerala Kaumudi, Kollam

Kerala Sabdham, Kollam.

M.R. Biju, "LDF's Repeat Performance: Kerala's Local Body Elections", *Economic and Political Weekly*, Vol. XXX, Nos. 41 and 42, October 14-21, 1995.

M.R. Biju, "Local Body Polls 2000 in Kerala: Warning Signs for the Left", *South Asian Journal of Socio-Political Studies*, Vol. I, No. 2, June-Dec. 2000.

M.R. Biju, "Local Body Polls 2005 in Kerala", *South Asian Journal of Socio-Political Studies*, Vol. VI, No. 2, January-June, 2006.

M.R. Biju, "Local Body Polls 2010 in Kerala: UDF Smashes LDF Fortresses", *Mainstream*, Vol. XLVIII No. 48, November 20, 2010.

M.R. Biju, "Local Body Polls in Kerala", *Mainstream*, Vol. XXXIX, No. 18, April 21, 2001.

Mathew A. Thomas, "When It Rains, It Pours", *The New Sunday Express*, 8th November, 2015.

N.V. Raveendranathan Nair, "Out the Carpet", *The New Sunday Express*, 8th November, 2015.

S. Anandan, "Wake-up Call to Both Fronts", *The Hindu*, 8 November, 2015.

The Hindu, Thiruvananthapuram.

The Malayala Manorama, Kollam.

The New Indian Express, Thiruvananathapuram.

Vinod Mathew, "A Politically Vibrant Message from the Grassroots", *The New Sunday Express*, 8th November, 2015.

Index